BARRON'S
FOREIGN LANGUA

D0390460

Mastering
SPANISH
Grammar

Margarita Görrissen

BARRON'S

First edition for the United States and Canada
© Copyright 2007 by Barron's Educational Series, Inc.
Original edition © Copyright 2005 by Ernst Klett Sprachen GmbH,
Stuttgart, Federal Republic of Germany. All rights reserved.

Author: **Margarita Görrissen**
English translation: **Kathleen Luft**

All inquiries should be addressed to:
Barron's Educational Series, Inc.
250 Wireless Boulevard
Hauppauge, NY 11788
http://www.barronseduc.com

ISBN-13: 978-0-7641-3657-3
ISBN-10: 0-7641-3657-7
Library of Congress Control Number: 2006929367

Printed in China
10 9 8 7 6 5 4 3

How to Use This Book

You're interested in improving your knowledge of Spanish grammar. Maybe you want to review, practice, and add to what you have already learned—or even just look something up quickly. *Mastering Spanish Grammar* will help you do all of that by way of simple explanations, arranged in a way that is clear and easy to understand, and plenty of helpful exercises. This book presents and discusses all the essential features of Spanish grammar.

How the Chapters Are Structured

First, in an introductory illustration accompanied by minidialogues, we present a selected aspect of Spanish grammar in an everyday context.

Clear, easy-to-understand rules, neatly arranged tables, and detailed sections on usage provide a quick overview of the fundamentals. Ample numbers of practical, real-life examples show you the right way to use the grammatical element in question.

In the many exercises that follow, you have a chance to practice and apply what you have learned. Here the level of difficulty of an exercise is indicated by asterisks:
* = easy exercise; ** = moderately difficult exercise; *** = difficult exercise.
This way you can easily monitor your own progress as you go.

In the marginal notes, you will find a great many helpful tips and information concerning correct usage:
▶ Introductory explanations of the grammatical subject
▶ Tips to help you learn and additional hints
▶ Important exceptions and stumbling blocks
▶ References to other grammar chapters
▶ Vocabulary aids and help with translation
▶ Pointers on differences in linguistic usage in Spain and Latin America

All the grammatical terms used in this book are listed in the overview on pages 276–277.

The index in the back of the book will help you find the right grammar information in a flash. To speed your search, important topics are given in red.

We wish you great success as you use this book as a reference tool and a means to improve and practice your Spanish!

Table of Contents

Contents

Contents

The Noun

¡Ahora Pedro tiene un problema! ②

La cartera, los cuadernos, el bolígrafo y los libros están en la mesa. ①

¡Las llaves y el dinero no están ahí! ③

Nouns denote a person, place, thing, or idea. Proper names of persons, places, or things are also nouns.

1. The satchel, the notebooks, the ballpoint pen, and the books are on the table.
2. Now Pedro has a problem! 3. The keys and the money are not there!

The Gender of Nouns

In Spanish, nouns are either masculine or feminine. There are no neuter nouns. One cannot predict the gender of a noun that denotes a nonliving thing. All nouns should be memorized with the definite article!

| el hotel | *the hotel* | la oficina | *the office* |
| el sol | *the sun* | la luna | *the moon* |

Generally, nouns that end in **-o** are masculine, and those that end in **-a** are feminine.

These are masculine:

Words of Greek origin that end in **-ma** are masculine:
<u>el</u> idioma, <u>el</u> progra-ma, <u>el</u> tema etc.

el chico	el hijo	generally, nouns that end in **-o**.
el libro	el dormitorio	
el coche	el avión	some nouns that end in **-e**
el viaje	el hotel	or a consonant.
el día	el mapa	some nouns that end in **-a**,
el tranvía	el sofá	including all international words
el problema	el clima	ending in **-ma**.
el Danubio	el Amazonas	rivers and oceans.
el Caribe	el Mediterráneo	
el amarillo	el verde	colors and numbers.
el lila	el ocho	

These are feminine:

la chica	la cama	generally, nouns that end in **-a.**
la mesa	la playa	
la noche	la parte	some nouns that end in **-e** or a consonant.
la llave	la catedral	
la habita**ción**	la ra**ción**	all nouns that end in **-ción**, **-sión**, **-dad**, and **-tad** as well as most ending in **-ud**.
la deci**sión**	la liber**tad**	
la e**dad**	la ciu**dad**	
la juven**tud**	la sal**ud**	
la mano	la radio	some nouns that end in **-o.**
la foto	la moto	
¿Es una **b** o una **p**?		letters of the alphabet.
Málaga es muy turística.		countries, cities, and islands ending in **-a**; the others (for example those ending in a consonant) are usually masculine.
Yo me voy a la **India** y al Japón.		
Fuerteventura es muy bonita.		
Como **el á**guila blanca es rara, **las** á**guilas** blancas están protegidas. **Las ha**das siempre ayudan en los cuentos, y así, **el ha**da buena salva muchas veces a la princesa.		Some nouns that begin with a stressed **-a** or **-ha** take the masculine article, because otherwise the pronunciation of the singular is unclear. In the plural, however, they use the feminine article **las**.

> La foto(grafía) and la moto(cicleta) only seem to be exceptions.

el águila – *the eagle*
el hada – *the fairy*

1. Nouns That Sound Identical or Similar But Differ in Gender

> ¡Hay mucho **capital** en la **capital**!

There is a lot of capital in the capital!

There are a few nouns that sound the same but differ in meaning, depending on whether they are masculine or feminine.

masculine		feminine	
el capital	*the capital (finances)*	**la** capital	*the capital (city)*
el policía	*the policeman*	**la** policía	*the police (force)*
el cura	*the priest*	**la** cura	*the cure*
el guía	*the guide (man)*	**la** guía	*the guide (woman)*

In some regions of Spain and Latin America, some nouns have a different gender. Examples are:

Spain	LA
la radio	el radio
la sartén	el sartén

There are a few words that are quite similar, but differ in gender and ending.

Watch out! Confusing these similar-sounding nouns can lead to unintentionally comical or embarrassing statements!

masculine		feminine	
el puerto	*the port*	**la** puerta	*the door*
el banco	*the bank*	**la** banca	*the bench; banking*
el bolso	*the handbag*	**la** bolsa	*the bag; the stock exchange*
el grupo	*the group*	**la** grupa	*the hindquarters*
los medios	*the media*	**las** medias	*the stockings*

2. Gender of Nouns Denoting Persons and Occupations

Mi tío es enfermero y mi tía es secretaria.

My uncle is a male nurse and my aunt is a secretary.

With nouns that denote persons or occupations, the grammatical gender is the same as the natural gender.

Regardless of the natural gender, a few words are always feminine:
la persona, la víctima *(the victim)*.

masculine	feminine	
el niñ**o**	la niñ**a**	Nouns whose masculine forms end in **-o** form the feminine by adding **-a**.
el hij**o**	la hij**a**	
el camarer**o**	la camarer**a**	
el señ**or**	la señ**ora**	If the masculine designation for a person or occupation ends in **-or**, the feminine forms ends in **-ora**.
el profes**or**	la profes**ora**	
el trabajad**or**	la trabajad**ora**	
el jef**e**	la jef**a**	Masculine designations for persons or occupations that end in **-e** usually have a feminine form ending in **-a**.
el dependient**e**	la dependient**a**	
el president**e**	la president**a**	
el **padre**	la **madre**	Some nouns have different designations for male and female persons or occupations.
el **hombre**	la **mujer**	
el **rey**	la **reina**	
el **príncipe**	la **princesa**	
el **actor**	la **actriz**	

3. One Form for Both Genders

La joven es estudiante y el joven es periodista.

The young woman is a student and the young man is a journalist.

Some nouns have only one form for both genders.

masculine	feminine	This group includes:
el estudiante el oyente	la estudiante la oyente	some nouns ending in **-nte**,
el turista	la turista	nouns ending in **-ista**,
el colega el guía	la colega la guía	nouns ending in **-a**,
el **joven** el **modelo**	la **joven** la **modelo**	and a few nouns that cannot be assigned to any group.

4. Gender of Nouns Denoting Animals

masculine	feminine		
el mosquito el lince el escorpión el sapo el pez	la mosca la liebre la araña la rana la serpiente	Often a single form denotes both male and female animals. It may be masculine or feminine.	la mosca – *the fly* la liebre – *the hare* la araña – *the spider* el sapo – *the toad* la rana – *the frog* el lince – *the lynx*
el lince macho la rana macho	el lince hembra la rana hembra	If you want to express the difference, add the word **macho** or **hembra**.	
el perro el gato el león el elefante	la perra la gata la leona la elefanta	For some animal species, there is a feminine form ending in **-a**. Then the masculine form is gender-neutral or denotes the male animal.	
el **toro** el **gallo** el **caballo** el **carnero**	la **vaca** la **gallina** la **yegua** la **oveja**	For some utility species, there are different terms for male and female animals.	

5. Gender of Nouns Denoting Plants

> ! Trees ending in **-a** are feminine: **la higuera** *(the fig tree)*, **la haya** *(the beech)*.

> ! But: **el plátano**, **el limón**, **el kiwi** are masculine.

el pino	el nogal	Most designations for trees and shrubs are masculine.
el naranjo	el peral	
el olivo	el romero	
la naranja	la pera	Almost all kinds of fruits are feminine.
la piña	la grosella	
la mandarina	la fresa	
el tulipán	la rosa	Flowers are masculine or feminine.
el jazmín	la margarita	

Noun Plurals

En las ciudad**es** hay muchos edifici**os** y muchas cas**as**.

In the cities there are many buildings and many houses.

Formation of the Plural

Singular	Plural	
el chic**o**	los chic**os**	If the noun ends in a vowel in the singular, attach an **-s** in the plural.
el dí**a**	los dí**as**	
la llav**e**	las llav**es**	
el hote**l**	los hotel**es**	If the noun ends in a consonant or a stressed **-í**, in the singular, add **-es** in the plural.
el seño**r**	los señor**es**	
el esqu**í**	los esquí**es**	
la ciuda**d**	las ciudad**es**	
la muje**r**	las mujer**es**	
el pe**z**	los pe**ces**	If the noun ends in **-z**, in the singular, replace that letter with **-ces** in the plural.
el lápi**z**	los lápi**ces**	
la lu**z**	las lu**ces**	
otra ve**z**	otras ve**ces**	
el avi**ón**	los avi**ones**	Nouns whose singular ends in a consonant and is stressed on the last syllable lose the written accent in the plural.
el alem**án**	los aleman**es**	
la habitaci**ón**	las habitaci**ones**	
el autob**ús**	los autobus**es**	
el examen	los ex**á**men**es**	Nouns whose singular ends in **-n** and is stressed on the next-to-last syllable acquire a written accent on the third-from-last syllable in the plural.
el joven	los j**ó**ven**es**	

el lunes la crisis	los lunes las crisis	Two-syllable nouns that end in **-s** preceded by an unstressed vowel in the singular do not change in the plural.
la gente — — — —	— **las vacaciones** **las tijeras** **las gafas** **las afueras**	Some nouns are commonly used only in the singular or only in the plural.

> Note that the days of the week are not capitalized: **el viernes** *(Friday / on Friday)*, **los viernes** *(Fridays / every Friday)*.

> In referring to the days of the week, it is common to use the articles.

Special Features of the Plural of Nouns Denoting Persons or Occupations

¿Tienen ustedes hijos, señores Roca?

①

Sí, tenemos un hijo y una hija.

②

1. Do you have children, Mr. and Mrs. Roca? 2. Yes, we have a son and a daughter.

Masculine nouns denoting persons or occupations that are used in the plural, depending on the context, designate either males or the entire group of males and females.

masc. Singular	fem. Singular	masc. Plural
el señor *the man/gentleman*	la señora *the woman/lady*	los señores *the gentlemen / Mr. and Mrs. / the gentlemen and ladies*
el hijo *the son*	la hija *the daughter*	los hijos *the sons / the children*
el padre *the father*	la madre *the mother*	los padres *the fathers / the parents*
el abuelo *the grandfather*	la abuela *the grandmother*	los abuelos *the grandfathers / the grandparents*
el hermano *the brother*	la hermana *the sister*	los hermanos *the brothers / the siblings*

> To refer to the entire family or to a married couple, simply use the plural of the article plus the family name, for example, **los Roca**. Do not attach an **-s** to the family name.

el profesor	la profesora	los profesores
the teacher (male)	*the teacher (female)*	*the teachers (male) /* *the teachers (m. & f.)*
el rey	la reina	los reyes
the king	*the queen*	*the kings / the king and queen*

The Noun as Part of a Sentence

¿Ves el coche nuevo de la profesora?

¡Sí! La profesora siempre compra coches deportivos, ¿verdad?

---

1. Do you see the teacher's new car? 2. Yes! The teacher always buys sports cars, doesn't she?

Unlike some other European languages, Spanish has abandoned all use of cases with nouns.

In Spanish the noun does not change in form, regardless of its role in the sentence.

Who?	**El tío** tiene un coche.
What?	**El coche** es grande.

The nominative is the subject of the sentence.

Whose?	El coche **del tío** es grande.
	El techo **del coche** es rojo.

The genitive (possessive) is expressed with the preposition **de** (+ article) + noun.

▶ **Verbs with the Dative**, p. 215

To / for whom?	Dale una foto **al tío**.
	Al tío le gusta.

The dative always involves the preposition **a**. It is used to express the indirect object of the verb and also with certain verbs.

▶ **The Preposition** *a*, p. 244

Whom?	¿Ves al tío?
What?	¿Ves el coche?

The accusative is the direct object of the verb and generally does not require a preposition. With persons, personified terms (such as **la orquesta**) or specifically defined animals (such as **mi perro**), the accusative is indicated by the preposition **a**.

1. Which article belongs with which noun? Put the nouns listed below in the appropriate columns. *

hoteles	mano	luna	avión
libro	problemas	sofás	decisiones
oficina	noches	habitaciones	libertad
Danubio	catedral	coches	llaves
ciudades	ocho	agua	mujer
sistema	camareros	farmacias	mapas

It is not always possible to tell the gender of a Spanish noun by its ending. Therefore, you always need to learn the article along with the noun!

el	la	los	las
libro			

2. What are the plural forms of these nouns?*

a) el vecino
b) la joven
c) el programa
d) el coordinador
e) la discusión
f) el domingo
g) la llave
h) el análisis

el vecino – *the neighbor*
el coordinador – *the coordinator*

a) los vecinos
b)
c)
d)
e)
f)
g)
h)

3. Translate the following. *

a) the mother—the father—the parents

la madre –

b) the son—the daughter—the children

Noun

c) the sister—the brother—the siblings

_____

d) Mr. Roca—Mrs. Roca—Mr. and Mrs. Roca

_____

e) the grandmother—the grandfather—the grandparents

_____

f) the man—the woman—the child

_____

4. What word is used for the female person or female animal? *

a) el hombre – *la mujer*   f) el dependiente – _____

b) el actor – _____   g) el príncipe – _____

c) el cantante – _____   h) el modelo – _____

d) el gato – _____   i) el toro – _____

e) el caballo – _____   j) el gallo – _____

5. Mark the correct article. **

a) (El)/La colega se llama Jordi Puig.

b) ¡Qué playa tan fantástica! Y por suerte, hasta aquí no han llegado los/las turistas.

c) Claro que puedes tomar el/la agua del grifo, no pasa nada.

d) ¡Huy! ¡No encuentro los/las llaves de casa!

e) ¡Qué bien! Yo lavando los platos y tú sentado cómodamente en el/la sofá! ¿Por qué no me ayudas un poco?

f) El/La edad de Lulú es ideal. Tiene mucha libertad, pero todavía no tiene responsabilidades.

g) Claro que no ignoramos los/las problemas, pero no perdemos el optimismo.

al agua del grifo –
the tap water

6. Which of the expressions on the right goes in each blank? Translate. **

a) • ¿Crees que podemos empezar nuevos negocios?

   ○ No, la empresa no tiene el capital_____ suficiente en este momento.

el capital / la capital

b) • ¡Aquí hay algo raro! ¡La caja fuerte está abierta!

   ○ ¡Huy! Mejor llamamos a _____ .

el policía / la policía

c) • Cristina es una chica muy inteligente.

   ○ Sí, es la mejor de _____ .

el grupo / la grupa

d) • ¿Has oído la noticia? ¡El equipo alemán no sigue en el campeonato de fútbol!

   ○ Claro, la noticia está ya en todos _____ .

los medios / las medias

e) • ¿Cómo sabes que hay un museo en este barrio?

   ○ Lo dice en _____ . Mira, aquí en la página 91.

el guía / la guía

f) • Asunción es una ciudad grande, ¿verdad?

   ○ Claro, es _____ de Paraguay y tiene más de 450 mil habitantes.

el bolso / la bolsa

g) • ¿Tienes hambre?

   ○ Sí. ¿Dónde has puesto _____ de papas fritas?

h) • ¿De quién son _____ azules?

   ○ De Paco. Son parte de su uniforme de deporte.

7. Which clauses belong together? Match the columns correctly. **

a) Esto es fácil, chicos,   1) Se llama Antonio.

b) Marcos practica todos los días;   2) sino las personas.

c) Lo más importante no son las cosas,   3) ¿dónde está el problema?

d) ¿Ya conoces al nuevo cura?   4) A ver, dame la mano izquierda.

e) ¿Te digo tu suerte?   5) quiere ser tenista profesional.

Noun Determiners

Aay, ¡necesito **un** dentista!

①

¿**Qué** dentistas conoces?

②

Pues **mi** dentista es muy bueno. Pero hay **varios** dentistas buenos en **el** centro.

③

Determiners are words that appear only along with nouns. They must be distinguished from pronouns, which can take the place of a noun.

1. *Ouch, I need a dentist!* 2. *What dentists do you know?*
3. *Well, my dentist is very good. But there are several good dentists in the center (of town).*

▶ **Pronouns**, p. 72

Nouns usually are accompanied by words that modify or more precisely define them, the so-called determiners. Generally they precede the noun and agree with it in number and gender. In addition to the articles, there are other determiners that can give more specific information about a noun.

definite article	• ¿Por qué no has comido **el** pan? ○ Me duele mucho **la** muela.
indefinite article	• ¿Me recomiendas un dentista? ○ Sí, aquí cerca hay **una** dentista muy buena.
possessive determiner	• **Mi** dentista está de vacaciones.
demonstrative determiner	○ Me duele **esta** muela. Mire, doctora, he tomado este analgésico.
interrogative or exclamatory determiner	• ¿**Qué** clase de analgésico es? ¿**Cuánto** tiempo lleva usted con este dolor?
indefinite determiner	○ Me duelen **todas las** muelas. Quiero **otro** medicamento.

Definite and Indefinite Articles

¿Dónde hay
un banco?

①

El Banco de Comercio
está en la esquina.

②

1. Where is there a bank? 2. The Bank of Commerce is on the corner.

As in English, the definite article restricts or particularizes a noun, and the indefinite article does not fix the identity of the noun, but refers to something general or new.

Spanish has definite and indefinite articles. They precede a noun and agree with this noun in number and gender. Since there are no neuter Spanish nouns, only masculine and feminine forms exist.

1. The Definite Article

Forms

	masculine	**feminine**
Singular	**el** coche	**la** casa
Plural	**los** coches	**las** casas

When **el** is combined with the prepositions **de** and **a**, it changes to **del** and **al**:

de	+	el	▶	**del**	Voy **del** trabajo directamente
a	+	el	▶	**al**	**al** curso de español.

Some feminine nouns use the masculine article in the singular to ensure that the pronunciation is clear: **el agua**.

▶ **Nouns**, p. 10

Use

El coche azul es de **la** chica alemana.
Voy en **el** autobús de las 8 **al** trabajo.

▌ The definite article is used with persons and things that are already known or have already been referred to.

¿Dónde está **el** museo de arte? El presidente va a abrir **la** sesión.

▌ – with persons or things that are unique.

No article is used with **Correos** *(the Post Office)*.

• Perdón, ¿está **la** señora Martínez?
○ No, **la** doctora Martínez ya no trabaja en esta oficina. Creo que ahora trabaja con **la** madre de su novio.

▌ – when speaking about persons or introducing them, and in the process using **señor**, **señora**, **señorita**, their title, or a kinship term.

In Spanish, using an article with someone's first name can be derogatory.

Definite and Indefinite Articles

Los (señores) García son mis amigos.

– in the plural with a surname, with or without title, to designate a married couple or a family.

Las llamas son animales andinos. **La** llama es muy inteligente.
Me gusta mucho **la** música andina. También me encanta **el** tango.

▶ **Verbs with the Dative**, p. 215

– in general statements about a category, class, or species. This is the case after verbs such as **gustar**, **interesar**, and **encantar**.

El amarillo me gusta mucho.

– with colors.

El inglés es una lengua muy útil.

– when making a statement about a language.

El desempleo es un problema serio.

– when speaking about an abstract topic.

In contemporary written Spanish, *Estados Unidos* is often referred to without the article.

El Mississipi es un río importante de **los** Estados Unidos.
(El) Perú, **(el)** Ecuador, **(el)** Paraguay, **(la)** Argentina y **(el)** Brasil son países latinoamericanos.

– with the names or rivers, lakes, mountain ranges, etc. and with some country names, but for most it is not required.

Only the definite article changes in form to indicate this plural:
el lunes – *on Monday* and **los lunes** – *Mondays / every Monday*

Empiezo a trabajar a **las nueve** de **la mañana**.
I start to work at nine in the morning.
A veces salgo **por la noche** y no vuelvo **hasta la madrugada**.
Sometimes I go out at night and don't come back until dawn.

– before referring to hours of the day or times of day.

la semana que viene – *the coming week*
el mes próximo – *next month*
el último verano – *last summer*
el año pasado – *the past year*

Este trabajo es para **la semana que viene**.
Tengo que entregarlo **el lunes**, pero **los lunes** no voy a la oficina.
El mes próximo voy al pueblo donde estuve **el último verano**.
Allí visité a unos amigos **el año pasado**.

– with a number of determinations of time. In particular, the article is used before time expressions if they are followed by a word that specifies them more precisely, such as **pasado**, **próximo**, **que viene**, **último** etc.

Mi hija Claudia tiene **el** pelo castaño y **los** ojos negros.

- frequently with **tener** in connection with physical features.

Me duele **la** cabeza. Me voy a poner **el** pijama.

- with parts of the body or articles of clothing in place of the possessive pronoun.

Julián es **el del** Instituto, sabes, **el de** la novia colombiana.

- with the preposition **de** + article + noun, to identify someone.

Tiene que torcer primero a **la** derecha y después a **la** izquierda.
- ¡Qué rico! Hoy hay pollo **al** ajillo y papas a **la** francesa.

- in certain fixed expressions.

- Tu hermana estudia **todo el** tiempo, ¿verdad?
○ Pobre, es que su profesor hace exámenes **todos los** días.
- Pero **toda la** clase es igual, **todas las** chicas estudian así.

- usually after the indefinite determiners **todo**, **toda**, **todos**, and **todas**.

> **Indefinite Determiners**, p. 37

Pablo toca **la** guitarra y juega **al** tenis.

- with **tocar** + instrument or **jugar** + game.

> In LA, frequently without an article:
>
> Pablo **toca guitarra y juega tenis**.

The definite article is not used:

¿Vas **en autobús** al trabajo?

- with means of transportation that lack a modifier.

- Buenos días, **señorita** López.
○ Hola, **Doctor** Pereda. ¿Cómo está?
- **Tío** Pepe, ¡qué gusto!

- before **señor**, **señora**, **señorita**, titles, or kinship terms in direct discourse.

Doña Lola es mi tía.

- with the honorific **don**, **doña**.

> Used with the definite article, **don**, **doña** is derogatory or ironic, also when the name is omitted:
>
> Ya llegó **la** doña.

Velázquez vivió en la época **de Felipe IV (Cuarto)**.

- with names of rulers.

> **Ordinal Numbers**, p. 259

Definite and Indefinite Articles

No **hablo inglés** ni **sé alemán**, pero hay libros **en español**. Creo que voy a **estudiar alemán** o a tomar un curso **de inglés**.

- generally, before names of languages after the verbs **hablar**, **saber**, **estudiar**, **aprender** and after the prepositions **en** and **de**.

Hoy **es martes**.

- with days of the week after the verb **ser**.

En diciembre voy a Chile. Es que quiero ir en **(la) primavera**.

- before the names of months. Not required before the names of seasons.

- Si estás **en casa**, mejor quédate **en cama**.

- in some fixed expressions.

The Use of *lo*

The neutral form **lo** is used only in the singular. It never precedes nouns.

- **Lo** fácil del español es la pronunciación.
- Sí, en francés no es **lo** mismo.

Lo is used to convert other types of words into nouns (substantives).

Me sorprende **lo** inteligente que eres y **lo** bien que sabes cantar.

- with adjectives or adverbs to express degree. **Lo** is translated here as *how*.

a lo mejor – *maybe, perhaps*
por lo pronto – *to start with*

A **lo** mejor no le decimos nada a Juan por **lo** pronto.

- in certain fixed expressions.

Por favor, envíenos los datos **lo** más rápidamente posible.

- in the construction **lo más / menos** + adverb + **posible** it means *as* + (adverb) *as possible*.

- No me gusta **lo del** viaje con mis padres. Es que **lo de** visitar museos con ellos es súper aburrido. Y tú, ¿adónde vas?
- Nada, **lo de** siempre, al lago con mis abuelos.

▶ **Indefinite Pronouns**, p. 93

- with **de** + noun, infinitive, or adverb it denotes facts, topics, or situations that are regarded as familiar.

- Deme **lo que** tiene y dígame **todo lo que** sabe.
- ¡Cómo! Pero, ¡**lo que** pide es increíble!

- in connection with **que** + verb it is translated as *what (that which)*.

2. The Indefinite Article

Forms

	masculine	feminine
Singular	**un** coche	**una** casa
Plural	**unos** coches	**unas** casas

> ❗ Feminine nouns with a stressed **a-** or **ha-**: see the definite article, for example, **un** águila *(an eagle)*, **un** hada *(a fairy)*.

Use

Quiero comprar **un** coche pequeño para ir a mi pueblo. En mi pueblo hay **un** bar nuevo que se llama "Paco".

▪ The indefinite article is used in the **singular** when speaking about an indefinite person or thing, or when introducing a topic.

En Murcia viven **unos** buenos amigos míos.

▪ The indefinite article is used in the **plural** when naming an indefinite quantity of things or persons. **Unos / unas** is translated as *some* or *a few*.

La ciudad de México tiene **unos** 20 millones de habitantes.
Necesitamos **unos** cien gramos de queso.

▪ – when stating a number or figure that is not exact. Then **unos / unas** is translated as *approximately* or *some*.

The indefinite article is not used:

Queremos comprar **coches** pequeños.

▪ – when speaking about several indefinite persons or things.

● ¿Tienes **coche**?
○ No, no necesito **coche**.

▪ – when speaking in general about something. In translation, the words *at all* may be added.

Camarero, ¡**otra** botella de **medio** litro, por favor!

▪ – before **otro** and usually before **medio**.

¡**Qué** suerte! ¿**Qué** tren has tomado para llegar tan pronto?

▪ – in exclamations or questions with **qué** + noun.

> To specify the object more closely, you need the article:
> **Tengo un coche azul.**
> **Necesito un coche grande.**

> ❗ **un medio litro**, **una media botella** are approximate statements of quantity; see above. Here, **un / a** means *approximately* or *about.*

Practice and Application

Definite and Indefinite Articles

1. Fill in the definite article wherever it is required. *

a) • Perdonen, ¿son ustedes __los__ señores Restrepo?

○ No, _____ señor, _____ señores Restrepo viven enfrente.

b) • Hola, _____ ingeniero Álvarez, ¿qué tal?

○ Muy bien, gracias, _____ señora García, ¿y usted?

c) • _____ profesor es _____ señor Jiménez.

○ ¿ _____ señor Jiménez? Pues no lo conozco.

d) • Oiga, _____ don Pablo, ¡teléfono! Es _____ señora Muñoz.

○ Gracias, _____ señorita Lozano.

e) • Soy amigo de _____ doctor Olivares.

○ ¡Ah, sí! Dicen que _____ doctor Olivares es un especialista famoso.

2. Translate the following statements made in a restaurant.

a) Another beer, please!

Por favor, ¡otra cerveza!

the restroom –
los servicios

b) Excuse me, where is the restroom?

_____

c) The best thing is the paella.

_____

d) I like paella very much.

_____

fizzy, carbonated –
con gas

e) Do you have fizzy mineral water?

_____

f) And another half liter of red wine, please.

_____

g) The check, please!

_____

3. Mark the correct answer. **

a) Perdón, ¿hay el (un) — banco por aquí?

b) En los El Los jueves tenemos siempre clase de español.

c) Camarero, ¿nos trae por favor — una las otra botella de Rioja?

d) ¿Has ido en el — del tren a Zamora?

e) Lo El — francés me gusta mucho, es muy musical.

f) Si quieres, conduzco yo. Para mí es el la lo mismo.

g) Juan toca muy bien la el de la guitarra.

4. These statements can be heard in an office. What Spanish words correspond to the English words in parentheses?

a) Lo siento, *(Mr. Lozada)* __el señor Lozada__ no ha llegado todavía.

b) ¿Por qué no han propuesto _____ *(another answer)*?

c) *(What you say)* _____ es una noticia fantástica.

d) No sé dónde está _____ *(Mrs. Reyes)*.

e) No necesitas ponerte _____ *(your* [fam.] *coat)*, no hace frío.

f) *(On Thursday)* _____ voy a ver al cliente de Bilbao.

lo siento – I'm sorry

proponer – to suggest
la solución – the solution, the answer

ponerse – to put on (clothing)
el abrigo – the coat
ir a ver – to visit, to (go) see
el cliente – the client, the customer

5. Decide whether an article is needed here, and if so, write it in the blanks below. **

a) __La__ señorita Luz es muy atractiva. Tiene __los__ ojos verdes y _____ pelo negro. Y tiene _____ trabajo muy interesante.

b) • ¿Ya ha llegado _____ profesor Gómez a _____ seminario?

   ○ No, llega en _____ tren _____ jueves a _____ diez de _____ mañana.

c) ¡Qué bien tocas _____ piano! ¿En _____ otoño das _____ concierto?

d) Vamos, Bertita, dile a _____ doctor todo _____ que te duele.

e) A mí _____ animales me encantan. Tengo _____ perro muy simpático.

f) ¡Qué rica ha estado _____ cena! ¿Pedimos _____ café?

Demonstrative Determiners

The Demonstrative Determiners

¿Ves ese autobús? ①

¿Este autobús rojo? ②

No, aquel autobús gris, el número 101. ③

The demonstrative determiners can be used to specify how close or far someone or something is.

1. Do you see that bus? 2. This red bus? 3. No, that gray bus, Number 101.

Demonstrative determiners are used to point out persons or things. Normally they precede the noun and agree with it in number and gender.

In Spanish, there are three ways of expressing the spatial, temporal, or psychological relationship to something or someone.

▶ **Adverbs**, p. 53

este (de aquí) **ese** (de ahí) **aquel** (de allí)	The demonstrative determiners often occur along with the adverbs **aquí** *(here)*, **ahí** *(there)* and **allí** *(there, over there)*.

Keep in mind that the masculine forms are not, as you might expect, **esto** or **eso**. These are neuter pronouns.

▶ **Demonstrative Pronouns**, p. 87

Forms

		Masculine		Feminine		adverb
Singular	**este**	autobús		**esta**	casa	(de aquí)
	ese	autobús		**esa**	casa	(de ahí)
	aquel	autobús		**aquella**	casa	(de allí)
Plural	**estos**	autobuses		**estas**	casas	(de aquí)
	esos	autobuses		**esas**	casas	(de ahí)
	aquellos	autobuses		**aquellas**	casas	(de allí)

Use

¿Me explicas **este** ejemplo de aquí?

▌ **Este, esta, estos**, and **estas** are used to refer to things or persons that are right next to the speaker.

Estos deberes de hoy están muy fáciles.
Esta tarde voy al dentista. **Este** año no he ido todavía.

▌ **Este** or **esta** is used with or in statements of time that are closely linked with the present.

● Con Luis hablé de política, aunque **este** tema no me interesa.
○ Yo no sé, ¡pero con **este** chico no se puede hablar de otra cosa!

▌ **Este, esta, estos**, and **estas** refer to a thing or person that has just been mentioned or is psychologically very close to the speaker (in a positive or a negative way).

¿Me muestra **esos** zapatos de ahí, por favor?

▌ **Ese, esa, esos**, und **esas** are used to speak about things or persons that are near the person or persons being addressed.

¿Cómo se llamaba **esa** película del otro día?
Esa mañana decidí casarme y me dije: "**Ese** día seré más feliz."

▌ **Ese, esa, esos**, and **esas** are used with or in statements of time that are not linked with the present.

No quiero contratar a Reyes porque no sé quién es **esa** persona.

▌ If you use **ese, esa, esos**, or **esas** to refer to a previously mentioned thing or person, you express a certain distance and sometimes even a derogatory attitude.

contratar – *to hire*

El mío es **aquel** abrigo gris de allí, el de atrás.

▌ **Aquel, aquella, aquellos**, and **aquellas** are used for everything located far away from the speaker and/or the person spoken to.

el abrigo – *the coat*
atrás – *at the back, behind*

En **aquellos** tiempos no había computadoras.
En **aquel** entonces mandábamos las felicitaciones por correo.

▌ Statements of time with **aquel, aquella, aquellos**, and **aquellas** refer to something far in the past.

Compare:
en ese entonces (*at that time, then*) with
en aquel entonces (*in those days*)

Possessive Determiners

The Possessive Determiners

> Possessive determiners indicate possession or belonging.

> Amigo **mío**, ¿cuál es **tu** número de celular?
> ①

> Quiero ponerlo en **mi** directorio.
> ②

1. My friend, what's your cell phone number?
2. I want to put it in my directory.

Spanish has unstressed possessive determiners, which always precede the noun, and stressed possessive determiners, which follow it.

1. Unstressed Possessive Determiners

Forms

Possessor \ Possession	Singular		Plural	
yo	**mi**	coche / casa	**mis**	coches / casas
tú	**tu**	coche / casa	**tus**	coches / casas
él / ella / usted	**su**	coche / casa	**sus**	coches / casas
nosotros / nosotras	**nuestro** coche / **nuestra** casa		**nuestros** coches / **nuestras** casas	
vosotros / vosotras	**vuestro** coche / **vuestra** casa		**vuestros** coches / **vuestras** casas	
ellos / ellas / ustedes	**su**	coche / casa	**sus**	coches / casas

> Only in the first and second person plural is a distinction made between masculine and feminine possession. The gender of the possessor, however, is never expressed.

Use

Estos son **mis** cuadernos y **mi** bolígrafo, y aquí están **vuestras** cosas.

Unstressed possessive determiners always precede the noun and agree with it in number. Only in the first and second person plural (*our*, *your* [fam.]) is there agreement in gender as well.

- ¿Son estas **sus** maletas?
- Son las maletas **de él / de Juan**, pero no las **de ella / de María**.

Su and **sus** have a great many possible meanings: For both, the possessor can be **él**, **ella**, **usted**, **ellos**, **ellas** or **ustedes**.
Su modifies possession in the singular and is translated as *his*, *her*, *their*, or *your*. **Sus** is used with possession in the plural and means *his*, *her*, *their*, and *your*.
If it is not clear who is meant, use **de** + noun or **de** + personal pronoun instead of **su** or **sus**.

No me puedo poner **la** chaqueta porque todavía me duele **el** brazo.

With articles of clothing and parts of the body, do not use the possessive determiner, as in English; instead, use the definite article.

2. Stressed Possessive Determiners

Forms

Possession / Possessor	Singular		Plural	
	masculine	feminine	masculine	feminine
yo	hijo **mío**	hija **mía**	hijos **míos**	hijas **mías**
tú	hijo **tuyo**	hija **tuya**	hijos **tuyos**	hijas **tuyas**
él ella usted	hijo **suyo**	hija **suya**	hijos **suyos**	hijas **suyas**
nosotros nosotras	hijo **nuestro**	hija **nuestra**	hijos **nuestros**	hijas **nuestras**
vosotros vosotras	hijo **vuestro**	hija **vuestra**	hijos **vuestros**	hijas **vuestras**
ellos ellas ustedes	hijo **suyo**	hija **suya**	hijos **suyos**	hijas **suyas**

▶ **Possessive Pronouns**, p. 88

Interrogative or Exclamatory Determiners

Use

¡Hijos **míos**! ¡Qué alegría!
¿Esos son amigos **tuyos**? ¿De verdad?

■ Stressed possessive determiners are less common than unstressed ones. They come after the noun and place special emphasis on the relationship of possession or belonging.

- ¿Quién es este chico?
- Es un amigo mío.

■ The construction indefinite article + noun + stressed possessive determiner denotes *one of several*.

> Here you need to be careful not to translate literally! *A friend of mine* is **un amigo mío** in Spanish.

The Interrogative or Exclamatory Determiners

¡**Cuánta** gente! ①

② ¿**En qué** restaurante habéis celebrado el fin de curso?

③ ¿**Qué** postres han probado?

> As determiners, **qué** and **cuánto** always accompany a noun.

▶ **Pronouns**, p. 72

1. How many people! 2. In what restaurant did you celebrate the end of the course?
3. Which desserts did you try?

The interrogative and exclamatory determiners are **qué** and **cuánto / -a / -os / -as**. They always have a written accent.

> In LA, **cuál / -es** is also used as a determiner, as in ¿**Cuál regalo te gusta más?**

> el camarón—*the shrimp*

Forms

	masculine	feminine
Singular	¡**qué** vino!	¡**qué** paella!
Plural	¡**qué** camarones!	¡**qué** carnes!
Singular	¡**cuánto** vino!	¡**cuánta** paella!
Plural	¡**cuánto**s camarones!	¡**cuántas** carnes!

Interrogative or Exclamatory Determiners

Use

- ¿**Qué** países latinoamericanos conoces?
- ○ He estado en Costa Rica. ¡**Qué** naturaleza tiene ese país!
- Sí, ¿verdad? Y me pregunto **qué** hombre ha viajado tanto como tú.

Qué is invariable and is usually translated as *what, what kind of,* or *which*. It is used with nouns denoting things or persons.

- ¿En **qué** problema piensas? ¿Por **qué** motivo estás preocupado?
- ○ Es que no sé de **qué** andén sale nuestro tren.

Frequently people also use a preposition + **qué** + noun.

el andén—*the train platform*

¿**Qué hora es**?	*What time is it?*
¿**A qué hora** nos vamos?	*At what time are we leaving?*
¡**Qué horas son estas** de llegar!	*How come you're arriving so late?*

In some fixed turns of speech, the translation varies.

- No hay nada en la nevera. ¡**Cuántas** cosas faltan!
- ○ Huy, ¡es verdad! ¿Y **cuánto** dinero nos queda hasta fin de mes?

The determiner **cuánto/-a/-os/-as** *(how much / many)* depends in number and gender on the noun and asks a question about the amount / quantity of something. As an exclamatory determiner, it expresses *how / how much / what a lot of*.

la nevera – *the refrigerator*

¿Con **cuántos** huevos preparas el flan? ¿Para **cuántas** personas es esta receta?

Frequent use is also made of the construction preposition + **cuánto/-a/-os/-as** + noun.

¿**Cuántos años** tienen?	*How old are you?*
¿**Cuánto tiempo** necesitas?	*How much time do you need?*
¡**Cuántas veces** tengo que decirlo!	*How many times do I have to say it!*

In some fixed expressions, the translation varies.

Practice and Application

1. At the airport you can hear the following utterances. Change the sentences from plural to singular. *

Note that the masculine singular is **este** and **ese**!

a) • ¿De quién son esas maletas? ¿De aquellos señores?

○ <u>¿De quién es esa maleta? ¿De aquel señor?</u>

b) Aquí están estos paraguas. ¿Son de aquellas jóvenes?

_____

c) Esos turistas han dejado estos mapas.

_____

2. Two friends are looking at a catalogue. Complete the sentences below with the correct endings. *

te matan –
(will) kill you

a) • ¡Mira! ¿Te gusta est_a_ moda? Est___ zapatos te matan.

b) ○ Pero mira, est___ zapatillas son muy bonitas. Y con est___ faldita

quedan muy bien, ¿no?

mono / -a – sweet, pretty

c) • Sí, est___ combinación es muy mona. ¿Ya has pedido algo por

est___ catálogo?

d) ○ Sí, es muy fácil. Hay que llenar est___ formulario, pones aquí

la prenda (de ropa) –
the garment

est_____ número, que es el de la prenda, y tu talla.

3. From your car, you're showing a visitor the places of interest in your city. Complete the sentences with the appropriate demonstrative determiners. *

Some demonstrative determiners are translated by this construction: article + possibly adverbs. Examples: the square over there, that building, etc.

a) Mira, Ángel, ___esa___ plaza es la Plaza Central. ¿Y ves _____

edificio antiguo? Es el Ayuntamiento.

b) En _____ esquina hay otro edificio interesante, ¿lo ves? _____

edificio amarillo es el museo de artesanías.

c) En _____ calles, detrás de _____ parque, hay varias tiendas de

recuerdos típicos.

d) _____ centro comercial es muy moderno. Y enfrente, ¿ves _____

casa? Ahí hay una pequeña galería de arte.

e) ¿Ya quieres comer? Podemos ir a uno de _____ restaurantes.

4. Put the sentences in the right order by writing the numbers 1–8 in the parentheses. *

a) ( ) • Sí, gracias. ¿Cuánto cuestan?

b) (1) • Buenos días. ¿Puedo ver esa chaqueta del escaparate, por favor?

c) ( ) • Mediana.

d) ( ) • No sé ... no mucho. Mmh. Pero me gustan aquellos pantalones de allí. ¿Los tiene en talla 40, en blanco o en gris?

e) ( ) ○ Huy, esta chaqueta ya sólo me queda en esta talla ...
Es talla pequeña. Pero mire, esa chaqueta de ahí es parecida, ¿no le gusta?

f) ( ) ○ A ver ... Esa marca es muy buena, por cierto ... ¡Sí, mire! Estos pantalones blancos son justo de su talla. ¿Se los quiere probar?   por cierto – *by the way*

g) ( ) ○ El precio está en esta etiqueta ... 49 euros.

h) ( ) ○ Por supuesto. Es esta chaqueta azul, ¿verdad? ¿Qué talla necesita?

5. Add the correct endings wherever necessary. *

a) • ¡Oye, Marisa! ¿Quién es es_e_ niño tan guapo que tienes ahí?

○ Est___ niño tan guapo es mi sobrinito Bruno. ¡Y ya va a la escuela!

b) Los abuelos siempre dicen que antes todo era mejor. Pero en aquel___ época no había ni teléfono, ni computadora, ni nada. ¡Qué horror!

c) • ¿A quién tengo que consultarle est___ asunto?

○ A aquel___ señor que está detrás del vidrio, en es___ oficina de ahí, ¿lo ve usted?

d) • Est___ aviones llegan siempre con retraso.

○ Sí, ¡es___ línea aérea es terrible!   la línea aérea – *the airline*
prestar – *to lend*

e) ¿Me prestas es___ diccionario? No sé cómo se traduce est___ palabra.

f) Est___ ejercicios son muy fáciles, pero aquel___ no.

g) • ¡Uff! ¿Qué es es___ música tan rara?

○ ¡Pero mamá, por Dios! Es la última canción de est___ grupo. ¡Es genial!

Practice and Application

Demonstrative, Possessive, and Other Determiners

6. Mark the unstressed possessive determiners in one color and the stressed ones in another color. *

a) • ¡Dios mío! ¿Es este su coche, señora?

○ No, es de una vecina mía. Ha entrado a la carnicería.

• Pues su vecina ha dejado a sus hijos en el coche, ¡y con este calor!

b) • Vuestros amigos han salido, pero pueden hablar con Inés, una compañera suya.

regresar – to return, to go / come back

○ ¡Muy bien! Pero, ¿cuándo regresan nuestros amigos?

7. Write the missing possessive determiners in the blanks. *

a) • Lucas, ¿dónde pasas ___tus___ vacaciones?

b) ○ Normalmente en Río, porque _____ padres tienen una casa allí. Y Matías y yo podemos llevar también a _____ amigos.

guapo / -a – good-looking

celoso / -a – jealous

c) • ¡Ah, sí! Oye, ¿cómo se llama esa amiga _____ tan guapa, la de la fiesta del otro día?

d) ○ Se llama Claudia, pero _____ novio es muy celoso.

e) • ¡Qué pena! Bueno, pero todas _____ amigas son muy hermosas. También esa compañera _____ de informática, sabes ... ¿Me das _____ número de teléfono?

f) ○ ¿De Raquel? Pues no tengo _____ datos, tienes que venir a _____ clase un día y le preguntas directamente.

8. You want to learn something about a Spanish-speaking country in Africa. Insert the correct interrogative determiners in the blanks. *

a) ¿_Cuántos_____ habitantes tiene Guinea Ecuatorial?

b) ¿_____ idiomas se hablan allí?

c) ¿A _____ horas de vuelo está Malabo, la capital?

d) ¿_____ sistema político tiene ese país?

e) ¿_____ gente habla español como idioma oficial en África?

The Indefinite Determiners

¿Practicas **algún** deporte?
①

Sí, **cada** día voy al gimnasio y hago **todos** los ejercicios en **varios** aparatos.
②

¡Qué horror! A mí **ningún** aparato me gusta. Prefiero **otras** cosas ...
③

1. Do you play some sport? 2. Yes, every day I go to the gym and do all the exercises on various workout machines. 3. How awful! I don't like any machine at all. I prefer other things ...

> Indefinite determiners have a general, indeterminate meaning. Usually they tell something about the quantity or distribution of persons or things.

Indefinite determiners are words such as **mucho/-a/-os/-as** *(much, many)*, **todos/-as** *(all)*, **ninguno/-a** *(no, not ... any)*, **cada** *(each, every)*, and others. Usually they precede the noun and agree with it in number and gender. Here are the most important ones:

▶ **Indefinite Pronouns**, p. 93

1. *mucho, poco, bastante, demasiado, suficiente*

Singular		Plural	
masculine	**feminine**	**masculine**	**feminine**
mucho sol	**mucha** luz	**muchos** días	**muchas** veces
poco sol	**poca** luz	**pocos** días	**pocas** veces
bastante sol	**bastante** luz	**bastantes** días	**bastantes** veces
demasiado sol	**demasiada** luz	**demasiados** días	**demasiadas** veces
suficiente sol	**suficiente** luz	**suficientes** días	**suficientes** veces

mucho – *much, many*
poco – *not much, little; not many, few*
bastante – *enough, quite a lot of*
demasiado – *too much*
suficiente – *enough, sufficient*

Use

- ¿Hay **suficiente** comida?
- A ver ... En la nevera hay **bastante** queso y **mucho** jamón. Pero hay **poca** leche y no hay **demasiados** yogures.

Mucho, poco, and **demasiado** agree with the noun in number and gender. **Bastante** and **suficiente** have only one form in the singular and add an **-s** in the plural.

Indefinite Determiners

2. *alguno – ninguno*

		Singular		Plural	
masc.	+	**algún**	sello	**algunos**	sellos
	–	**ningún**		**ningunos**	
fem.	+	**alguna**	carta	**algunas**	cartas
	–	**ninguna**		**ningunas**	

Use

- • ¿Hay **(alg)una** película buena? Aquí hay **(alg)unos** anuncios ...
- ○ Pues a mí **ninguna** película me parece interesante.

▌**Alguno**, **alguna** means *some*, *any*, and the plural **algunos**, **algunas** means *some* or *a few*. **Ninguno** is used almost exclusively in the singular and means *no*, *not ... any*. Often the indefinite article **un / -a** is used instead of **alguno / -a**.

▶ **Negation**, p. 227

- • ¿Hay **algún** problema?
- ○ No, no hay **ningún** problema.

▌Before masculine singular nouns, **alguno** and **ninguno** are shortened to **algún** and **ningún**.

el recado = el mensaje – *the message*

No he recibido **ninguna** llamada ni tampoco **ningún** recado.
No he recibido llamada **alguna** ni tampoco recado **alguno**.

▌In rare cases, **alguno** or **alguna** is used to replace **ningún** or **ninguna** after the noun in negated sentences. This serves as emphasis, and then it is translated as *no / not ... any at all*.

Fixed Phrases:

en alguna / ninguna parte	*somewhere/nowhere*
alguna vez	*sometime*
ninguna vez	*at all*
algún día	*some day*
algunos días	*(on) some days*
de alguna manera, de algún modo	*somehow*
de ninguna manera, de ningún modo	*in no case*
sin ninguna duda = sin duda alguna	*without any doubt*

3. *todo / -a / -os / -as*

	masculine	**feminine**
Singular	**todo el** pastel	**toda la** tarta
Plural	**todos los** pasteles	**todas las** tartas

Use

- **Todo el** día he pensado en **todas las** cosas que tengo que hacer.
○ Tranquilo, recuerda que **toda la** gente tiene problemas y que **todos los** caminos llevan a Roma.

Usually the definite article is used between the determiner **todo / -a / -os / -as** and the noun. **Todo el** and **toda la** mean *all, whole* in the singular and *every* or *all* in the plural.

- **Toda mi** vida he querido hacer un viaje al Caribe.
○ Mira, **todos estos** catálogos tienen viajes bastante baratos.
- ¡Huy! ¡Qué precio! ¡Esta sí que es **toda una** oferta!

toda una oferta – *a genuine offer*

The indefinite article, a possessive determiner, or a demonstrative determiner can also appear between the determiner **todo/-a/-os/-as** and the noun, however.

- En **toda** Alemania, **todo** accidente debe ser reportado a la policía.

reportar – *to report*

Without additional determiners, **todo** + noun is used almost exclusively in formal Spanish, with the meaning *every*, or with geographic names that are not further specified, with the meaning *all (of)*.

Fixed Phrases:

todos los días	*every day*
todo el día	*all day*
todo el mundo	*everybody, everyone*
a todas horas	*continually, at all hours*
en todas partes	*everywhere*
de todas maneras, de todos modos	*at any rate, anyway*
en todo caso	*in any event, in any case*
a toda costa	*at all costs, at any price*
todo tipo de, toda clase de	*all kinds of*

Indefinite Determiners

4. *más / menos / tanto / -a / -os / -as*

	invariable masculine	feminine	variable masculine	feminine
Sing.	**más** dinero	**más** suerte	**tanto** dinero	**tanta** suerte
Plural	**menos** amigos	**menos** fiestas	**tantos** amigos	**tantas** fiestas

Use

- Ya no hay **más** cerveza.
○ Yo ya compro **menos** cerveza. No es bueno tomar **tanto** alcohol.

Más *(more)* and **menos** *(less)* are invariable; **tanto / -a / -os / -as** *(so much, so many)* agrees with the noun in number and gender.

- Tengo **más** dinero **que** tú.
○ Posiblemente, pero tienes **menos** suerte **que** yo. Y yo tengo **tantos** amigos **como** tú.

You can use **más / menos ... que** *(more / less ... than)* and **tanto / -a / -os / -as ... como** *(as much / many ... as)* to compare nouns.

la suerte – *luck*

▶ **Comparison of Nouns**, p. 62

5. *otro / -a / -os / -as, demás*

Unlike English, Spanish never uses the indefinite article before **otro**!

Use

- Pepe, ¿abres **otro** vino?
○ Lo siento, ya no hay, pero puedo darte **otra** cosa.

Otro / -a / -os / -as agrees in number and gender with the noun. It means *another, other*.

- ¡Pero había **otras dos** botellas! ¿Dónde están?

If a numeral comes before the noun, **otro** precedes it. Spanish differs here from English (*two other*).

- ¿Quién se ha terminado **las demás** botellas de cerveza?
○ Yo no, seguramente **la demás** gente.

The other can be expressed with the definite article + **otro / -a / -os / -as** or **demás**. **Demás** is invariable.

Fixed Phrases:

otra cosa / persona	*something / somebody else*
otra vez	*(once) again*
¡Otra vez será!	*Some other time!*
otro día	*another time*
el otro día	*the other day*
en otro lugar / sitio	*somewhere else*
por otra razón, por otro motivo	*for another reason, for a different reason*

6. *cada*

Use

Aquí **cada** persona trabaja independientemente.

■ **Cada** is invariable and is always singular. It is translated as *each, every*.

Cada día hay una pequeña reunión para informar a los demás y **cada dos** semanas hay una reunión más larga con presentaciones.

■ If **cada** is followed by a time expression with or without a numeral, this expresses a regular interval.

Fixed phrases:

cada vez	*every time*
cada vez más	*more and more*
a cada rato	*all the time*

7. *cualquier / a*

Use

A Angélica **cualquier** música latina le encanta.

■ **Cualquier** is invariable and always precedes the noun in the singular. It means *any*.

No podemos llevar un regalo **cualquiera**.

■ After an indefinite noun in the singular, the invariable form **cualquiera** means *just any* or *any ordinary* or *common thing* or *person*.

41

Indefinite Determiners

Fixed Phrases:

cualquier cosa	*anything (whatsoever)*
cualquier persona	*anyone (whosoever)*
cualquier día	*any day (at all)*
cualquier cantidad (de)	*any amount (of)*
a cualquier hora	*at any time*
en cualquier momento	*at any moment*
en cualquier parte	*anywhere*
de cualquier manera / modo	*any way; any old how*

8. *mismo / -a / -os / -as*

el mismo gusto –
the same taste

> ### Use
>
> - Tenemos **el mismo** gusto, nos gustan **los mismos** cantantes.
> - Claro, y sobre todo, **la misma** canción...
>
> **Mismo / -a / -os / -as** is placed between the definite article and the noun and agrees with the noun in number and gender. It is translated as *same*.
>
> - ¡Cómo! ¿El jefe **mismo** te ha dado la noticia?
> - Sí, ¡González **mismo**! Mi compañera **misma** lo ha visto.
>
> If **mismo / -a / -os / -as** follows the subject or pronoun, it is emphatic and means *myself*, *yourself*, etc. or *even*.

9. *varios, diferentes, distintos, diversos*

> ### Use
>
> Tengo **varios** amigos en **diferentes** países de Latinoamérica.
> Ya he estado en **distintas** ciudades y he visitado **diversos** lugares.
>
> **Varios** (*several*), **diferentes** (*different*), **distintos** and **diversos** (*varied, diverse*) always precede a noun in the plural and agree with it in gender.

1. Insert the indefinite determiners on the right in these minidialogues. *

a) • ¡Tengo __mucha__ hambre! ¿Tienes _____ dulce?

○ Sí, mira, aquí tengo _____ caramelos. Toma.

b) • ¿Perdone, está Araceli?

○ Aquí no hay _____ persona con ese nombre. Se equivoca.

c) • Necesito _____ cosa para protegerme del sol, hay

_____ luz y con los lentes de contacto ...

○ Pero Alfonso, si tienes _____ gafas de sol, ¿por qué no has traído unas?

algún
cualquier
demasiada
mucha
ninguna
tantas
varios

2. In these statements of a difficult customer in a travel agency, fill in the blanks with the correct indefinite determiners. *

a) Quiero volar con *(another)* _____otra_____ línea aérea. Esta es muy impuntual.

b) ¿No hay *(another)* _____ hotel más céntrico?

c) Resérveme por favor *(other)* _____ excursiones, estas salen muy temprano por la mañana.

d) ¿Me puede recomendar *(other)* _____ lugares de interés? En el catálogo hay muy pocas infomaciones.

e) ¡Creo que prefiero ir a *(another)* _____ agencia de viajes!

3. Fred has started a language course in Barcelona and is writing down his first impressions in an e-mail. Fill in the blanks with the appropriate forms of **todo**. *

a) Por fin estoy en Barcelona. _____Todo el_____ ambiente me encanta.

b) _____ compañeros de la escuela son alumnos internacionales.

c) Tenemos seis horas de clase y _____ profesoras son muy simpáticas.

d) Quiero explorar _____ ciudad y conocer _____ los bares y discotecas.

e) Voy a salir _____ las noches con _____ compañeros.

f) Creo que dormiré muy poco durante _____ estancia, ¡pero puedo descansar a la vuelta!

todo el
toda la
todos los
todas las

el ambiente –
the atmosphere
dormiré –
future of dormir
la estancia – *the stay*
la vuelta – *the return (trip)*

Practice and Application

Indefinite Determiners

4. Which determiner is the right one here? You decide. **

a) • ¿Tienes (alguna)/ninguna pastilla contra el dolor?

○ Lo siento, pero no tengo algún/ningún medicamento aquí.

b) • Quería comprar algún/ningún libro para las vacaciones, pero alguna/ninguna novela de las que vi me gustó.

○ Qué raro, yo pienso que hay algunas/ningunas muy buenas...

c) • ¿Has estado alguna/ninguna vez en un restaurante senegalés?

○ No, no conozco algún/ningún restaurante africano. ¿Y tú?

d) • Perdone, ¿hay alguna/ninguna playa por aquí?

realmente –
really; actually,
in fact

○ Sí, pero para llegar no hay algún/ningún camino realmente.

5. Pilar is remembering the summer trips of her childhood. Which endings are missing in her story? **

a) Cad_a_ vez íbamos al mism___ lugar, siempre al mism___ pueblo, pero con diferent___ personas.

b) En much___ ocasiones íbamos con tod___ mis tíos y sus familias, así había vari___ primas de la mism___ edad y no había ning___ problema para pasar el tiempo.

c) La casa era pequeña pero tenía suficient___ espacio, aunque en cada habitación dormía bastant___ gente.

trepar – *to climb*

d) Cerca había algun___ playas con much___ rocas para trepar y vari___ cuevas para explorar.

e) Tod___ las niñas íbamos juntas, por eso ning___ adulto se preocupaba.

f) Algun___ veces venía algun___ abuela u otr___ amiga de mi madre, pero era más aburrido porque no traían a ning___ niño.

g) A mí me gustaba estar con mi abuela Dorotea porque algun___ noches me leía cuentos y otr___ veces me contaba sobre su vida, ¡sabía tant___ cosas!

Adjectives

¿Me opero? Tengo los labios demasiado **delgados** y los ojos muy **pequeños**, ¿no crees?

①

¡Qué va! Eres una mujer muy **guapa**, ¡tienes una cara **perfecta**!

②

With adjectives, you can describe the characteristics of persons and things.

1. Should I have an operation? My lips are too thin and my eyes are very small, don't you agree?
2. No way! You're a very pretty woman, you have a perfect face!

Agreement of Adjectives

The gender and number of adjectives is always determined by the noun they modify. That is true even when the noun and the adjective are separated by a verb like **ser**, **estar**, or **parecer**.

▶ **The Noun**, p. 10

	masculine		feminine	
Singular	**el** sombrero blanc**o**		**la** chaqueta blanc**a**	
Plural	**los** sombreros blanc**os**		**las** chaquetas blanc**as**	

The adjective agrees with the noun even when the two are separated by a verb: **Est<u>as</u> chaquetas me parecen car<u>as</u>.**

Only a few color adjectives that are derived from nouns are invariable; they include **lila**, **naranja**, **rosa**, and **violeta**. Even when **claro**, **oscuro**, or a noun (such as **vino**) give more information about the color, the color adjective remains unchanged.

- ¿Te gustan los coches **violeta** o **amarillo limón**?
- No, pero los coches **rojo vino** o **azul oscuro** son muy bonitos.

claro – *light*
oscuro – *dark*
amarillo limón – *lemon yellow*
rojo vino – *wine red*

If an adjective refers to two or more nouns, the following rules apply:

Juan lleva chaquet**a** y corbat**a** blanc**as** y sombrer**o** y zapat**os** blanc**os**.

If the nouns are identical in gender, use the corresponding masculine or feminine form in the plural.

Juan lleva corbat**a** y sombrer**o** blanc**os**.

If the nouns differ in gender, take the masculine plural form, and ensure that the noun directly preceding the adjective is not feminine, to avoid "dissonance."

Agreement of Adjectives

1. Feminine Form of Adjectives

This also applies to past participles (such as **cerrado**), when used as adjectives.

▶ **Past Participle,**
  p. 187

holgazán – *lazy, idle*
pequeñín – *teensy-weensy*
dormilón – *sleepyhead*

masculine	feminine	
guapo	guapa	Adjectives whose masculine form ends in **-o** form the feminine with **-a**.
bonito	bonita	
cerrado	cerrada	
conservador	conservadora	Adjectives that end in **-dor**, **-án**, **-ín**, and **ón** also add **-a** in the feminine form and may lose the written accent in the process.
holgazán	holgazana	
pequeñín	pequeñina	
dormilón	dormilona	
francés	francesa	Adjectives of nationality whose masculine forms end in a consonant add an **-a** in the feminine form as well.
alemán	alemana	
español	española	
andaluz	andaluza	
agradable	agradable	All other adjectives have the same form for both genders.
fácil	fácil	
optimista	optimista	
belga	belga	This also applies to adjectives of nationality that end in **-a**, **-e**, **-í**, or **-ú**.
canadiense	canadiense	
israelí	israelí	
hindú	hindú	

Note: Adjectives denoting nationality are not capitalized in Spanish!

2. Adjective Plurals

trabajador –
hard-working, industrious
cortés – *polite, courteous*

Singular	Plural	
simpático	simpáticos	If an adjective ends in an unstressed vowel, add an **–s** in the plural.
trabajadora	trabajadoras	
grande	grandes	
fácil	fáciles	If an adjective ends in a consonant, **-í**, or **-ú**, you generally add **-es**.
trabajador	trabajadores	
iraní	iraníes	
joven	jóvenes	
cortés	corteses	With **-án** and **-és**, the written accent is omitted in the plural.
catalán	catalanes	
feliz	felices	If an adjective ends in **-z**, the plural ending is **-ces**.
audaz	audaces	

audaz – *audacious, bold*

Placement of Adjectives

¿Conoces **muchas** marcas de vinos **chilenos**?

①

Sí, los vinos **tintos chilenos** son fantásticos.

②

1. Do you know many brands of Chilean wines? 2. Yes, the Chilean red wines are fantastic.

Generally, adjectives follow the noun they modify.

These precede the noun:

¡**Otra** botella! Hay que brindar, porque vamos a ganar **mucho** dinero.
– **mucho**, **poco**, **tanto**, **demasiado**, **varios** and **otro**.
Hablas con Adriana **todo el** día, aunque la ves **todos los días**.
– **todo** + definite article.
¡Qué **rica** ensalada!
– adjectives in exclamations with ¡**Qué** + adjective + noun!
¡Es una **estupenda** receta!
– adjectives to which you want to give special emphasis.

brindar – *to drink a toast*

In an exclamation with **qué**, you can also place the adjective after the noun, but then **tan** or **más** must precede it:
¡<u>Qué</u> ensalada <u>tan/más</u> rica!

Some adjectives indicate differences in meaning by means of their placement.

antiguo	*former*	un **antiguo** colega
	old (historic)	un pueblo **antiguo**
cierto	*certain*	un **cierto** tiempo
	true	una noticia **cierta**
medio	*half*	**medio** litro
	average	la temperatura **media**
mismo	*same*	el **mismo** día
	herself	la jefa **misma**
nuevo	*new (further)*	la **nueva** idea
	new (not old)	la casa **nueva**
pobre	*poor (pitiable)*	un **pobre** hombre
	poor (impoverished)	un hombre **pobre**
simple	*simple, easy*	una **simple** respuesta
	naïve, innocent	una personalidad **simple**
triste	*gloomy, dismal*	una **triste** historia
	sad	una historia **triste**
viejo	*old (of long standing)*	una **vieja** amiga
	old (elderly)	una mujer **vieja**

No indefinite article is used before **otro** and **medio**!

▶ **Indefinite Determiners**, p. 37

The adjective that logically is more closely related to the noun is mentioned first. For example: **una iglesia <u>protestante</u> barroca**.

estupendo – *fantastic, wonderful*
casero – *homemade*

If several adjectives refer to the same noun, they usually follow the noun, with the exceptions of **mucho**, **poco**, **todo**, which always precede it, and those adjectives that change their meaning by preceding the noun. For example: Tengo **muchos viejos** amigos **españoles simpáticos**.

If the speaker wishes to put special emphasis on one or more characteristics, he / she places the corresponding adjectives before the noun. The other adjectives follow the noun, as here: Esta es una **estupenda** y **fácil** receta **casera** del pastel de queso.

Shortening of Some Adjectives

¿Y este precio?
¡Aquí hay un **gran** error!

①

¿O es un **mal** chiste?

②

1. And this price? There's a big mistake here! 2. Or is it a bad joke?

▶ On **algún**, **ningún**: Indefinite Determiners, p. 38

▶ On **primer**, **tercer**: Ordinal Numbers, p. 259

Bueno, when placed after the noun and referring to persons, means *good-natured*: **Eres un <u>buen</u> amigo y una persona <u>buena</u>.**

1. *buen, mal, algún, ningún, primer, tercer*

Some adjectives lose the **-o** when they precede a masculine singular noun. If they follow the noun, they retain their ending. This is the case for the following:

Este es un **buen** ejemplo.	bueno	▶	buen
Jorge es un **mal** amigo.	malo	▶	mal
¿Hay **algún** banco por aquí?	alguno	▶	algún
No hay **ningún** banco por aquí.	ninguno	▶	ningún
Vivo en el **primer** piso.	primero	▶	primer
Vivo en el **tercer** edificio.	tercero	▶	tercer

The feminine form and the plural of these adjectives are not shortened: la primer**a** vez, los buen**os** ejemplos.

2. *gran*

● Leonardo es un **gran** artista.
○ Sí, la Mona Lisa es una **gran** obra de arte.
● Pero no es un cuadro **grande**, ¿verdad?

If **grande** in the singular precedes the noun, it is always shortened. Then it means *great*. But if it follows the noun, it is not shortened and means *big, large*.

Differences in Adjectival Constructions

Sometimes Spanish and English differ in the use of adjectives and adjectival constructions.

Use

*a **gold** ring*	un anillo **de oro**

The material used is expressed with the preposition **de** + noun.

*a **little** boy*	un niño pequeñ**ito**/un niñ**ito**

Little and *big* often are expressed with the suffixes **-ito** / **-ote**.

*to make **warm***	**calentar**
*to get **cold***	**enfriarse**
*to get **better** / **worse***	**mejorar**/**empeorar**

Some English verb + adjective constructions are expressed by a Spanish verb.

the main course	el plato **principal**
the inner courtyard	el patio **interior**

In some phrases, the order of noun and adjective is reversed.

Soy una persona **deportista** que usa siempre ropa **deportiva**.
I'm a sporty person who always wears sporty clothing.

Sporty in the sense of *athletic* has two equivalents in Spanish: For persons, use **deportista**, for things, use **deportivo**.

*an **un**important subject*	un tema **poco importante**

Some English adjectives with the prefix *un-* are translated with **poco** + adjective, if Spanish lacks an equivalent term with the prefix **in-**.

> Adjectives too can be shortened or lengthened, as in these examples: **pequeñito** *(very small)*, **grandote** *(very big)*.

Practice and Application

Adjectives

alegre
barato
corto
feo
interesante
moderno
negro
pequeño
rico
viejo

1. Find the opposites in the list on the left. *

a) blanco _____negro_____   f) caro _____

b) nuevo _____   g) aburrido _____

c) triste _____   h) bonito _____

d) grande _____   i) antiguo _____

e) pobre _____   j) largo _____

2. Conjure up a menu with six tapas from this jumble. *

fritas con tomate – aceitunas – picantes – ensalada – jamón – manchego – queso – sardinas – papas – mixta – negras – serrano

_____

_____

3. Emily describes her *au pair* family. Add endings where necessary. *

Some Spanish adjectives resemble English words but have different endings.
Examples:
conservador— *conservative*, **serio—** *serious*, and **catastrófico—** *catastrophic*.

encantador – *enchanting*
amable – *kind, nice*
cariñoso – *loving, affectionate*
bajita – *rather short*
atender – *to attend, to help*
hostil – *hostile*
inquieto – *restless*
mono – *sweet, charming, nice* (colloquial)
precioso – *lovely, beautiful*

a) La familia es encantador___ y todos son muy amabl_____. Charo, la madre, es muy cariños___a___ y alegr_____. Es una mujer rubi___ y bajita con los ojos muy azul_____. Trabaja medi_____ día y además atiende a la abuela, que vive aquí también y ya está muy mayor_____.

b) El padre es un poco más seri___. Es bastante conservador_____, pero no es hostil___. Es alt___ y delgad___ y siempre lee revistas económic___. Creo que trabaja en una empresa internacional_____ y que piensa que su trabajo es súper important_____.

c) Los niños son muy pequeñ_____ y creo que son muy inquiet_____ y activ_____. ¡Su habitación siempre está en un estado catastrófic___! Pero ellos son muy mon_____, Carlitos es moren___ y un poco gordit___ y Laurita es rubi___ como su mamá y tiene los ojos más precios_____ que he visto. ¡Seguro que voy a estar muy ocupad_____ con ellos!

4. Alberto works in a laundry and sorts the clothes by color. Write down the articles of clothing with the appropriate color. *

a) rojo: 3 blusa, 1 pantalones
b) azul marino: 2 pantalones
c) marrón: 1 chaqueta
d) blanco: 5 camisa
e) verde: 1 blusa, 1 suéter
f) naranja: 1 vestido

a) tres blusas y unos pantalones rojos, _____

_____

_____

_____

_____

5. In these minidialogues, translate the adjectives in parentheses. *

a) • ¿Qué tal tu ____nueva____ *(new)* jefa?

   ○ Bien, parece muy _____ *(hard-working)*.

b) • Niños, ¡son muy _____ *(lazy)*! ¡Siempre frente a la tele!

   ○ Pero estamos mirando un documental _____ *(scientific)*.

c) • ¿Por qué estás _____ *(sad)*, Cristóbal?

   ○ No, no; sólo estoy un poco _____ *(tired)*.

d) • Estos ejercicios son muy _____ *(easy)*.

   ○ Y además son _____ *(useful)* y _____ *(amusing)*.

new – nuevo
hard-working – trabajador
lazy - holgazán
scientific – científico
sad – triste
tired- cansado
easy – fácil
useful – útil
amusing – divertido

6. Many things are advertised in the newspaper. Match the nouns with the appropriate adjectives. *

OFREZCO

a) cámaras
b) guitarra
c) computadora
d) préstamos
e) cajas
f) antena
g) perrita

1) clásica española
2) cariñosa pastor alemán
3) rápidos y fáciles
4) portátil
5) parabólica
6) digitales
7) fuertes

el préstamo – *the loan*
la caja fuerte – *the safe, strongbox*
el perro pastor alemán – *the German shepherd dog*
portátil – *portable*
parabólico – *parabolic*

Practice and Application

Adjectives

7. Which is the correct position for the adjectives below? Draw a line through the incorrectly placed adjectives. *

a) Es la primera vez ~~primera~~ que estoy aquí.

b) Este es un buen restaurante buen.

el chiste – *the joke*
¡Pare! – *Stop!*

c) ¡Eso me parece un mal chiste mal!

d) ¡Mmmh! ¡Qué buena receta buena!

e) Pare por favor enfrente del tercer edificio tercer a la izquierda.

f) ¡No tengo ningún problema ningún!

g) ¡Esa es una gran película grande!

8. Colors convey meanings that depend on a country's culture. Fill in the blanks below. **

el abeto – *the fir (tree)*

a) El abeto es el árbol de la Navidad porque siempre es ___verde___.

b) Cuando amas a alguien le regalas rosas _____.

c) En la primavera los narcisos son _____.

el luto – *mourning*
el velo – *the veil*
la pureza – *the purity*
el varón – *the male*
el semáforo – *the traffic light(s)*
alto – *stop*
el extintor (de fuego / de incendios) – *the fire extinguisher*
la esperanza – *the hope*

d) Como señal de luto, en nuestra cultura la gente lleva ropa _____.

e) Las novias llevan un vestido y un velo _____ como símbolo de pureza.

f) Cuando nace un bebé, muchas personas les regalan a las niñas vestidos _____ y a los niños varones, suéteres _____.

g) La luz _____ de los semáforos significa "alto"; la luz _____ pide poner atención y la luz _____ nos permite seguir.

h) Los extintores de fuego siempre son _____.

i) ¿De qué color es la esperanza? Es _____, naturalmente.

Adverbs

**Afortunadamente,
hoy** vamos a llegar **muy
rápido** a la playa.

① ②

Sí, porque la carretera
no está **tan** llena.

> Adverbs modify or
> describe everything
> other than nouns
> and pronouns. For
> example, they can
> describe an action (a
> verb) or an attribute
> (an adjective).

1. Fortunately, we're going to get to the beach very quickly today.
2. Yes, because the road is not so crowded.

Spanish has both original adverbs and adverbs that are derived
from an adjective. They tell, for example, when, how, where, in what
manner, and whether something occurs. Adverbs are always invariable
and modify

– a verb,	La profesora explica **bien**.
– another adverb,	Sabe motivar **muy** bien.
– an adjective,	El curso es **muy** interesante.
– or an entire clause or sentence.	**Naturalmente** aprendo mucho.

Original Adverbs

Adverbs that are not derived from an adjective are known as original
adverbs. They have no typical form or ending, but they are easier to learn
when they are divided up into the following groups:

1. Adverbs of Time

- ¿Vamos al cine **hoy** o **mañana**?
- **Ahora** no lo sé, **luego** te digo.

Original Adverbs

Adverbs of time tell when something happens.

In some regions of LA, **recién** is used in the sense of *just* with verbs, as in **Recién ha salido.** Otherwise it is used only before past participles, as in **recién nacido** (*newborn*), **recién casado** (*newlywed*).

ahora	now	entonces	then, at that time
hoy	today	mañana	tomorrow
antes	formerly, before	después	later, then, next
ya	already	todavía	still, yet
luego	then, later	pronto	soon
siempre	always	nunca	never
temprano	early	tarde	late
ayer	yesterday	anoche	last night, yesterday evening
mientras	during	recién	just

2. Adverbs of Place

- El museo, ¿está **lejos**?
- No, no. Está **cerca**. ¿Lo ve? **Allí enfrente**, señor.

Adverbs of place describe where something happens or where it is located.

▶ Demonstrative Determiners, p. 28

aquí / acá	here	allí / allá	there
cerca	near, close	lejos	far (away)
delante	in front	adelante	forward
detrás	behind	atrás	at the back, behind
dentro	inside, indoors	fuera	outside, out
adentro	inside	afuera	outside
arriba	up	abajo	below, downstairs
encima	on top	debajo	underneath, below
junto / al lado	next to	enfrente	opposite, facing
alrededor	round, around		

3. Adverbs of Quantity and of Degree

▶ On **muy – mucho** and **tan – tanto**: see pp. 62, 64, 67

- Julia es **muy** inteligente.
- Es **demasiado** inteligente para mí; sólo habla de filosofía.

These adverbs tell to what extent an attribute is present or with what intensity an action is performed.

Don't confuse the following adverbs: **bastante** = *fairly, quite, rather; enough* **suficiente** = *enough; plenty*

mucho	a lot, very much	poco	not (very) much, little
muy	very	tan(to)	so much
algo	quite, somewhat	nada	not at all
demasiado	too (much)	bastante	fairly, quite, rather
más	more	menos	less
casi	almost	sólo	only
además	moreover	excepto	except
suficiente	enough; plenty		

4. Adverbs of Manner

- **Así** lo haces **bien**.
- ○ No sé... Pienso que lo hago **mal**.

Adverbs of manner tell how something happens or is done.

bien	*well, fine*	mal	*badly, wrong*
regular	*so-so*	fatal	*awfully, terribly*
rápido	*quickly, fast*	despacio	*slowly*
así	*like this, this / that way*	hasta	*even*

5. Adverbs of Negation, Affirmation, and Conjecture

- Pepe **ya no** va a nadar, ¿verdad?
- ○ **No**, pero yo **sí**. **Quizá** voy mañana.

With the help of these adverbs, you can affirm or deny something, or express a supposition or probability.

sí	*yes; indeed*	no	*no, not*
también	*also, too*	tampoco	*neither, not ... either*
ni	*neither*	quizá(s)	*perhaps, maybe*

Derived Adverbs Ending in *-mente*

Adverbs that are derived from an adjective are formed by attaching the ending **-mente** to the feminine form of the adjective.

▶ Feminine Forms of the Adjective, p. 46

adjective	adverb
tranquilo	tranquilamente
fácil	fácilmente
probable	probablemente

If an adjective has a written accent, it is retained in the verb as well.

De aquí se llega a la estación **fácil**, **cómoda** y **rápidamente**.

If several derived adverbs are used for an attribute and / or a sentence, then only the last one takes the ending **-mente**. The others are expressed by using the feminine form of the adjective.

bueno	**bien**	These adverbs are irregular.
malo	**mal**	

Note:
1. After **ser**, never use **bien** or **mal**!
2. When applied to persons, **estar bien / mal** means *to be well / ill.*

Adjectives as Adverbs

> Silvia, ¡ven **rápido**! ¿Ya sabes que Víctor vuelve **pronto** a casa?

①

> ¿Qué? ¡Pepa, no te oigo, habla más **alto**! ¿No puedes hablar más **claro**?

②

---

1. Silvia, come quickly! Do you already know that Victor is returning home soon?
2. What? Pepa, I can't hear you, talk louder! Can't you speak more clearly?

> The written accent differentiates the adverb **sólo** (*only*) from the adjective **solo** (*alone*).

Some adverbs have the same form as the masculine adjective, but remain invariable. They include **rápido** (*quickly, fast*), **pronto** (*soon*), **alto** (*loudly*), **claro** (*clearly, plainly*), **limpio** (*fairly [fair play]*), **sólo** (*only*), **mucho** (*a lot, very much, often*), and **poco** (*a little, not very much, rarely*).

Some of these also have an additional derived form ending in **-mente**, including **rápido / rápidamente, sólo / solamente**.

Differentiating Between Adjective and Adverb

> ▶ **Adjectives**, p. 45

In Spanish, the adjective differs fundamentally from the adverb. This distinction is important, because adjectives must agree with the nouns they modify. Adverbs, on the other hand, are invariable. Compare the following:

Adjectives:
María es una **buena** <u>cocinera</u>.
Prepara <u>recetas</u> muy **buenas**, pero **pocas** son **fáciles**.

Adverbs:
María <u>cocina</u> **bien**.

presumir – to boast

<u>Prepara</u> **bien** las recetas. <u>Presume</u> **poco** y <u>hace todo</u> **fácilmente**.

Adverbial Expressions

> Yo voy a nadar **con frecuencia**.

①

> Trato de ir a la piscina **por lo menos una vez por semana, por lo general** los jueves.

②

---

1. I go swimming frequently. 2. I try to go to the swimming pool at least once a week, usually on Thursdays.

Sometimes Spanish uses an **adverbial expression** instead of an adverb consisting of a single word. Here are some examples:

a veces	*sometimes*	a menudo	*often*
a tiempo	*on time*	a propósito	*intentionally*
cada vez más	*more and more*	con curiosidad	*curiously*
con frecuencia	*frequently*	con cuidado	*carefully,*
con gusto	*gladly*		*cautiously*
de inmediato	*immediately*	con calma	*calmly*
de memoria	*by heart, from*	de repente	*suddenly*
	memory	de verdad	*really*
de vez en cuando	*from time to time*	de cerca / lejos	*closely / from*
en general	*in general*		*a distance*
en absoluto	*not at all*	en seguida	*at once*
los sábados	*every Saturday*	en realidad	*in fact,*
no ... hasta	*not until*		*actually*
por cierto	*by the way*	muchas veces	*often*
por la mañana	*in the morning*	nunca más	*never again*
por suerte	*luckily*	por fin	*at last*
por supuesto	*of course*	por lo general	*in general*
sobre todo	*above all*	por desgracia	*unfortunately*
rara vez	*rarely*	tal vez	*perhaps, maybe*

These days, **en seguida** usually is written as one word: **enseguida**.

Placement of the Adverb

Usually adverbs and adverbial expressions are placed

– before the adjective,	Lulú es **muy** impuntual.
– at the front of the sentence,	**Frecuentemente** calcula
– before the adverb,	**muy** mal su tiempo.
– and after the verb.	Viene **tarde con frecuencia**.

When several adverbs modify a verb, there are various possibilities:

Ahora solamente queremos hacer un viaje corto.
Ahora queremos hacer **solamente** un viaje corto.
Ahora queremos hacer un viaje corto **solamente**.
Solamente queremos hacer un viaje corto **ahora**.
Solamente queremos hacer **ahora** un viaje corto.

Compare **Es una frase bien dicha.** *(It is a well formulated sentence.)* and **Has dicho bien la frase.** *(You have formulated the sentence well.)*

You just have to make sure not to interrupt a verb unit, including the following:

auxiliary verb + participle
ir a, **tener que** + infinitive
modal verb (such as **saber**, **poder**, **querer**, **deber**) + infinitive.

English and Spanish: Adverb or Verb Construction?

▶ **Present Perfect**,
p. 119

▶ **Modal Verbs**,
p. 104

▶ **Special Verbs**,
p. 202

Sometimes Spanish uses a verb construction where English uses an adverb—and sometimes not. Compare and contrast the following:

Me gusta ir en tren. *I like taking the train.*	**me gusta** + infinitive
Está lloviendo aquí. *It's raining here.*	**estar** + present participle
El tren **acaba de llegar**. *The train has **just** arrived.*	**acabar de** + infinitive
Sigue lloviendo. *It's **still** raining.*	**seguir** + present participle *still*
Prefiero esperar en la estación. *I prefer to wait in the station.*	**preferir** + infinitive
¡Por fin! Ha **dejado de llover**. *At last it's stopped raining!*	**dejar de** + infinitive
No **tardo en** llegar a casa. *I'm not coming home **late**.*	no **tardar en** + infinitive *not ... late*
¡Oh! ¡**Vuelve a** empezar a llover! *Oh! It's starting to rain **again**!*	**volver a** + infinitive *again*
¡Aquí no **suele llover** tanto! *It **usually** doesn't rain so much here!*	**soler** + infinitive *usually*

1. Fill in the blanks in these minidialogues with the appropriate adjectives or adverbs. *

a) • ¿Y qué tal Enrique? ¿Es un __buen__ trabajador?

 ○ Sí, trabaja _____ y es muy agradable además.

b) • Mira, María habla _____ con sus amiguitas.

 ○ Me encanta. Siempre parece muy _____ esa niña.

c) • A Jorge le encantan las motos _____.

 ○ Sí, pero es peligroso. Me parece que conduce demasiado _____.

d) • ¿Cómo es Casares, es un lugar _____?

 ○ Exactamente. Ahí podemos pasar _____ las vacaciones.

e) • Ese director es muy _____.

 ○ Sí, sus películas describen _____ a los jóvenes y eso me

 pone de _____ humor.

> Remember to shorten the adjectives **bueno** and **malo** before masculine singular nouns!

a) bueno

b) alegre

c) rápido

d) tranquilo

e) malo

2. Write the numbers 1–8 in the parentheses below, arranging the sentences to create a dialogue that you might hear in an office. *

( ) ¿Está aquí el Sr. Salgado?

( ) ○ Está **bien**, **muchas** gracias. Es usted muy **amable**.

( ) Pero **por supuesto** puede dejarme los papeles.

(1) ○ **Buenos** días, Srta. Perea.

( ) **Sólo** traigo estos papeles para él.

( ) Está en una reunión **urgente**.

( ) • No, **lamentablemente** no está, pero vuelve **pronto**.

( ) Yo se los doy **luego personalmente**.

3. Now mark the adjectives above in one color and the adverbs or adverbial expressions in another color. *

Adverbs

4. **Bien** or **bueno**? That is the question in these classified ads. *

la capacitación –
the training

el directivo –
management

el taller – *the garage, workshop*

a) Puesto de directivo. Buen_____ salario, cursos de capacitación.

b) Piso amueblado, _____ comunicado, _____ precio.

c) Aprenda a hablar _____ inglés. _____ profesores, _____ preparados.

d) Taller mecánico, _____ servicios, todas las marcas.

5. Soccer is a weekly passion for people in Latin America and Spain. In the article below, the adverbs or adverbial expressions are missing. We have given you the first letter of each word to help you find the right answers. **

a menudo – a tiempo – al final – bien – caóticamente – Casi – con mucho gusto – de repente – En realidad – Hoy – lamentablemente – mucho – Por fin – por la tarde – Por lo general – Por supuesto – Pronto – rápido – sobre todo – también – todavía – totalmente

el polideportivo – *the sports center*

la pasión – *the passion*

el equipo del barrio – *the neighborhood team*

el partido – *the match, game*

tardar – *to take a long time*

colocarse – *to position oneself*

el primer tiempo – *the first half*

marcar un gol – *to score a goal*

el ganador – *the winner*

la asfixia – *shortness of breath*

el fútbol dominical – *Sunday soccer*

a) Los domingos __por la tarde__, el aparcamiento del polideportivo del barrio se llena t_____. **b)** P_____ será el momento del deporte y, a_____, de la pasión. **c)** H_____ hay que vestirse r_____, t_____ quieren tomar una foto del equipo del barrio antes del partido. **d)** Se nota que no lo han hecho m_____, tardan en discutir hasta que se colocan b_____. **e)** P_____ se deciden, porque hay que empezar a_____. **f)** P_____ estos deportistas del pueblo juegan un poco c_____, pero c_____. **g)** C_____ al terminar el primer tiempo, d_____ alguien marca un gol. **h)** P_____, las caras de los ganadores están rojas de felicidad, pero t_____ de asfixia. **i)** En el segundo tiempo l_____ caen dos goles más; a_____ el equipo del barrio ha perdido. **j)** Da igual. E_____ el fútbol dominical es, s_____, el momento de los amigos y de pasar un rato divertido.

6. This portion of a novel describes the first meeting between Rafa, who works in a bookstore, and Soledad. Choose the appropriate adverbs or adverbial expressions. **

a) (Ya)/Todavía era un poco antes/tarde , pero Rafa estaba poniendo después/todavía unos libros en la estantería cuando, de pronto/ pronto se acercó el dueño de la librería con una chica.

la estantería – *the shelves, bookcase*
el dueño – *the owner*

b) • Mira, Rafa, Soledad trabajará aquí contigo desde mañana/ por la mañana .

○ Y a ella le dijo enseguida/tal vez:

c) • Mira, Soledad, este es Rafa, de quien ya te he hablado luego/ antes . Lleva mucho/algo trabajando en el negocio y lo conoce perfectamente/en absoluto .

el negocio – *the business*
la duda – *the question; the doubt*

d) Hasta/Así se conocieron. Los primeros días, Soledad tenía dudas constantemente/enseguida y nunca/siempre Rafa le ayudaba muy generalmente/amablemente .

e) Por lo general/Poco a poco empezó una amistad que muy pronto/ después se convirtió en otra cosa ...

la amistad – *the friendship*
convertirse – *to turn into*

7. From the business news, you gather the following information. Fill in the blanks with adjectives or derived adverbs. **

a) El año pasado se crearon 170 mil empleos ____temporales____ .

b) Muchas empresas pueden dar nuevos puestos, pero sólo _____ .

c) Las mujeres participan _____ en el mundo laboral.

d) Un 44,7 % de la población _____ son mujeres.

e) En las empresas hay reuniones _____ para analizar la situación.

f) Los jefes se reúnen _____ con los representantes del sindicato.

g) Las pequeñas empresas ganan más si las asesoran _____ .

h) También es mejor para las empresas familiares tener la dirección en manos _____ y no necesariamente en las de algún pariente.

a–b temporal

c–d activo

e–f regular

g–h profesional

temporal – *temporary*
regular – *regular*
el sindicato – *the union*
asesorar – *to advise*
el/la pariente – *the relative*

Comparisons, Degree Words, and Intensifiers

Adjectives, adverbs, nouns, and verbs can all be compared, and equal and unequal degrees can be expressed.

Aunque Simón es **mucho mayor** que Lola, se entienden **tan** bien **como** otras parejas **más jóvenes**.

①

Sí, porque él es tan joven de corazón **como** ella. Es la persona **más simpática** que conozco.

②

1. Although Simón is much older than Lola, they get along as well as other younger couples.
2. Yes, because he is just as young at heart as she is. He is simply the nicest person I know.

Comparison of Nouns

1. Comparative Degree: Inequality and Equality

Yo tengo	**más**	dinero	/	**menos**	suerte	**que** tú.
Voy a	**más**	lugares	/	**menos**	fiestas	

Inequality is expressed with **más** (*more*)/ **menos** (*less*) + noun + **que** (*more / less … than*).

Yo tengo	**tanto**	dinero	/	**tanta**	suerte	**como** tú.
Voy a	**tantos**	lugares	/	**tantas**	fiestas	

Equality is expressed with **tanto** / **-a** / **-os** / **-as** + noun + **como** (*as much / many … as*).

Tanto is used as a determiner in comparing nouns, and it agrees with them in number and gender.

▶ **Indefinite Determiners**, p. 37

2. Superlative Degree: The Highest Degree

María es	**la que**	tiene	**más**	dinero	**de**	todos
Mis primos son	**los que**	tienen	**menos**	problemas.		

The highest degree of comparison is expressed by means of a relative clause.

3. Comparison with *más / menos / tanto* as Pronouns

- ¿Suerte? Yo tengo **tanta como** cualquiera.
- ¡Qué va!, yo creo que tienes **más que** muchos.

If the context is clear, you can make a comparison even without a noun.

¡Qué va! – *No way!, Come on!*

Comparison with Numbers and Quantities

Esto cuesta **más de** cien euros, pero es **menos del** doble.

With numbers and quantities, Spanish uses **más / menos de**; elsewhere, *more / less than* is **más / menos que**.

- ¿Tienes dinero? **No** necesito **más de** diez euros.
- Lo siento, **no** tengo **más que** cinco.

In negated sentences, **más / menos de** + number / quantity means *at most / at least*, while **no más que** can be translated as *only*.

▶ más / menos del doble, **Definite Article**, p. 21

Comparison of Adjectives and Adverbs

1. Comparative Degree: Inequality and Equality

Adjectives must continue to agree with the noun in number and gender, and adverbs are always invariable. Otherwise, comparison of adjectives and adverbs is quite similar.

Pepe es **más** fuerte pero **menos** simpático **que** tú.
Estas chicas son **más** guapas **que** las otras.
Lola hace deporte **más** frecuentemente **que** Clara.
Clara corre **menos** rápido **que** Lola.

Inequality is expressed with **más / menos** + adjective / adverb + **que** (*more / less ... than*).

Eres **más** simpática y corres **más** rápido **de lo que** yo creía.

In the comparative degree, **de** is used instead of **que** if the adjective or adverb is followed by a relative clause with **lo que** + verb.

In comparing adjectives and adverbs, you specify whether a characteristic or the manner of an action is superior, inferior, or equal.

Adjectives whose meaning contains a comparison, such as **anterior** *(previous)*, **posterior** *(later)*, etc., do not form the comparative degree.

tan guapo como –
as good-looking as

Pepe es	**tan**	simpático	**como**	Luis.
Estas chicas son		guapas		las otras.
Pepe hace deporte	**tan**	frecuentemente	**como**	Luis.
Los chicos corren		rápido		Lola.

Equality is expressed with **tan** + adjective / adverb + **como**.

Elena es guapa **como** su madre y corre rápido **como** el rayo.

Tan is not part of comparisons of equality that are to be expected or have a logical connection.

Without the comparison word **como**, **tan** means *so*: ¡Hablas <u>tan</u> bien inglés! ¡Soy <u>tan</u> feliz! *(You speak English so well! I'm so happy!)*

2. Superlative Degree: The Highest Degree

Lola es	**la**	**más**	simpática	(**del** grupo).
Estos chicos son	**los**	**menos**	guapos	(**de la** clase).

With adjectives, the highest degree of comparison is expressed not by a single form, but by simply placing the definite article before the comparative form. The group in which the comparison is made is preceded by **de**.

Compare with English: *the **prettiest** thing (in the world).*

▶ **Main Clauses and Dependent Clauses**, p. 232

Nicolás es	**el** (chico)	**que** corre **más** rápido **de** todos.
Mis hijas son	**las** (chicas)	**que** corren **menos** rápido.

The superlative of the adverb is formed by using a relative clause.

3. Superlative Degree with *-ísimo*

Tengo que hablar **clarísimo** contigo.
①

Este asunto es **urgentísimo**. ¡Necesitamos resultados **urgentísimamente**!
②

---

1. I have to speak extremely plainly with you.
2. This business is most urgent. We need results with the utmost urgency!

▶ **Adverbs with Adjectival Form**, p. 56

The ending **-ísimo** expresses a very high degree of a quality or of comparison. This form is called the "absolute superlative." It is often used for adjectives, and the principle of agreement with the noun in number and gender continues to apply.

In adverbs with adjectival form, such as **rápido**, **pronto**, **alto**, **claro**, etc., and with **mucho** and **tanto**, this ending is more common than in adverbs ending in **-mente**. In the latter, the ending **-ísimamente** replaces the final vowel of the adjective. These adverbs too, as always, are invariable.

guap**o**	▸ guap**ísimo**	If the word ends in a vowel or an unstressed diphthong, replace it with **-ísimo**.
inteligent**e**	▸ inteligent**ísimo**	
limp**io**	▸ limp**ísimo**	
jove**n**	▸ joven**císimo**	If an adjective ends in **-n** or **-r**, use **-císimo**.
trabajado**r**	▸ trabajador**císimo**	
fácil	▸ facil**ísimo**	For other adjectives, simply add **-ísimo**.
difícil	▸ dificil**ísimo**	
amable	▸ amabil**ísimo**	A few adjectives have an irregular form ending in **-ísimo**.
antiguo	▸ antiqu**ísimo**	
mucho	▸ much**ísimo**	Some indefinite determiners or indefinite pronouns also have a form ending in **-ísimo**.
poco	▸ poqu**ísimo**	
tanto	▸ tant**ísimo**	

Some forms undergo an orthographic change in order to retain their pronunciation:

blan**c**o	▸ blan**qu**ísimo	**c** ▸ **qu** before **i**
lar**g**o	▸ lar**gu**ísimo	**g** ▸ **gu** before **i**
feli**z**	▸ feli**c**ísimo	**z** ▸ **c** before **i**

> **!**
> These have no form ending in **-ísimo**:
> 1. Adjectives with great intensity of meaning, such as **fantástico**, **enorme**, etc.
> 2. The adverb with the adjectival form **sólo**.
> 3. **Malísimo** is often replaced with **pésimo**.

> ▸ **Indefinite Determiners** and **Indefinite Pronouns**, pp. 37, 93

4. Irregular Forms of Comparison in Adjectives

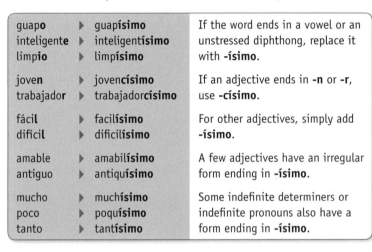

① Los dibujos de Gloria son **buenos**, pero los de Lourdes son **mejores**.

② Es que Lourdes es **mayor** que Gloria, aunque Gloria es **más grande**.

---

1. *Gloria's drawings are good, but Lourdes's are better.*
2. *It's because Lourdes is older than Gloria, although Gloria is taller.*

Some adjectives have an irregular form of comparison that is identical for both genders. In the plural, **-es** is added:

> **!**
> **más** and **menos** have no plural!

Comparison of Adjectives and Adverbs

> Note:
> The adverb of degree **más** is omitted with these irregular forms.

	irregular	regular
mucho	**más**	—
poco	**menos**	—
bueno	**mejor**	más bueno
malo	**peor**	más malo
grande	**mayor**	más grande
pequeño	**menor**	más pequeño/-a
alto	**superior**	más alto
bajo	**inferior**	más bajo

> Human body height usually is described with the adjectives **alto / bajo**.

Mi hijo **menor** es muy **alto**, pero mi hija **mayor** es bastante **baja**.
My youngest son is very tall, but my oldest daughter is quite short.

Some adjectives have both irregular and regular comparative forms, and they differ in meaning: In reference to persons, the irregular forms **mayor / menor** mean *older / younger*, and **mejor / peor** mean *better / worse*. The regular forms, however, refer to height or size: **más grande / pequeño** mean *taller / shorter*, and **más bueno / malo**, *nicer / meaner*. **Superior** and **inferior** refer to superiority and inferiority, usually with respect to the quality of a thing.

> Gabriela es **la** (hija) **menor** (**de** la familia).
>
> ▌The superlative is formed by adding the definite article and possibly **de** to indicate the frame of reference.

Fixed phrases:

una persona mayor	*an older person*
mayor / menor de edad	*of full (legal) age / underage, minor*
lo mejor / lo peor	*the best / the worst*

5. Irregular Forms of Comparison in Adverbs

Antes practicaba **mucho**, pero ahora entreno **más**.

Eso está **bien**. ¡Cada vez juegas **mejor** al tenis!

②

---

1. In the past I used to practice a lot, but now I train more.
2. That's fine. You're playing tennis better and better!

Adverbs have only a few irregular forms of comparison:

mucho / muy	▶	**más**
poco	▶	**menos**
bien	▶	**mejor**
mal	▶	**peor**

> **Más bien** is a fixed phrase and means *rather.*

Even in comparisons of equality, **mucho** is an exception. The construction used is **tanto como**, and it directly follows the verb, as here:

En casa mi marido hace **tanto como** yo.

Intensification with *muy* and *mucho*

¡Tienes **muchos** libros!

①

Sí, es que me gusta mucho leer. ¡Es **muy** interesante!

②

> **Tan** *(so)* and **tanto** *(so much)* are used like **muy** and **mucho**.

1. You have a lot of books! 2. Yes, because I very much like to read. It's very interesting!

Very and *a lot, very much* can be expressed in Spanish with the words **muy** and **mucho**. When do you use which?

> **Muy** never precedes **mucho**! Instead, use the superlative **muchísimo**.

Use

Las clases son **muy** interesantes. El profesor sabe explicar **muy** bien.

■ **Muy** *(very, very much)* comes before an adjective or an adverb.

Tengo **muchas** clases y **muchos** cursos.
Tengo **muchas** más clases que tú.

■ **Mucho** *(much / many / a lot)* used as a noun determiner is variable, even if **más / menos** comes between it and the noun.

- Estudio **mucho**.
- ○ Eres **mucho** más aplicado que yo. Pero no eres **mucho** mejor.
- ¿Te gusta estudiar?   ○ Sí, **mucho**.

■ **Mucho** *(very much, a lot)* is invariable when it functions as an adverb, that is, after verbs, before adjectives or adverbs in a comparison, or when standing alone, for example, as an answer.

> ▶ **Indefinite Determiners**, p. 37

Practice and Application

Comparisons, Degree Words, and Intensifiers

1. Complete these comparisons. **

lamentablemente –
regrettably
la cosecha – *the harvest*

a) En las empresas todavía hay más jefes __que__ jefas y las mujeres
   lamentablemente no ganan tant____ dinero _____ los hombres.

b) Este verano ha habido menos lluvia _____ normalmente y por eso
   no tendremos tant____ cosechas _____ siempre.

c) Tú piensas que no tengo tant____ dificultades _____ tú, ¡pero yo
   sé que tú no tienes tant_____ problemas _____ yo!

2. At a fashion show, two women in the audience are exchanging
comments. Fill in the endings and the missing terms of comparison. *

a) ● Me parece que la túnica gris es más bonit_a_ _que_ la azul, ¿y a ti?

b) ○ También. Y el vestido rojo me parece menos anticuad___ _____
   el marrón.

c) ● ¡Mira ese modelo deportivo! Hoy en día la ropa de materiales

el algodón –
the cotton
la lana – *the wool*

   sintéticos es tan fresc___ _____ la de algodón.

d) Claro, pero encuentro los suéteres de algodón más cómod___ _____
   los de lana.

e) ¡Uff! ¿Qué es esto? ¡Este abrigo es tan horribl___ _____ el otro!

3. Below are a few tips on ways to reinforce your knowledge of a
language. Select the appropriate words. *

a) La (mejor)/ mayor manera de aprender un idioma es viajar al país.

hoy en día – *nowadays*
aun – *even*
los subtítulos –
the subtitles
alquilado/-a – *rented*

b) Hoy en día los viajes son mucho menor / menos caros de / que antes.

c) También hay cursos que ofrecen más / mayor servicios que / como
   otros por el mismo precio.

d) Pero aun si se queda en casa, mirar en idioma original y con
   subtítulos películas alquiladas en DVD es más / tan fácil de / que
   nunca.

4. Which sentences go together? Make the correct matches. *

a) Pedro siempre llega a tiempo.

b) ¡Esta torta tiene mucha azúcar!

c) ¿Ya conoces a Minerva?

d) ¡Mira el precio de estos relojes!

e) ¡Qué difícil situación!

f) ¿Quieres más cava?

1) ¡Hombre, sí! Está durísima.

2) ¡Qué barbaridad! Están carísimos.

3) Sí, es puntualísimo.

4) Gracias, está riquísimo.

5) Está dulcísima, ¿verdad?

6) ¿La secretaria? Es amabilísima.

a tiempo – *on time*
¡Qué barbaridad! –
*What nonsense! /
How awful!*
el reloj – *the clock*
el cava – *the champagne,
sparkling wine*

5. Sibling rivalries probably exist everywhere! Fill in the blanks with appropriate comparative forms. *

a) • Yo tengo muchos juguetes.   ○ Yo tengo más.

b) • ¡Mi dinosaurio es muy malo!   ○ El mío es _____ .

c) • ¡La abuela te da pocos regalos!   ○ ¡A ti te da _____ !

d) • Este CD es muy bueno.   ○ Este es _____ .

e) • Mi cuarto es muy grande.   ○ El mío es _____ .

f) • Tú siempre serás el menor.   ○ Y tú, _____ .

serás – *you* (fam.)
will be, fut. of, **ser**

6. Did you know that Argentina has more psychologists than any other country? In the text below, there are 10 words too many. Mark out the superfluous ones! ***

a) En Buenos Aires hay más q̶u̶e̶ de 15.000 psicólogos. **b)** Se dice que los argentinos siempre han estado tan mucho cómodos con los tratamientos como igual con su tradición de beber mate. **c)** Además, hoy los precios por consulta son mucho más baratos que de antes. **d)** Después de la crisis económica, las terapias son muy más necesarias que nunca. **e)** Gracias a ellas, aun la gente que ha perdido mucho de dinero o su puesto de trabajo no está tan deprimida que como antes de los tratamientos. **f)** Si en casa hay mucha que tensión, también el rendimiento escolar de los chicos es más peor. **g)** Hoy la economía por suerte está mejor que de hace unos años y sin duda, el trabajo de los psicólogos ha ayudado para lograr una actitud positiva.

el mate – *yerba mate
(tea)*
el tratamiento –
the treatment
la consulta – *the
doctor's appointment*
la tensión –
the stress, tension
el rendimiento –
the performance
lograr – *to achieve*
la actitud – *the attitude*

Comparisons, Degree Words, and Intensifiers

7. We heard these statements in a travel agency. Translate the comparisons. **

a) Esta fotocopiadora trabaja *(more silently than)* <u>más silenciosamente</u> <u>que</u> la del segundo piso.

la campaña –
the campaign
eficiente – *efficient*

b) Durante la campaña podemos hablar *(less calmly than)* _____ _____ nunca, porque hay mucho estrés en el ambiente.

c) ¡Eres muy eficiente! Algunos de mis colegas no reaccionan *(as quickly as)* _____ tú cuando les pido ayuda.

d) Los productos anunciados en los periódicos se van a vender *(better than)* _____ los del portal web porque llegan a más público.

el público –
the public

e) Los clientes no compran *(as much as)* _____ antes. Hoy tenemos que trabajar *(harder)* _____.

8. In the faculty room, two colleagues are talking about their pupils. Compare the pupil named first with the one mentioned second. *

a) Enrique canta muy bien. Pepe canta bien.
   <u>Enrique canta mejor.</u>

b) Sonia hace deporte. Sara hace muchísimo deporte.
   _____

c) Juliana hace deberes. Carlitos no hace deberes casi nunca.
   _____

d) Pedro ha hecho dos presentaciones. María ha hecho tres.
   _____

e) La letra de Eduardo es horrible. La letra de Gonzalo es fea.

la letra – *here: the handwriting*

   _____

Comparisons, Degree Words, and Intensifiers

9. In the home of the extended Méndez family, a lot of comparisons are made! Replace the underlined words with the **-ísimo** form. Write it in the space provided. **

a) ¡Qué horror, Paco! ¡Siempre pones la radio **muy alto**! ___altísimo___

b) Queda **muy claro** que no puedes ir a la fiesta, Antonia. _____

c) ¡Jimena, la abuela llama **muy raramente**; por lo menos salúdala! _____

d) Mamá, ¿cuándo compras los nuevos libros? Los necesito **muy pronto**. _____

e) ¿Por qué protestas **tanto**, Miguelito? ¡Si sólo te voy a bañar! _____

10. Two former school friends meet in the street. Insert the correct comparative form in the blanks. *

a) • ¡Cristina! ¿Qué tal? ¿Qué sabes de los compañeros del Instituto?

   ○ Pues, José Luis es director de banco. Trabaja ___mucho___, incluso los fines de semana hace _____ horas extra.

b) • Claro. Ser _____ importante significa también tener _____ trabajo. ¿Y Rocío?

c) ○ Rocío, que es ama de casa, organiza _____ actividades para sus hijos. También participa _____ en grupos de padres.

d) • ¡Qué bien! ¿Sabes algo de Joaquín?

   ○ Sí, Joaquín está _____ enfermo, ha sufrido _____ operaciones.

e) • ¡Pobre! Ha tenido una vida _____ dura. ¡Qué pena! ¿Y de Laura?

f) ○ Laura trabaja en una agencia de viajes _____ grande. Habla _____ lenguas y eso, claro, es _____ práctico para su trabajo.

   • ¿Y tú? ¿Trabajas cerca de aquí?

g) ○ Sí, _____ cerca. Soy vendedora en la tienda "Maxx". Como es _____ céntrica, veo a _____ gente. _____ veces veo también a los ex-compañeros y hablo _____ con ellos de los viejos tiempos ...

incluso – even

myeho

mucha

muchos

muchas

muy

sufrir – to suffer

Pronouns

① ¿Con **quién** vas al cine?

Yo creo que con mis amigas, porque a **ellas les** gusta el mismo actor que a **mí**. ②

Bueno, ¡que **te** diviertas! ③

> Pronouns take the place of nouns. They are used, for example, to avoid repetition. They must not be confused with determiners, which accompany the subject.

> ▶ **Determiners**, p. 20

1. With whom are you going to the movies? 2. With my girl friends, I think, because they like the same actor I do. 3. Okay, have fun!

Personal Pronouns

Personal pronouns take the place of persons, groups of persons, or things. They can play various roles in the structure of a sentence.

1. Subject Pronouns

① Silvia, ¿eres **tú**?

Sí, ¡soy **yo**! ②

> Subject pronouns are much less common in Spanish than in English.

1. Silvia, is it you? 2. Yes, it's I!

Subject pronouns answer the question *Who?* In Spanish, they are used only for persons, never for things. That is, the pronoun *es* cannot function as the subject.

> 1. In LA, **vosotros/ vosotras** is replaced by **ustedes: Niños, ¿qué quieren ustedes?**
> 2. In Argentina, Paraguay, and Uruguay, **vos** is used instead of **tú**, and with its own verb form besides: **¿Me escuchás vos?**

Forms

	Singular		Plural	
1st Person	**yo**	*I*	**nosotros / nosotras**	*we*
2nd Person	**tú**	*you*	**vosotros / vosotras**	*you*
3rd Person	**él**	*he*	**ellos / ellas**	*they*
	ella	*she*		
	usted	*you*	**ustedes**	*you*

Use

- ¿Dónde estás?
- ¿Dónde está la oficina?
- ○ Estoy en la oficina.
- ○ Está en el centro.

Since the subject is usually recognizable by the verb endings, Spanish only rarely uses subject pronouns for persons and never uses them for things.

- Señora López, ¿qué profesión tiene **usted**?
- ○ Soy enfermera. Y **ustedes**, ¿qué profesión tienen?

The formal or polite form of the pronoun *you* is **usted** in the singular. The corresponding verb is in the third person singular. If several people are being addressed, use **ustedes** with the third person plural form of the verb.

- ¿Quién viaja a Bilbao, el señor Díaz o **usted**?
- ○ **Él** viaja mañana, **yo** no.
- Ah. ¿Y quién es el señor Díaz?
- ○ Soy **yo.**

Subject pronouns are needed to differentiate various persons or to emphasize them. Placing the subject pronoun after the verb serves to emphasize it; otherwise, in declarative statements the subject pronouns usually precede the verb.

Reportera: Chicas, **¿vosotras** pagáis cuando salís con amigos?
Elena: **Nosotras** sí, por supuesto.
Julián: Así son las chicas modernas: **ellas** pagan lo suyo.
Pero si **nosotros** las invitamos, pagamos **nosotros.**

For *we*, *you* (fam. pl.), and *they*, a feminine form is used when one is speaking exclusively about women: **nosotras, vosotras, ellas.** However, if the group includes at least one man, the pronouns **nosotros, vosotros,** and **ellos** are used.

The written accent is used to distinguish the pronouns **tú** and **él** from the possessive determiner **tu** and the definite article **el.**

1. **Usted** and **ustedes** are used relatively often as indications of politeness.
2. On signs, etc., you often find the abbreviations **Ud./Vd.** for **usted**, and **Uds./Vds.** for **ustedes.**

Ello

Estamos en una crisis. **Ello** significa que tenemos que gastar menos.

Rarely, a form of the subject pronoun in the neuter is also used: **Ello** is translated as *this* and refers to a set of facts, a situation, or even an entire sentence.

Instead of **ello**, the demonstrative pronoun **esto** is also used.

Personal Pronouns

2. Stressed Pronouns After Prepositions

When a pronoun is the object of a preposition, Spanish uses a different set of pronouns, known as prepositional pronouns.

> ¿Por qué te ríes de mí?

①

> ¡Qué va! Me río contigo.

②

1. Why are you laughing at me? 2. Come on! I'm laughing with you.

Forms

The written accent differentiates the prepositional pronoun **mí** from the possessive determiner **mi**: **mi** casa.

Person	Singular			Plural	
1.	a / para	**mí**	**conmigo**	a / para / con	**nosotros / nosotras**
2.	a / para	**ti**	**contigo**	a / para / con	**vosotros / vosotras**
3.	a / para / con	**él**		a / para / con	**ellos**
	a / para / con	**ella**		a / para / con	**ellas**
	a / para / con	**usted**		a / para / con	**ustedes**

Use

After **entre, según, incluso**, and **menos**, the subject forms are used for persons.

Por **mí** podemos salir. ¿Los problemas? ¡Ya no pienses en **ellos**!

After a preposition (**a, de, en, para, por, sin**, etc.), the prepositional pronouns are identical with the subject pronouns except in the first and second persons singular, which have the forms **mí** (with a written accent) and **ti** (with no written accent).

● ¿Vienes **conmigo** a comer?
○ No, lo siento. Ya le he dicho a Pepe que voy **con él** más tarde.

The preposition **con** combines with the special pronouns for the first and second persons singular to form **conmigo** and **contigo**.

● Estos chocolates son **para** ti y **para** mí, ¿vale?

Normally the preposition is repeated before each pronoun.

▸ **Duplication of Accusative and Dative Pronouns**, p. 78

● Ana quería ver esta película, pero no ha venido.
○ **A mí** esto **me** llama mucho la atención. **A ella le** interesaba mucho.
● ¿Llamamos a su madre para preguntar?
○ ¿Por qué no **la** llamamos **a ella** directamente al celular?

Direct and indirect objects frequently are reinforced or more precisely defined by using **a** + stressed pronoun.

3. Direct Object Pronouns

> ¿Me quieres?
> ¿Aceptas este anillo?

> ¡Sniff! Claro
> que lo acepto…,
> ¡y claro que te quiero!

① ②

> Direct object
> pronouns are also
> called accusative
> pronouns. They
> answer the questions
> *Whom?* or *What?*

1. *Do you love me? Will you accept this ring?*
2. *Sniff! Of course I'll accept it … and of course I love you!*

Forms

Direct object pronouns take the place of a direct object, that is, a noun
that receives the action of a transitive verb. Usually they immediately
precede the verb. **Me**, **te**, **nos**, and **os** substitute for persons, while **lo**
and **la** replace things and persons.

> In the third person
> plural and in the
> polite forms of
> the accusative
> pronoun, Spanish has
> both masculine and
> feminine forms.

	Singular		Plural	
1st Person	**me**	*me*	**nos**	*us*
2nd Person	**te**	*you*	**os**	*you*
3rd Person	**lo (le)**	*him, it*	**los (les)**	*them*
	la	*her, it*	**las**	*them* (fem. only)
	lo / la	*you*	**los / las**	*you*

Use

Lo

- ¿Y el libro?   ○ No **lo** encuentro. Tengo que buscar**lo**.
- ¿**Lo** tiene Pepe?   ○ No sé, no **lo** he visto. Voy a llamar**lo**.

Lo takes the place of a male person or thing in the accusative.

- Estamos en una crisis.   ○ Ya **lo** sé, pero no es tan grave.

Lo substitutes for a set of facts, a situation, or an entire sentence.

> In the countries
> where **vos** is used,
> the corresponding
> object pronouns are
> the same as for **tú**:
> **¡A vos no te veo!**

- ¿Es usted <u>el jefe</u>? ○ Yo no **lo** soy, **lo** es el señor Pardo.
- Esto es <u>fácil</u>, ¿verdad? ○ Claro que **lo** es.

Lo takes the place of a noun or an adjective after **ser** or **estar**.

La, los, las

- ¿Y <u>la llave</u>? ○ No **la** encuentro. Tengo que buscar**la**.
- ¿La tiene Lina? ○ Quizá, pero no **la** he visto. Voy a llamar**la**.

La substitutes for a female person or feminine thing in the accusative.

- ¿Y <u>los libros</u>? ¿Y dónde están <u>la lapicera y el lápiz</u>?
- ○ No **los** encuentro. Tengo que buscar**los**.
- ¿Los tienen <u>los chicos</u>?
- ○ Quizá, pero no **los** he visto. Voy a llamar**los**.

Los stands for several persons or things in the accusative, of which at least one is masculine.

- ¿Dónde están <u>las llaves</u>?
- ○ No **las** encuentro. Tengo que buscar**las**.
- Quizá las tienen <u>las chicas</u>.
- ○ Puede ser, pero no **las** he visto. Tengo que llamar**las**.

Las stands for several female persons or feminine things in the accusative.

- ¿Hay <u>una oficina de turismo</u>? ○ Sí **la** hay, está muy cerca.
- ¿Hay <u>hoteles buenos</u> aquí? ○ Sí **los** hay, y muy buenos.

Lo, **la**, **los** or **las** replace a noun with **hay**.

Le / Les as accusative objects:

- ¿Conoces <u>a Juan</u>? ○ Sí, **le** conozco.
- ¿Conoces <u>a los señores Pérez</u>? ○ Sí, **les** conozco.

In some regions of Spain, **lo** and **los** are replaced by **le** and **les** as direct object pronouns, but only for male persons.

Les invitamos cordialmente a la celebración de aniversario.

In other regions too, this usage is widespread in written formal language.

4. Indirect Object Pronouns

> Estos quesos **me** gustan. ¿**Me** compras uno?

①

> No, ¡ya no **te** compro nada más hoy! ¡Hemos gastado demasiado!

②

1. I like these cheeses. Will you buy me one?
2. No, I'm not buying you anything else today! We've spent too much!

Forms

	Singular		**Plural**	
1st Person	**me**	*to/for me*	**nos**	*to/for us*
2nd Person	**te**	*to/for you*	**os**	*to/for you*
3rd Person	**le**	*to/for him, her*	**les**	*to/for them*
	le	*to/for you*	**les**	*to/for you*

Only in the third person do the indirect object pronouns differ from the direct object pronouns.

In the singular, no distinction based on gender is made.

Use

Si Paquito **nos** trae buenas notas, **le** vamos a comprar una bicicleta.

The indirect object pronouns substitute for indirect objects.

• A Daniel este pintor **le** interesa mucho. ¿**Os** gustan sus cuadros?
○ Pues no sé... Algunos **me** parecen muy raros.

They are used with verbs that express affect, such as **gustar**, **encantar**, **interesar**, **molestar**, **parecer**, **doler**, and **faltar**.

▶ **Verbs with the Dative**, p. 215

• **Me** es imposible comprar la casa, el dinero no me alcanza.
○ No importa, cariño, ¡este piso **nos** basta!

They also are used in some impersonal expressions: **ser (im)posible / necesario / suficiente, alcanzar, bastar,** etc.

cariño – *darling*

• ¿**Le** puedo preguntar algo?
○ Claro, Doña María, **la** escucho.

It is not always possible to predict which case follows a verb.

In Spanish, these are used with the dative: **preguntar** (*to ask*), **mentir** (*to lie to*); these are used with the accusative: **seguir** (*to follow*), **felicitar** (*to congratulate*), and **escuchar** (*to listen to*).

5. Duplication of Accusative and Dative Pronouns

A Juan no **lo** veo.
¿Ha salido?

①

A mí no **me** ha
dicho nada.

②

Eso no **lo** entiendo.
¡**Al jefe** no **le** va a
gustar nada!

③

---

1. I don't see Juan. Has he left? 2. He didn't say anything to me.
3. I don't understand that. The boss isn't going to like it at all!

Accusative and dative objects can be "duplicated" in Spanish, with the same sentence containing both an object (a noun or stressed pronoun) and an unstressed pronoun. In such cases, the unstressed pronoun always precedes the verb.

Use

el triciclo – *the tricycle*

Le vamos a comprar una bicicleta **al niño / a Paquito**.
A las niñas les vamos a regalar triciclos, porque son más pequeñitas.

▪ Generally the third person singular or plural indirect object pronoun is duplicated, even if the noun or proper name is mentioned in the same sentence. The dative object can be placed at the beginning or at the end of a sentence.

In English, you can achieve the same effect by raising your voice for emphasis.

El libro lo he leído en un solo día.
A Susana y a Gloria no **las** voy a invitar.

▪ If you want to reinforce or emphasize the direct object, place it at the beginning of the sentence and duplicate it with an object pronoun.

Note: **a** + stressed pronoun can never be used without duplication! For example, **me** and **la** are required in <u>A mí</u> esto no <u>me</u> parece bien and <u>A ella</u> no <u>la</u> veo.

A mí esto no **me** parece bien. ¿Qué **os** parece **a vosotros**?
A ella no **la** voy a consultar.

▪ Object pronouns are duplicated with **a** + stressed pronoun when you want to emphasize a contrast or your opinion.

Mi hija siempre **lo** cuenta **todo**.

▪ If **todo** is used as a direct object, it usually appears along with **lo**.

6. Reflexive Pronouns

Yo siempre **me** ducho con agua fría. ①

Así **me** pongo fuerte contra la gripe. ②

Reflexive pronouns are a special type of object pronouns.

▶ **Reflexive Verbs,** p. 216

1. I always shower with cold water. 2. That way I harden myself against the flu.

Forms:

(yo)	**me**	llamo
(tú)	**te**	llamas
(él, ella, usted)	**se**	llama
(nosotros / -as)	**nos**	llamamos
(vosotros / -as)	**os**	llamáis
(ellos, ellas, ustedes)	**se**	llaman

With the exceptions of the third person singular and plural, **se**, the reflexive pronouns are identical to the object pronouns.

Use

- ¿**Os** divertís?　　○ ¡Sí! ¡Nunca **nos** hemos divertido tanto!

The form of the pronoun is determined by the subject of the reflexive verb.

Hoy los chicos se escuchan a **sí** mismos y no se ponen de acuerdo entre **sí**!

After a preposition, use the form **sí**. **Entre sí** means *between / among themselves.*

Mis amigos siempre llevan el móvil **consigo**.

The preposition **con** merges with the pronoun to form **consigo**.

No siempre es fácil, pero **uno se** acostumbra.

In impersonal statements, use **uno / -a se**.

el (teléfono) celular – *the cell(ular) phone*

acostumbrarse a algo – *to get used / become accustomed to something*

79

7. Placement of Object and Reflexive Pronouns

A pronoun in a sentence

> ¿A <u>Juana</u>? No **le** he enviado un e-mail, **la** veo en el colegio.
> ¡No **la** llames! Hoy **se** queda para la clase de deporte.

Generally, object and reflexive pronouns precede the conjugated verb. With compound tenses, therefore, they precede the auxiliary verb **haber**.

When pronouns are attached, the verb often acquires a written accent, to preserve the original stress: **búscalo**, **escribiéndola**.

> ¿La <u>carta</u>? Felipe está escribiéndo**la**. / Felipe **la** está escribiendo.
> ¿La <u>leche</u>? Voy a comprar**la**. / **La** voy a comprar.

With the present participle as well as infinitive constructions, such as modal verb + infinitive, **ir a** + infinitive, or **tener que**, the pronouns can be attached to the participle or to the infinitive. However, they also can precede the conjugated verb.

> Busca <u>a Pedro</u>.   ¡Búsca**lo**!

With the affirmative imperative, the pronouns must be attached.

Several Pronouns in One Sentence

Reflexive or dative pronouns always <u>precede</u> the accusative!

> • Las manos, ¿**te las** has lavado ya?
> ○ **Me las** estoy lavando. / Estoy lavándo**melas**.

The reflexive pronoun precedes the direct object pronoun: **me lo**, **te la**, **se los**, **se las**, etc.

> • Los zapatos azules, ¿**me los** dejas?
> ○ No, lo siento, hoy no **te los** puedo dejar / hoy no puedo dejár**telos**.

The indirect object pronoun precedes the direct object pronoun: **me lo**, **te la**, **nos las**, **os los**, etc.

	lo ▶ se lo	
	la ▶ se la	
le / les +	los ▶ se los	
	las ▶ se las	

> • ¿Quién **le** ha regalado las rosas a Carmen?
> ○ **Se las** ha enviado un amigo, y el CD **se lo** he regalado yo.

If the indirect object pronouns (dative) **le** and **les** precede the direct object pronouns (accusative) **lo**, **la**, **los**, **las**, then **le** and **les** are replaced with **se**.

1. Translate the following. *

a) Where is the car? Is it out of order?

¿Dónde está el coche? ¿No funciona?

b) Mr. Mata, you live far away, don't you? I do too.

_____

c) Jesús and María have been working for a month. She works in a bank and he in a supermarket.

_____

desde hace un mes – for a month

d) • This painting is very interesting. ○ Yes, it is very modern.

_____

e) • The new colleague?
   ○ I'm not she, that's she. I'm only visiting.

_____

estar de visita – to be visiting

2. Verónica is talking with a friend at a party. Fill in the gaps in their conversation with the missing pronouns. *

a) • Estos son mis hijos. He tenido que venir con __ellos____ porque hoy no ha venido Nuria, mi "canguro".

"la canguro" – in Spain, "babysitter"

b) ○ ¿Cuánto tiempo lleva Nuria con _____ de "canguro", Verónica?

c) • Tres meses. Pero entre _____ y _____ a veces es un poco informal.

d) ○ Pues yo tengo una "canguro" excelente. Mira, es esa chica que está detrás de _____. Si quieres, puedes hablar con _____.

3. Which sentences go together? Make the correct matches. *

a) ¡Huy, qué manos tan sucias, hijito!

b) Esta falda me queda muy bien.

c) La sopa está demasiado sosa.

d) A mí no me gusta el nuevo colega.

e) La situación está muy difícil.

f) ¡Qué rica está la tarta de fresas!

1) ¿Me das un poco para probarla?

2) No lo creo, yo soy optimista.

3) Ahora me las lavo, mamá.

4) ¿Se la paso a la caja?

5) ¡Hombre, pero si no lo conoces!

6) ¿Le falta sal? ¿Te la paso?

Practice and Application

4. Translate the words in parentheses, using preposition + pronoun. **

a) • A Juan lo veo, pero María, ¿dónde está? *(Her)* _A ella_ no la veo.

○ Hombre, *(you)* _____ te lo digo, ¡yo sé que no va a venir!

b) • Martha, ven *(with me)* _____. Tenemos que solucionar

el conflicto *(between you and me)* _____, sin

nadie más.

○ No, Pablo, yo ya no quiero hablar más *(with you)* _____.

¡*(For me)* _____, ya todo está dicho!

c) • ... Y de pronto vi a un hombre *(behind us)* _____, comisario.

○ No, Loreto, estaba *(ahead of you)*_____, pero como estaba

oscuro...

5. Translate the words in **bold**, using the corresponding direct object pronouns in this interview. *

a) • Yanbal, **tus admiradoras** te aman, ¿no es así?

○ Pues sí, afortunadamente, y yo _las_ amo a ellas también.

b) • Dime, ¿compones tú mismo **todas tus canciones**?

○ No, algunas _____ compone mi hermano, que también es del grupo.

c) • ¿Conoces desde hace mucho tiempo a todos los miembros?

○ Bueno, **a mi hermano** _____ he conocido de toda la vida, jeje, y a

Chalo y a David _____ conozco desde la escuela.

d) • ¿Cuándo van a hacer **la próxima gira** para presentar **los nuevos temas**?

la gira – *the tour*

○ _____ vamos a hacer el mes que viene. _____ queremos hacer por

todo el país, así todos ustedes _____ van a conocer muy pronto.

6. Write down the last answer in Exercise 5, using a different placement of the pronouns.

_____

_____

_____

7. Duplicate the objects in **bold** by using unstressed pronouns. *

a) No, señor Cano. No _les_ he podido enviar los paquetes **a los clientes**.

b) **A mí** _____ encanta la pizza. ¿Vamos a un restaurante italiano?

c) ¿Por qué no _____ das de comer **al gato**? Tiene hambre.

d) Y ahora, ¿por qué esa cara, hijito? **¿A ti** qué _____ duele?

e) El profesor _____ va a explicar la gramática **a vosotros**, no a mí.

f) Yo ya no _____ presto dinero **a mis compañeros**, porque nunca pagan.

g) **A nosotras** Leticia no _____ ha presentado a su novio, no lo conocemos.

h) Nacho está muy nervioso. Es que _____ va a pedir un aumento **a su jefe**.

el aumento – *the raise (in pay)*

i) ¿Quién _____ ha traído este pastel **a los niños**? ¡Mmmh! Está muy rico.

8. Insert reflexive pronouns in the blanks below. *

a) Mario siempre _se_ prueba toda la ropa de la tienda, ¡es horrible!

b) Uff, ¡_____ aburrimos mucho en vacaciones! No hay nada que hacer.

c) La verdad es que _____ preocupo demasiado y por eso no _____ decido.

d) ¿Por qué _____ ponéis así? Tenemos que relajar_____ un poco, ¿no?

e) • ¿Ya _____ despides? ¿No _____ quedas un poco más de tiempo?

f) ○ No, _____ tengo que ir porque a esta hora _____ va el último tranvía.

Have you noticed what roles **se** can play? 1. a reflexive pronoun, 2. an indirect object pronoun when immediately followed by **lo, la, los,** or **las,** and 3. the impersonal **se** structure, referring to people in general. For example, **¿Cómo se escribe?**

9. Translate and "duplicate" the underlined objects. **

a) I don't see <u>Laura</u> anymore.

_____.

el tranvía – *the trolley car*

b) We pay <u>these bills</u> immediately.

_____.

c) <u>You</u> are the only ones I love so much!

_____.

Practice and Application

10. Fill in the blanks with the missing pronouns. *

Note the following
sequences:
me / te / se +
lo / la / los / las.

a) • ¿Mamá, me compras un helado?

○ Sí, claro que __te__ __lo__ compro, Juanito.

b) • ¿Nos da esas revistas por favor, señor?

○ Sí, ahora _____ _____ doy, señores.

c) • ¿Me prestas dinero, María?

○ No, no _____ _____ puedo prestar porque no tengo.

d) • Camarero, ¡otras dos cervezas, por favor!

○ Sí, señores, enseguida _____ _____ traigo.

e) • ¿Nos recomienda usted este restaurante?

○ Sí, _____ _____ recomiendo, señoritas.

f) • ¿Nos das los libros, Pepe?

○ Claro, chicos, ahora _____ _____ doy.

11. Replace the underlined words in these newspaper headlines with
pronouns. **

In newspaper head-
lines, there often is
no duplication of
dative objects, in
order to save space
and be concise.

La empresa CF vende <u>aparatos médicos</u> a bajo costo <u>a países pobres</u>.

▶ ¿A cuánto __se__ __los__ vende?

La Seguridad Social anuncia <u>más ayudas</u> <u>a las familias</u>.

▶ ¡Siempre _____ _____ anuncia!

El gobierno no <u>nos</u> mandará <u>más tropas</u>.

▶ ¿Seguro no _____ _____ mandará?

Los ciudadanos piden <u>una explicación</u> <u>al Ministro</u>.

▶ ¡Hombre, claro que _____ _____ piden!

Los médicos recetan <u>demasiadas medicinas</u> <u>a sus pacientes</u>.

▶ ¿Por qué _____ _____ recetan?

12. Use the words on the right to fill in the blanks below. Pay close attention to the placement of the pronouns. **

a) • ¿De dónde has sacado ese vestido tan sexy?

○ _Me lo he comprado_____ en la playa.

comprado ~~he to~~ me

b) • ¿Le han gustado las blusas a María?

○ No sé, _____ ahora mismo.

está las probando se

c) • ¡Qué bonito bolígrafo! Es muy original.

○ Si lo quieres, _____.

regalar lo puedo te

d) • ¿Dónde está Carolina? ¿Se ha ido con Ramón?

○ Sí, justamente _____ al cine.

ha con ido él se

e) • Señorita, ¿ya está lista la carta para firmarla?

○ Ya casi, señor López. En un minuto _____
a su oficina.

a voy la se llevar

13. In which of the sentences in the previous exercise is there another possible sequence for the pronouns? Rewrite the sentences, and note their letters in the parentheses. **

___) _____

___) _____

___) _____

14. In this brochure on Argentina, find the correct pronouns. **

a) Argentina (te)/se invita a conocer el país y a sus habitantes. ¿Has pensado alguna vez en los argentinos y en las diferencias culturales?

Keep in mind: Subject pronouns are used only for persons!
Lo / la are not subject pronouns!

b) Es muy interesante pensar en las/ellas para entender los/ellos mejor.

c) Todos sabemos que —/los comen mucha carne y también que lo/la exportan a otros países.

d) Quizá usted conoce la tradición del mate pero, ¿sabía usted que —/lo toman en un ritual de amigos que proviene de los gauchos?

e) Quizá por esas tradiciones se/— tienen otras prioridades que nos/nosotros : para les/ellos lo más importante es vivir la vida.

Personal Pronouns

f) La capital del país es Buenos Aires. La / — tiene 12 millones de habitantes. Sus habitantes te / se llaman "porteños".

g) Buenos Aires es una ciudad enorme. ¡En ella / nos hay mucho tráfico!

h) El clima en Buenos Aires es agradable, pero en otras regiones de Argentina, lo / — es muy diferente.

i) Argentina es un país muy variado y grande. A ti / tu , ¿ te / les gustaría visitar se / lo también?

15. Enrique, the hero of our novel, is wondering how he can better cope with the separation from his beloved, Luisa. Add the missing pronouns and a written accent wherever necessary. ***

a) Enrique puso la foto que Luisa __le__ había dado delante de _____ en su escritorio y _____ miró con amor.

b) "Ahora siempre estarás con_____," _____ dijo.

c) Luego _____ _____ repitió a _____ mismo:

d) "Sí, ahora _____ siempre estará con_____, pero _____ pregunto si también tiene mi foto con_____ todo el tiempo."

escanear – *to scan*

e) Entonces decidió escanear una foto de los dos y mandar_____ anexa en el siguiente emilio.

el emilio – *colloquial: the e-mail*

f) Así Luisa podría convertir_____ en protector de pantalla, y Enrique estaría con _____ todo el tiempo.

el protector de pantalla – *the screen protector*

g) "¡Qué buena idea", _____ felicitó Enrique a _____ mismo.

The Demonstrative Pronouns

¿Qué coche te gusta
más, **este** o **ese**?

①

A mí me encanta **aquel**
rojo convertible.

②

1. Which car do you like more, this one or that one? 2. I adore that red convertible.

Most forms of the demonstrative pronouns and demonstrative determiners are identical. They agree in number and gender with the noun they replace.

▶ **Demonstrative Determiners**, p. 28

Forms

	masculine	feminine	neuter	adverb
Singular	este	esta	esto	(de aquí)
	ese	esa	eso	(de ahí)
	aquel	aquella	aquello	(de allí)
Plural	estos	estas		(de aquí)
	esos	esas		(de ahí)
	aquellos	aquellas		(de allí)

Previously, the masculine and feminine forms had a written accent to differentiate them from the demonstrative determiners. Nowadays the accent is no longer required. Only the singular neuter forms never have a written accent.

Use

Quería queso de **este**, aceitunas de **esas** y cacahuetes de **aquellos**.

The spatial, temporal, or psychological distance between the speaker and a designated thing or person is expressed with a corresponding demonstrative pronoun.

De mis hijas Beatriz y Ana María, **esta** se parece a su padre, y **aquella** se parece a mí.

If you indicate two previously mentioned nouns, **aquel** refers to the first one (*former*), while **este** refers to the second (*latter*).

• ¿Qué es **eso**?
○ **Esto** es una máquina para hacer helado.

Esto, **eso**, and **aquello** always refer to facts or to things that have yet to be defined.

1. **Esto**, **eso**, and **aquello** are never placed with a noun!
2. Common turns of phrase with **eso** are: **Eso es** (*that's true / good idea*), **eso sí** (*that's right / that's for sure*), **por eso** (*therefore*).

el cacahuete – *the peanut*

The Possessive Pronouns

> Possessive pronouns take the place of nouns. They indicate possession or belonging.

▶ **Possessive Determiners**, p. 30

¿Y este loro?
Es igual al **mío**. El **mío** ya
dice algunas palabras.

Pues el **mío** es
más listo que el **tuyo**,
no sólo habla, ¡además
canta!

---

1. *And this parrot? It's just like mine. Mine already says a few words.*
2. *Well, mine is smarter than yours, it not only speaks, it sings as well!*

The forms of the possessive pronouns correspond to those of the stressed possessive determiners. They agree in number and gender with the noun they replace.

Forms

> As in the case of the possessive determiner, the gender of the owner or possessor is not expressed.

possession / possessor	Singular masculine	feminine	Plural masculine	feminine
yo	(el) **mío**	(la) **mía**	(los) **míos**	(las) **mías**
tú	(el) **tuyo**	(la) **tuya**	(los) **tuyos**	(las) **tuyas**
él ella usted	(el) **suyo**	(la) **suya**	(los) **suyos**	(las) **suyas**
nosotros nosotras	(el) **nuestro**	(la) **nuestra**	(los) **nuestros**	(las) **nuestras**
vosotros vosotras	(el) **vuestro**	(la) **vuestra**	(los) **vuestros**	(las) **vuestras**
ellos ellas ustedes	(el) **suyo**	(la) **suya**	(los) **suyos**	(las) **suyas**

Use

- ¿De quién es este libro, es **tuyo**?   ○ Sí, es **mío**.
- No he escuchado bien. ¿De quién es?   ○ ¡**Mío**!

With **ser** or alone, possessive pronouns indicate the possessor of a thing or show belonging.

- Mi coche no tiene aire acondicionado. ¿Vamos en **el tuyo**?

Otherwise, the possessive pronoun always is accompanied by the definite article.

The Interrogative or Exclamatory Pronouns

¿A **quién** buscamos?
Hay mucha gente.
①

Sí, ¡**cuánta**!
No se ve nada.
②

> In contrast to the interrogative and exclamatory determiners, the pronouns are used without a noun.

> ▶ **Interrogative and Exclamatory Determiners**, p. 32

1. Whom are we looking for? There are a lot of people. 2. Yes, what a lot! You can't see anything.

Forms

	thing	person	selection	quantity
Singular masc.		**quién**	**cuál**	**cuánto**
fem.	**qué**			**cuánta**
Plural masc.		**quiénes**	**cuáles**	**cuántos**
fem.				**cuántas**

Interrogative and exclamatory pronouns always have a written accent.

> **Qué** never stands for persons.

Use

- ¿**Qué** haces? ¿**Qué** lees? ¿En **qué** piensas?
- ¡**Qué** te has creído! ¿Eres la policía para preguntar tanto?

▌ **Qué** *(what)* is invariable and stands exclusively for things or facts.

- ¿Para **qué** necesitas esto?
- ¿De **qué** me hablas? ¿Por **qué** preguntas?

▌ With prepositions, the translation varies:
para qué *(what for, for what)*, **por qué** *(why)*, **de qué** *(about what)*.

> The answer to **por qué** is **porque** (one word, with no written accent).

- ¿**Quién** es, a **quién** estás llamando, con **quién** hablas?
- Pero, ¡con **quién** me he casado! Siempre quieres saberlo todo.

▌ **Quién/-es** stands for persons who are not known or not determined. If you know in advance that you are asking about several persons, use **quiénes**.

> Since **quién / -es** substitutes for persons, the direct object must be preceded by the preposition **a**.

> ▶ **The Noun as Part of a Sentence**, p. 16

The preposition **a** also precedes **cuál / -es** as the direct object when it substitutes for persons: **¿A cuál de tus hermanos quieres más?**

- ¿**Cuál** te gusta más, esta o aquella?
- Me da igual. ¿Tú **cuál** de las dos prefieres?

Cuál / -es *(which)* is used only as an interrogative pronoun. It asks about a person or a thing and serves to make a selection from a group. If the group is not clear, it is expressed by **de** + noun, number, or pronoun.

¿**Cuál** es la capital de Bolivia?
¿**Cuál** es su apellido materno? ¿**Cuál** es su número de teléfono?

Cuál / -es is used to ask about something that you take for granted, for example, that every country has a capital and a currency, or that every person has a given name and surname, an address, and a telephone number.

- ¿**Quién** ha ido contigo al cine?
- Un amigo.
- ¿**Cuál**? / ¿**Qué** amigo?

- *Who went with you to the movies?*
- *A friend.*
- *Which one? What friend?*

If the question of identity has already been answered, you can continue your questioning by using either the pronoun **cuál** or the determiner **qué** + noun.

dejar pobre / s –
to make poor

- ¿**Cuánto** necesita Mario al mes? ¿Dos mil euros?
- Sí, es terrible, nos va a dejar pobres. ¡**Cuánto** gasta este chico!

Cuánto / -a / -os / -as *(how much / many)* agrees in number and gender with the noun and asks about number or quantity. As an exclamatory pronoun, it expresses a great many things (*how, how much*).

In some fixed phrases, the translation varies.

¿**Cuánto** dura / tarda la película?	*How long is the film?*
¿**Cuánto** llevas aquí?	*How long have you been here?*
¿**Cuánto** mide?	*How tall are you?*
¿**Cuánto** pesa?	*What do you weigh?*
¿**Cuánto** cuesta?	*How much does it cost?*
¿**Cuánto** es (en total)?	*How much is it (all together)?*
¿**A cuánto** están los tomates?	*How much do the tomatoes cost?*

Demonstrative, Possessive, Interrogative, and Exclamatory Pronouns

1. Who made each of the statements below, the saleswoman in the boutique (la vendedora = V) or the customer (la cliente = C)? *

a) ¿Por qué no se prueba este? Es la última moda.　　(V)

b) Quería ver ese rojo, el de la izquierda.　　( )

c) Aquel no lo tengo en otra talla, lo siento.　　( )

d) Mire usted, esos de ahí están rebajados.　　( )

e) Aquella no la tiene en azul, ¿verdad?　　( )

f) No, con esto que traigo realmente no combina.　　( )

g) ¡Esta me encanta! Me la llevo.　　( )

2. In a bar. Fill in the endings of the demonstrative pronouns. *

el bar –
the bar, pub, snack bar

a) • Hola, Paco. Me das por favor unas sardinas, de es_as__ con tomate.

b) ○ Yo quiero queso. Es____ manchego de ahí tiene muy buena pinta.

tener buena pinta –
to look tasty or attractive

c) • Y nos das un vaso de vino tinto, de aque____ del otro día, ¿sabes?

d) □ De es___ ya no me queda. Pero tengo est___, también muy bueno.

e) • Vale, probaremos de es___.

f) □ Aquí está todo. Est_____ es para ti... Y est___ para la señorita.

3. Complete these minidialogues in an airplane by using the appropriate possessive pronouns. *

a) • ¿De quién es este bolso? ¿Es ___suyo___, señor?

○ No, el _____ está debajo de mi asiento.

b) • Estas tazas son _____, ¿verdad, niños? ¿Quieren más chocolate?

○ ¡Sí, sí! Esas tazas son _____. La blanca es la _____.

c) • Miriam, ¿esa revista es _____? ¿Me la dejas un momento?

○ No es _____. Las _____ son estas, si quieres leerlas...

d) • Imposible dormir contigo aquí en mi asiento, hijo. ¡Vete al _____!

○ Es que el _____ está muy atrás y ahí se mueve más el avión, mami.

el asiento – *the seat*
atrás – *at the back*

mía　　suyo

mía
mías

mío　　mío

vuestras

nuestras

tuyo　　tuya

Practice and Application

4. Saint George's Day, La Diada de Sant Jordi, is also a day for giving books in Catalonia. Many authors, such as Imma Monsó, autograph their books and chat with their readers. Find the correct pronouns below. **

lo mío – *my thing*

a) – Me encanta (mi)/mío trabajo, – dice, – y también mis/míos lectores. **b)** Ese día nos dicen sus/suyas opiniones sobre nuestras/nos novelas y sus/suyos personajes, y nos piden las nuestras/nos sobre muchos temas: **c)** "Los padres de José son como los mis/míos . Dime, ¿los tus/tuyos son así también?" **d)** "Yo soy divorciada y la relación con mi/mío marido es terrible. ¿Cómo Charo puede vivir con el suo/suyo en tu/tuya novela?" **e)** "Es usted muy feminista. ¿Cuándo vosotras las mujeres aceptaréis vos/vuestras tareas?" y más cosas así... **f)** El día es muy intenso, pero al final me alegro de volver a lo más/mío .

5. Write the correct interrogative pronouns in the blanks. *

cambiar – *to change*
el titular – *here: the requester*

a) Perdone, ¿ __cuál__ es la caja para cambiar cheques de viaje?

b) • Esta es, señor. ¿ _____ quiere cambiar?

   ○ 500 pesos.

c) • ¿ _____ es el titular, usted?

d) ○ Sí. ¿Por _____?

   • Es que necesito su documento de identidad.

6. Here you have six very different situations. Which word is missing: **qué** or **cuál**? *

a) ¿ __Qué__ me pongo, falda o pantalones?

b) Mi amor, ¿ _____ tienes, _____ te pasa?

c) ¿ _____ es la moneda de Costa Rica?

d) Tengo queso manchego y suizo. ¿ _____ prefieren?

e) ¿ _____ hacemos? ¿Vamos al parque o al gimnasio?

f) ¿ _____ es su correo electrónico?

The Indefinite Pronouns

¿**Algo** más?

No, creo
que es **todo**.

¿No te parece
suficiente?

① ② ③

> Indefinite pronouns
> refer to no particular
> persons or things.

1. Anything else? 2. No, I think that's all. 3. Don't you think it's enough?

Most of the indefinite pronouns correspond to the indefinite determiners, but are used without a noun.

> Only the indefinite
> pronouns **algo**,
> **alguien**, **nada**, and
> **nadie** do not exist
> as determiners.

Indefinite Pronouns Referring to Number or Quantity

▶ **Indefinite
Determiners**, p. 37

1. *mucho, poco, bastante, demasiado, suficiente*

Singular		Plural	
masculine	feminine	masculine	feminine
mucho	**mucha**	**muchos**	**muchas**
poco	**poca**	**pocos**	**pocas**
bastante	**bastante**	**bastantes**	**bastantes**
demasiado	**demasiada**	**demasiados**	**demasiadas**
suficiente	**suficiente**	**suficientes**	**suficientes**

Use

- ¿Hay **suficiente** en la nevera?
- A ver... Quesos hay **bastantes**. Pero postres hay **pocos** y helados no hay **demasiados** tampoco.

Mucho, **poco**, and **demasiado** agree with the noun in number and gender. **Bastante** and **suficiente** have only one form in the singular, and to form the plural they add an **-s**.

Indefinite Pronouns

2. *alguien – nadie*, *algo – nada*, *alguno – ninguno*

> If a "negative" indefinite pronoun follows a verb, **no** or another term of negation (such as **tampoco**) must precede it.

¿Ya nadie quiere **nada**?

①

Bueno, yo sí. Dame **alguna** de esas manzanas que están en la mesa.

②

1. Nothing else?
2. Okay, I do. Give me one of those apples that are on the table.

		thing	person	thing / person	
				masculine	feminine
Singular	+	algo	alguien	alguno	alguna
	–	nada	nadie	ninguno	ninguna
Plural	+			algunos	algunas

Use

- Te pasa **algo**, ¿verdad?   ○ ¡Qué va! No me pasa **nada**.

Algo (*something*) and **nada** (*nothing*) substitute for things.

- ¿Has visto a **alguien**?   ○ No, no he visto a **nadie**.

Alguien (*somebody; anybody*) and **nadie** (*nobody; anyone*) substitute for persons.

- Aquí están las fotos. ¿Nos sirve **alguna** para la presentación?
○ ¡Uff! Creo que no nos sirve **ninguna**.

Alguno / -a / -os / -as refer to things or persons. They agree in number and gender with the noun they replace. **Alguno** means *someone*, while the plural is usually translated as *some* (*people*). **Ninguno** is almost always used in the singular and means *nobody, no one*.

- ¿Puede venir **alguno de** ustedes?
○ Lo siento, pero en este momento no puede ir **ninguno del** grupo.

Alguno or **ninguno de** + pronoun / article + noun means *one* or *none of*.

> There are only a very few phrases in which **ningunos / -as** occurs in the plural, such as **No tengo ningunas ganas.** (*I absolutely don't want to.*)

3. *uno / -a*

Uno tiene que tener cuidado. **Una** también, por supuesto.
Uno or **una**: *always remember your sex.*

Uno / -a as a pronoun means *one* in an impersonal sense.

Unos van, **otros** vienen.

The plural **unos / -as** means *some*.

Unos / -as often is used to contrast with **otros** (*others*).

4. *todo / -a / -os / -as*

Vivo en Barcelona porque hay de **todo**. ¡Es que quiero **todo** o nada!

The pronoun **todo** in the masculine singular means *everything, all*.

- ¿Vamos **todos** al cine?
- ¿Te doy un trozo de esta pizza?

○ Sí, pero antes quiero comer.
○ **La** quiero **toda**, ¡tengo hambre!

Otherwise, **todo / -a / -os / -as** agrees in number and gender with the noun it replaces, and it means *everything, all* in the singular and *all* in the plural. Together with the first or second person plural of the verbs, it can be rendered as *all of us, we all* or *all of you, you all*.

Fixed phrases:

sobre todo	*above all*
después de todo	*after all*
del todo	*completely, to the full*
así y todo	*even so*
de todo un poco	*some of everything*

If **todo / -a / -os / -as** is the direct object, generally it is duplicated, with the accusative pronoun **lo / la / los / las** preceding the verb.

▶ **Duplication of Personal Pronouns**, p. 78

5. *tanto / -a / -os / -as*

¿Por qué has comprado **tanto**? Si aquí ya no vivimos **tantos**, ¿no?

The pronoun **tanto** means *so much / many* and agrees in number and gender with the noun it replaces.

Other Indefinite Pronouns

1. *otro/-a/-os/-as, demás, cada uno/-a*

- Si todavía quedaba vino en la botella, ¿por qué has abierto **otra**?
○ Porque ahora mismo vienen Laura y las **otras** para brindar contigo.

Otro/-a/-os/-as agrees in number and gender with the noun. It means *other, another, another one*.

- Anda, ¡sirve copas para **las demás**! **Lo demás** no importa ahora.

Demás is invariable and always is accompanied by the definite article. It means *the rest*.

Aquí **cada uno** de nosotros ayuda en la cocina.

Cada uno/-a means *each one, every one*. The group can be indicated by using the preposition **de**.

Spanish never uses the indefinite article before **otro**!

Fixed phrases with **uno** and **otro**:

unos y otros	*all the parties, everybody concerned*
uno u otro	*either one*
uno al otro	*each other*

2. *cualquiera, varios*

- No podemos invitar a **cualquiera**.

Cualquiera almost always is singular and means *whatever, any one, anybody*.

Hoy vinieron todas las primas y **varias** me preguntaron por ti.

Varios/-as *(several)* is always plural and agrees in gender with the noun it replaces.

If preceded by the indefinite article, it has a derogatory meaning: **Es un cualquiera.** *(He's a nobody.)* The plural form **cualesquiera** is very rare.

3. *mismo/-a/-os/-as*

Siempre es **lo mismo** contigo, tus excusas siempre son **las mismas**.

Lo mismo means *the same thing*. Otherwise, **mismo / -a / -os / -as** always appears with the definite article and agrees in number and gender with the noun. It is rendered as *the same*.

Relative Pronouns

El hotel **que te recomiendo** está muy cerca de la playa.
①

Las playas **a las que** puedes ir desde allí están muy limpias.
②

---

1. *The hotel that I recommend to you is very near the beach.*
2. *The beaches to which you can go from there are very clean.*

Relative clauses are usually introduced by relative pronouns. But the relative determiner **cuyo** and a few relative adverbs can assume this function. For the sake of simplicity, we list all of them here.

> Relative pronouns introduce a dependent clause and usually have an antecedent in the main clause.

1. Relative Pronouns

Relative pronouns take the place of a noun. If they substitute for a person as the direct object, they are preceded by the preposition **a**.

▶ **Main Clauses and Dependent Clauses**, p. 232

Forms

	thing	person	thing / person masculine	feminine	fact(s) neuter
Singular	**que**	**quien**	**el que** **el cual**	**la que** **la cual**	**lo que** **lo cual**
Plural	**que**	**quienes**	**los que** **los cuales**	**las que** **las cuales**	

> In contrast to interrogative pronouns, relative pronouns have no written accent.

▶ **Interrogative Pronouns**, p. 89

Relative Pronouns

Before a relative clause, use a comma only if the clause gives additional information and does not serve the purpose of identification: **El pisco, que es de Perú, es popular en toda América.**

Quien appears in many sayings and bits of folk wisdom: **Quien busca, encuentra.** (*He who seeks, finds.*)

Use

Este es el chico **que** sabe cocinar. La sopa **que** hace es estupenda, pero la receta con **que** la prepara es un secreto.

Que is invariable and can refer to persons as the subject and to things as the subject or direct object. With things, it often follows the prepositions **a**, **con**, **de**, and **en** as well.

Luz no es la única a **quien** he consultado. **Quienes** saben más son María y Raúl; ahora son ellos en **quienes** confío para solucionar esto.

Quien seems more formal than **que**. **Quien** refers to one person, **quienes** to several persons. After longer prepositions, preference is given to **el que**, **la que**, **los que**, and **las que**.

La hermana de Pablo es la única a **la que** quiero y con **la que** deseo casarme. Con ella quiero ir al lugar **del que** te he hablado tanto ...

El que, **la que**, **los que**, and **las que** agree in number and gender with the antecedent. They are used in place of **que** or **quien**, especially when additional antecedents would be a possibility, or after prepositions.

Este es el cliente **del cual** le he hablado. Estuvimos juntos en aquella conferencia en León después de **la cual** me invitó a visitar su fábrica.

El cual, **la cual** ... are used in place of **el que**, **la que** ..., especially in formal contexts or after longer prepositions.

- Los visitantes no han llegado, **lo que / lo cual** nos preocupa.
- Tranquila. He oído en la radio que hubo un accidente, por **lo que / por lo cual** podría haber un atasco en las carreteras.

As the subject, **lo que** and **lo cual** are translated as *what*, but after prepositions the translation varies. They replace contents or statements in a preceding clause.

- **Lo que** te voy a decir es muy importante.
- **Todo lo que** dices es importante para mí.

For contents and statements that refer to a subsequent clause, Spanish uses **(todo) lo que** exclusively.

el atasco – *the traffic jam*
por lo que / cual – *here: because of which*

▸ **Definite Article**, p. 21

2. Relative Determiners *cuyo/-a/-os/-as*

	masculine	feminine
Singular	**cuyo**	**cuya**
Plural	**cuyos**	**cuyas**

A la presentación vendrán una pintora **cuyos** ▸ cuadros han sido expuestos en Nueva York y un director **cuyas** ▸ películas han recibido premios en San Sebastián.

Cuyo agrees with the following noun, not with the antecedent in the main clause.

The relative determiners **cuyo/-a/-os/-as** are used primarily in formal contexts. They agree in number and gender with the following noun. If they accompany a person as the direct object, they are preceded by the preposition **a**.

3. Relative Adverbs

Mira el plano, estas son las ruinas **adonde** vamos. Son de la época **cuando** los mayas tenían mucho poder.

①

Pues el camino por **donde** vamos me parece peligroso.

②

No te preocupes, el guía conoce la manera **como** hay que llegar. Esta es la región **donde** trabaja siempre.

③

---

1. Look at the map, these are the ruins to which we're going. They're from the time when the Mayas had a lot of power. 2. Hmmm, the road by which we're going seems dangerous to me. 3. Don't worry, the guide knows the way to get there. This is the area in which he always works.

Relative adverbs are invariable. **Donde** (*where*) refers to location, to a place. It is also used in connection with prepositions, one of which is attached to the adverb: **adonde**. **Cuando** (*when*) refers to time, and **como** (*how*) is an adverb of manner.

Indefinite and Relative Pronouns

1. Translate the words in parentheses below. *

a) • Parece que no hay *(no one)* ____nadie_____ aquí.

   ○ A ver... ¡Hoooola! ¿Hay *(anybody)* _____ en casa?

b) • ¿Tienes hoy *(something)* _____ que hacer?

   ○ No, *(nothing)* _____. Podemos salir

    juntos a tomar algo, si quieres.

c) • ¿Ha llamado *(anyone)* _____ esta mañana?

la llamada – *the call*

   ○ Pues ha habido dos llamadas. ¿Por qué, esperas *(anybody)*

   _____ en especial?

de tu parte – *from you*   d) • Pepe no está. ¿Le digo *(anything)* _____ de tu parte?

   ○ No, *(nothing)* _____, gracias. Yo llamo más tarde.

2. Paco is a waiter. He can't go to sleep because everything the customers said to him during the day is running through his head. What did they say? Choose the correct words below. **

a) Ya no quiero (nada) – alguien – algo más, muchas gracias.

b) Esta puerta ya está cerrada, ¿hay una otra – la otra – otra en otro lado?

c) ¡Uff! Lo siento, pero no tengo billetes pequeños, tengo que pagarle con algunos – uno – todo de cien.

d) En este barrio no conozco a uno – ninguno – nadie . Por eso vengo a conversar contigo...

¡Qué ilusión! – *How exciting!*   e) ¡Qué ilusión! ¡Por fin tenemos tanto – suficiente – demasiado para comprar el coche! ¿Qué te parece?

f) Ponme lo mismo – mismos – demás del otro día. ¿Cómo dices que se llama ese cóctel?

3. Mirna has read two questionable health tips in the newspaper. She is outraged and has torn up the pages. What did she read there? Arrange the words below to form complete sentences. ******

a) Las dietas – ayudan – a nadie – no

 <u>Las dietas no ayudan a nadie.</u>

b) azúcar – consumo de – preocuparse por – reducir el – Uno no debe

 _____

c) suficientes – Las vitaminas de – los alimentos naturales – no son

 _____

d) de la gente – es necesario – ¿Ejercicio? – tanto! – hace demasiado, ¡no – La mayoría

 _____

 _____

e) tres aspirinas – A cualquiera – le ayuda tomar – diarias

 _____

4. Sweets are popular all year round in Spain. Complete the passage below with the appropriate pronouns. We've given you the first letter of each missing word to get you started. *******

alguien – Algunos – cada uno – Cualquiera – demasiado – muchos – nada – nadie – nadie – otros – pocos – suficientes – tantas

a) En Chile hay _muchos_ días festivos y para c _____ hay platos especiales. **b)** A _____ se preparan típicamente en casa, pero las posibilidades de comprarlos son s _____ como para que n _____ tenga que quedarse sin comerlos. **c)** C _____ conoce las empanadas, pero p_____ saben que hay t _____ diferentes. **d)** En Navidad parece que los chilenos siempre comen d _____ , pero nadie desea privarse de rosquillas, chocolates, mazapanes y muchos o _____ dulces. **e)** En los festejos de Año Nuevo n _____ se resiste al *cola de mono* y n _____ es tan apreciado como los excelentes vinos de ese país. Los chilenos son un pueblo goloso: ¿hay a _____ que lo dude?

la empanada – *a turnover with a filling of ground meat, onions, olives, and minced hard-boiled egg*
la rosquilla – *doughnut*
el mazapán – *marzipan*
dulces – *sweets*
cola de mono – *eggnog and rum*
goloso – *sweet-toothed*

Practice and Application

Indefinite and Relative Pronouns

a) que

b) donde

c) quien

d) adonde

5. Below is a short article about a famous chef. Where do the relative pronouns belong? Add an arrow to indicate the spot ↓.*

a) Juan Mari Arzak es un cocinero famoso ↓ vive en San Sebastián.

b) El restaurante trabaja es muy conocido por su cocina tan original.

c) Su mujer, trabaja en su restaurante, es su mejor colaboradora.

d) El restaurante Arzak es un lugar van clientes de todo el mundo.

6. Claudia, now in her first apartment, is talking to her mother on the phone. Reword the sentences below to create main and dependent clauses, and fill in the relative pronouns. **

a) Por fin estoy en el apartamento. ¡He soñado con el apartamento tanto tiempo! ▶ ¡Por fin estoy en el apartamento <u>con el que he soñado tanto tiempo</u> !

b) He encontrado a una vecina en el pasillo. La vecina me ha saludado muy amablemente. ▶ Una vecina, _____

_____

c) Ahora estoy en el salón. Desde el salón se escucha el ruido de los pájaros del parque. El parque está enfrente del edificio. ▶ _____

_____

7. Below is some information about Cuba and tourism. Complete the sentences with the appropriate relative pronouns. **

como
cuya
cuyo
cuyos
lo que
que
que
que
que/quienes

a) Los cubanos, <u>cuya</u> situación ha sido muy difícil desde los años 90, siempre encuentran maneras _____ mejorar sus pequeños presupuestos. **b)** Algunos venden cosas _____ fabrican o preparan, otros arreglan aparatos _____ valor es ya histórico, otros prefieren llevar en el taxi a los turistas, _____ sólo piensan en disfrutar sus vacaciones. **c)** Es el reciente desarrollo del turismo _____ le ha permitido a muchas personas viajar a Cuba. **d)** Descansan en las aguas cristalinas del Caribe y en las playas blancas _____ son ya de leyenda. **e)** Sin embargo, cuando pasean por el centro de La Habana, _____ edificios fotografían con entusiasmo, muchos de estos turistas no ven la vida tan dura _____ tienen los cubanos.

el presupuesto – *here: the budget*

el Caribe – *the Caribbean*

Verbs

Types of Verbs

On the basis of their function in the sentence, verbs can be broken down into three categories:

> Verbs can express actions, processes, and perceptions or describe circumstances.

1. Complete Verbs

Complete verbs, on their own, say something about a subject. They are

– transitive if they require a direct object (*whom* or *what*).	**Leo** un libro. *I read a book.*
– intransitive if they require no object.	**¿Salimos**? *Are we going out?*
– intransitive with a dative if they are accompanied only by an indirect object.	El hotel **me gusta**. *I like the hotel.*
– reflexive if the subject and object are the same (I = myself).	**Me despido.** *I say good-bye.*
– impersonal if they occur only in the third person singular.	**¡Llueve** otra vez! *It's raining again!*

> The verb plays a central role in the sentence. It determines both the message of a sentence and the placement of the individual elements of the sentence.

▶ **Word Order**, p. 230

2. Auxiliary Verbs

Auxiliary (helping) verbs assist in the formation of other verb constructions.

– **haber** + past participle creates the compound tenses, such as the present perfect.	**He** dormido bien. *I slept well.*
– **ser** + past participle results in the passive.	Lima **fue** fundada en 1535. *Lima was founded in 1535.*
– **estar** + present participle results in a verbal periphrasis.	**Estoy** estudiando. *I am studying.*

▶ **Present Perfect**, p. 119

▶ **Passive**, p. 240

▶ **Verbal Periphrasis**, p. 191

3. Modal Verbs

Modal verbs are a special type of auxiliary (helping) verbs. Generally they precede the infinitive of another verb and clarify the relationship between the subject and the activity by expressing intention, possibility, permission, capability, or necessity:

– **querer**	*to want, wish*	**Quiero** divertirme.
– **poder**	*to be able to, can*	**Puedo** llamar a Genaro.
– **saber**	*to know how to*	Pero no **sabe** bailar.
– **tener que**	*to have to, must*	**Tiene que** aprender.

Verb Forms

The verb stem expresses the meaning of the verb. The ending adds additional information, such as the conjugation group to which the verb belongs (**-ar**, **-er**, **-ir**), who the subject is, etc.

Stem—Ending			Stem—Ending		
com	er	*– to eat*	**viv**	ir	*– to live*
beb	er	*– to drink*	**mor**	ir	*– to die*

1. Unconjugated Forms

The past participle is variable only in its function as an adjective or in a passive construction.

▶ **Unconjugated Forms of the Verb,** p. 182

Unconjugated verb forms usually are invariable and cannot form an independent sentence. Their endings tell nothing about the person, number, and tense of the verb or about its mood (mode). They are:

– the infinitive	comp**rar**
– the present participle	compr**ando**
– the past participle	compr**ado**

2. Conjugated Forms

Conjugating a verb means inflecting it to reflect person, number, voice, tense, and mood. All this information can be derived from the verb endings:

		Stem	Ending
– person:	first (I)	compr	
– number:	singular	teng	**o**
– tense:	present	prueb	
– mood:	indicative		

Mood

Furthermore, the ending of a Spanish verb tells whether the activity is an objective fact for the speaker (indicative); whether it is a hypothetical action or condition, that is, a wish, a fear, etc. (*subjuntivo*, or subjunctive); whether it is something that might happen (conditional); or whether it is a command (imperative).

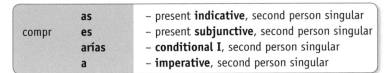

compr	as	– present **indicative**, second person singular
	es	– present **subjunctive**, second person singular
	arías	– **conditional I**, second person singular
	a	– **imperative**, second person singular

In addition, all the moods (except the imperative) convey information about the time of the action, such as the present. Each verb tense is characterized by certain endings for the various persons.

▶ **Tenses of the Indicative**, p. 106

▶ **Tenses of the Subjunctive**, p. 158

Regular and Irregular Verbs

Depending on the infinitive ending, there are three conjugation groups: **-ar**, **-er**, and **-ir**. Each of these groups follows a certain conjugational pattern for the various tenses.

Most irregular verbs can be divided into groups. That is, even with irregular forms there are certain regularities. This makes learning them easier!

Regular Verbs

hablar	▶ hablo	– have the same stem as the infinitive for all persons and tenses.
aprender	▶ aprendes	
escribir	▶ escribes	– follow the patterns of the personal endings for their conjugation group.

Group Verbs

cerrar	▶ cierro	– depending on the tense, have a stem change for certain persons.
jugar	▶ juegas	
conocer	▶ conozco	– follow the patterns of the personal endings for their conjugation group.
hacer	▶ hago	

Irregular Verbs

| estar | ▶ estoy | – can display both a stem change and divergent personal endings. |
| ser | ▶ eres | |

Verbs that are irregular in the present tense are not necessarily so in other tenses. For example, **cerrar** and **conocer** are regular in the *indefinido* and in the future.

Verbs based on other verbs display the same irregularities in conjugation, for example, **escribir** (*to write*) and **describir** (*to describe*), **probar** (*to test, try*) and **comprobar** (*to check*), **reír** (*to laugh*) and **sonreír** (*to smile*), etc.

Tenses of the Indicative

The indicative indicates that what is asserted is objectively true for the speaker.

Overview

Vivo en un pueblo pequeño. *I live in a small village.*	Present
Nunca **he vivido** en una ciudad. *I have never lived in a city.*	Present Perfect
Antes **vivía** con mis padres. *In the past I lived with my parents.*	Imperfect
Pero ayer **me mudé**. *But yesterday I moved.*	*Indefinido* (Preterit)
Siempre **había querido** algo propio. *I had always wanted something of my own.*	Past Perfect
Decoraré a mi gusto. *I'll decorate according to my taste.*	Future
En un mes **habré terminado**. *In one month I will have finished.*	Future Perfect

Present

> Normalmente **recibo** e-mails de mis amigos y los **respondo** enseguida.

Normally I get e-mails from my friends and answer them immediately.

> Actions and habits in the present as well as facts not dependent on time are expressed in the present tense.

1. Regular Verbs

For all the regular verbs in a group, the following endings and stress patterns apply:

> Subject pronouns are seldom used in Spanish, because the person can be identified by the verb ending.
>
> ▶ **Subject Pronouns**, p. 72

Infinitive	comp<u>rar</u>	vend<u>er</u>	discut<u>ir</u>
(yo)	comp<u>ro</u>	ven<u>do</u>	discu<u>to</u>
(tú)	comp<u>ras</u>	ven<u>des</u>	discu<u>tes</u>
(él / ella / usted)	comp<u>ra</u>	ven<u>de</u>	discu<u>te</u>
(nosotros / -as)	comp<u>ramos</u>	vend<u>emos</u>	discut<u>imos</u>
(vosotros / -as)	comp<u>ráis</u>	vend<u>éis</u>	discut<u>ís</u>
(ellos / ellas / ustedes)	comp<u>ran</u>	ven<u>den</u>	discu<u>ten</u>

Here is a selection of regular verbs:

> Only the irregular verbs **ser (soy)**, **estar (estoy)**, **dar (doy)**, **ir (voy)**, **saber (sé)** and the auxiliary verb **haber (he)** have no **-o** in the first person singular.

-ar			
ayudar	to help	bajar	to descend, go down
cambiar	to change	entrar	to enter
esperar	to expect; to hope; to wait	estudiar	to study
ganar	to earn; to win	hablar	to speak
limpiar	to clean	llamar	to call
llegar	to come	llevar	to take; to carry
pagar	to pay	pasar	to pass
preguntar	to ask	preparar	to prepare
tomar	to take	viajar	to travel

-er			
aprender	to learn	beber	to drink
comer	to eat	creer	to believe
escoger	to choose	leer	to read
responder	to answer, reply	vender	to sell

-ir			
abrir	to open	escribir	to write
decidir	to decide	discutir	to argue; to discuss
permitir	to permit	recibir	to receive
subir	to climb, go up	vivir	to live

> 1. Most Spanish verbs end in **-ar**.
> 2. **Creer** and **leer** have two e's, except in the first person: **crees**, **leemos**.

> ▶ For **escoger**: orthographic change, p. 109

Present

2. Verb Groups with Vowel Change: o ▶ ue, e ▶ ie, e ▶ i

In the dictionary, these verbs are usually indicated with (*ue*), (*ie*), or (*i*).

¿**Puedes** venir, por favor?

①

No, ahora no **quiero**, estoy ocupado.

②

1. Can you come, please? 2. No, I don't want to now, I'm busy.

1. Only in **jugar** (*to play*) does **u ▶ ue**.
2. Among the stem-stressed forms, **oler** (*to smell*) acquires an **h**: **huel**o, **huel**es, **huel**e, olemos, oléis, **huel**en.

Group Infinitive	o ▶ ue poder	e ▶ ie pensar	e ▶ i repetir
(yo)	**pue**do	**pie**nso	rep**i**to
(tú)	**pue**des	**pie**nsas	rep**i**tes
(él, ella, usted)	**pue**de	**pie**nsa	rep**i**te
(nosotros /-as)	po**de**mos	pen**sa**mos	repe**ti**mos
(vosotros /-as)	po**déis**	pen**sáis**	repe**tís**
(ellos, ellas, ustedes)	**pue**den	**pie**nsan	rep**i**ten

In these groups, the stem vowel changes only in the forms that are stressed on the stem. Here is a selection:

o ▶ ue

alm**o**rzar	to have lunch	c**o**ntar	to count; to tell
c**o**star	to cost	d**o**rmir	to sleep
enc**o**ntrar	to find	m**o**rir	to die
m**o**strar	to show	m**o**ver	to move
p**o**der	to be able, can	pr**o**bar	to taste, try
rec**o**rdar	to remember; to remind	s**o**ñar	to dream
v**o**lar	to fly	v**o**lver	to return

e ▶ ie

c**e**rrar	to close	desp**e**rtar	to wake (up)
emp**e**zar	to begin	enc**e**nder	to light; to switch on
ent**e**nder	to understand	m**e**ntir	to lie
qu**e**rer	to want; to love	p**e**nsar	to think
p**e**rder	to lose	pr**e**ferir	to prefer
recom**e**ndar	to recommend	s**e**ntir	to feel

e ▶ i

corr**e**gir	to correct	el**e**gir	to choose; to elect
m**e**dir	to measure	p**e**dir	to ask (for); to order
r**e**ír	to laugh	rep**e**tir	to repeat
s**e**guir	to continue; to follow	s**e**rvir	to serve

Only **querer** + person means *to love*, as here: ¡**Te quiero mucho**!

All **e ▶ i** verbs belong to the **-ir** conjugation group.

3. Orthographic Changes in the First Person Singular

In order to preserve the pronunciation of the infinitive in all forms of the verb, the spelling often is adapted. This is true of the first person singular of some verbs. In the other persons the stem of the infinite is retained. Below are examples, the rules, and additional verbs.

• ¿Esco**ges** tú el menú? ○ Claro, lo esco**jo** enseguida.		Verbs ending in **-ger** or **-gir**: **g ▶ j** before **o**.	
coger	*to take*	elegir (i)	*to choose; to elect*
proteger	*to protect*	recoger	*to pick up; to gather*
• ¿Te conven**ces**? ○ No, no me conven**zo**.		Verbs ending in **-cer** or **-cir**: **c ▶ z** before **o**.	
cocer (ue)	*to cook*	torcer (ue)	*to twist; to bend*
• ¿Quieres se**gui**rme? ○ ¡Claro que te si**go**!		Verbs ending in **-guir**: **gu ▶ g** before **o**.	
distinguir	*to distinguish, tell apart*	conseguir (i)	*to get, obtain*
extinguir	*to extinguish, put out*	perseguir (i)	*to persecute; to pursue*

> Watch out! In some countries of LA, **coger** has a sexual meaning and its use can lead to embarrassing misunderstandings! If you want to *take* something, use only **tomar** in LA.

4. Verb Groups with an Expanded Stem

> Yo **distribuyo** folletos. Además, mi trabajo **incluye** llamar a los clientes.

I hand out brochures. Moreover, my job includes calling the customers.

Group **y** Infinitive	distribuir
(yo)	distri<u>buyo</u>
(tú)	distri<u>buyes</u>
(él, ella, usted)	distri<u>buye</u>
(nosotros / -as)	distri<u>buimos</u>
(vosotros / -as)	distri<u>buís</u>
(ellos, ellas, ustedes)	distri<u>buyen</u>

With verbs ending in **-uir**, in the forms stressed on the stem the **i** changes to **y** and is retained as part of the stem in conjugation. Additional verbs:

construir	*to build*	destruir	*to destroy*
incluir	*to include*	influir	*to influence*
huir	*to flee*	sustituir	*to replace, substitute for*

Present

5. Verb Groups with a Shift in Stress

In dictionaries, (*i*) and (*ú*) are used to indicate these groups. Not every verb with a diphthong belongs to this category, however. For example, **cambiar**, **limpiar**, and others are regular.

> Anita **continúa** trabajando hasta muy tarde y **envía** las cartas.

Anita keeps on working until quite late and sends out the letters.

Group	í		ú
Infinitive	enviar	prohibir	continuar
(yo)	envío	prohíbo	continúo
(tú)	envías	prohíbes	continúas
(él, ella, usted)	envía	prohíbe	continúa
(nosotros/-as)	enviamos	prohibimos	continuamos
(vosotros/-as)	enviáis	prohibís	continuáis
(ellos, ellas, ustedes)	envían	prohíben	continúan

In these groups, the stress on the diphthong is shifted. The **i** and the **u** acquire a written accent in the form stressed on the stem.

With these verbs, **oi** and **eu** are perceived as diphthongs, even though the vowels are separated by an **h**, as in **prohibir**, **rehusar**.

í			
confiar	*to confide*	vaciar	*to empty*
esquiar	*to ski*	guiar	*to guide, lead*
ú			
acentuar	*to stress, emphasize*	continuar	*to continue*
reunir	*to collect, gather*	rehusar	*to refuse*

6. Verb Groups with an Irregular First Person Singular

① **Traigo** comida china.

② Mmh, no la **conozco**. ¿**Pongo** la mesa?

1. I'm bringing Chinese food. 2. Mmm, I'm not familiar with it. Shall I set the table?

Depending on the context, **poner** has a lot of meanings, including *to set, to lay, to put.*

zc	g		ig
conocer	poner	hacer	traer
conozco	pongo	hago	traigo
conoces	pones	haces	traes
conoce	pone	hace	trae
conocemos	ponemos	hacemos	traemos
conocéis	ponéis	hacéis	traéis
conocen	ponen	hacen	traen

These irregularities affect only the first person singular; the other persons in the present tense are regular in their conjugation.

zc			
conducir	*to drive; to conduct*	conocer	*to know*
obedecer	*to obey*	ofrecer	*to offer*
parecer	*to seem*	producir	*to produce*
reconocer	*to recognize*	traducir	*to translate*
g			
hacer	*to do; to make*	poner	*to put, place*
salir	*to leave, go out*	valer	*to be worth*
ig			
caer	*to fall*	traer	*to bring*

7. Individual Verbs with an Irregular First Person Singular

These verbs are at variance with the infinitive in the first person singular.

dar	saber	ver	caber
doy	**sé**	**veo**	**quepo**
das	sabes	ves	cabes
da	sabe	ve	cabe
damos	sabemos	vemos	cabemos
dais	sabéis	veis	cabéis
dan	saben	ven	caben

The forms **dais** and **veis** have no written accent because they are monosyllabic.

8. Highly Irregular Verbs

María, ¿**eres** tú? ¿Dónde **estás**? ¿**Voy** a buscarte?

María, is it you? Where are you? Shall I pick you up?

Only a very few verbs are highly irregular.

ser	ir	estar	haber
soy	voy	estoy	he
eres	vas	estás	has
es	va	está	ha
somos	vamos	estamos	hemos
sois	vais	estáis	habéis
son	van	están	han

1. With **estar**, the stress is divergent.
2. **Haber** is conjugated only as an auxiliary verb. As an independent verb it is impersonal and has only one form: **hay**.

111

Present

9. Verbs with Several Irregularities

¿**Tienes** tiempo mañana?
①

②
¿Qué **dices**?
No te **oigo**.

1. Do you have time tomorrow? 2. What are you saying? I can't hear you.

There are a very few verbs with two irregularities.

g, ie		i + g	ig, y
tener	**venir**	**decir**	**oír**
tengo	vengo	digo	oigo
tienes	vienes	dices	oyes
tiene	viene	dice	oye
tenemos	venimos	decimos	oímos
tenéis	venís	decís	oís
tienen	vienen	dicen	oyen

Tener, venir, and **oír** have one irregularity in the first person and another one in the remaining persons. **Decir** has two irregularities simultaneously, in the first person.

Use

Los abogados **trabajan** mucho. Yo **trabajo** más de ocho horas.

The present is used to indicate repetitive actions and general circumstances in present time.

La palabra "periódico" **significa** *newspaper*.

– to describe facts that are not dependent on time.

La próxima vez **pagas** tú, ¿vale?

– to represent future actions or events as certain.

Ahora mismo **buscas** las llaves del coche.

– to indicate that a command is absolutely essential.

Estábamos a medio lago cuando de pronto, ¡se **termina** la gasolina!

– to relate past events in an especially vivid way.

¡Qué raro! Pepe **toma** té.

– sometimes for individual actions or events that are in the process of occurring, instead of the construction **estar** + present participle.

If something is in the process of occurring, you can use the progressive form: **estar** + present participle. **Ella está tomando té.**

▶ Verbal Periphrasis, p. 191

Verb—Present Indicative

1. Match the verbs on the right with the appropriate persons. *

a) yo: _____sonrío_____

b) tú: _____

c) él / ella / usted: _____

d) nosotros / -as: _____

e) vosotros / -as: _____

f) ellos / ellas / ustedes: _____

~~sonrío~~ vivís
sé sueñas ven
distribuís prefiere
dais recordamos
puedo hacen
vamos bebes
conocéis trabajan
sigue habla vemos
encuentras voy

2. Read the article, which tells how young families can be helped to get a home of their own without having a lot of money. Write down the basic form in which the verbs in red can be found in a dictionary. *

a) En Mijas, que está en la Costa del Sol, muchas familias jóvenes que no ganan mucho dinero pueden comprar ahora una casa propia. **b)** El Ayuntamiento regala terrenos en los que empresas constructoras construyen edificios para viviendas. **c)** Para ellos significa un negocio seguro, y por eso ofrecen un buen precio. **d)** Un apartamento que mide 90 metros cuadrados cuesta sólo 60 mil euros. **e)** Esta iniciativa tiene ya casi un año y todos parecen contentos.

ganar – to earn
la casa propia –
home of one's own
el Ayuntamiento –
the City Council
la empresa
constructora – *the*
construction company
la vivienda – *the*
dwelling
el negocio – *the*
business
contento – *happy,*
pleased

a) _____estar_____, _____, _____, _____

b) _____, _____; c) _____, _____

d) _____, _____; e) _____, _____

3. Find the verbs that are opposites in meaning. *

a) construir ◀▶ _____destruir_____

b) buscar ◀▶ _____

c) preguntar ◀▶ _____

d) abrir ◀▶ _____

e) subir ◀▶ _____

f) comprar ◀▶ _____

g) entrar ◀▶ _____

h) dormir ◀▶ _____

i) traer ◀▶ _____

j) empezar ◀▶ _____

bajar
cerrar
despertar
~~destruir~~
encontrar
llevar
responder
salir
terminar
vender

Practice and Application

4. Place the verbs from Exercise 3 in the correct group. *

a) regularly: ___buscar,_____

_____

b) o ▸ ue _____   e) g _____

c) e ▸ ie _____   f) ig _____

d) y _____

5. Do you like radio interviews? Fill in the blanks with verbs in the present tense. *

a) estar, tener, tener

b) tener, ver, venir, querer, dormir

c) ser, ser

d) seguir, jugar, querer

e) ser, decir

f) creer, ser, aprender, salir, dar, significar, costar, ser, comer

g) oír, poder, contar, repetir, llamar, escuchar, volar

a) • Aquí, de Radio Uno, nosotros __estamos__ haciendo una entrevista con gente que _____ animales. Perdone, ¿usted _____ algún animalito?

b) ○ Yo sí, _____ un gato, pero casi no lo _____. Sólo _____ cuando _____ comer... Bueno, y también _____ en la casa.

c) • Es que los gatos _____ muy independientes... Y tú, pequeñita, ¿ese perrito, _____ tuyo?

d) ▫ Sí. Nerón me _____ a todas partes. Yo siempre _____ con él y por eso me _____ más que a nadie.

e) • Ustedes _____ los mejores amigos, ¿verdad? ¿Y qué _____ tu mamá de Nerón?

f) ✳ Yo _____ que los perros _____ algo muy bueno, así los chicos _____ a ser responsables. Claro que yo _____ con el perro todas las mañanas, le _____ su comida, en fin, _____ trabajo. Y también _____ un poco de dinero. Por suerte Nerón _____ pequeño y no _____ mucho.

g) • ¡Bien, bien! Y ustedes que nos _____, amigos y amigas, _____ llamar al 11 23 ahora y nos _____ sus experiencias y opiniones. ¿Vale? Les _____ el número: 11 23. ¡Hasta ahora! Y mientras ustedes _____, nosotros _____ la canción "Pájaro que _____"...

la entrevista –
the interview
independiente –
independent
tuyo – *your*
nadie – *no one*
el mejor amigo –
the best friend
por suerte – *fortunately*
vale – *all right*
el pájaro – *the bird*

6. Practice makes perfect! Fill in the missing words in the table. *

Infinitive	yo	tú	él/ella/usted	nosotros/nosotras	vosotros/vosotras	ellos/ellas/ustedes
a) estudiar	estudio	estudias	estudia	estudiamos	estudiáis	estudian
b)		vendes				
c)	escribo					
d) estar						
e)				hacemos		
f)			viene			
g)						van
h)					sabéis	

7. Two friends are thinking about what they will do in the evening. Connect the two columns to create a dialogue. *

a) • Esa película es muy buena.   1) Tengo mucha sed.

b)   Pero es para mayores de 18.   2) ¿Tienes ganas de ir?

c) ○ 21. El cine empieza a las 9.   3) ¡Es que además tengo sueño!

d) • Pero antes, vamos a beber algo.   4) ¿Tienes hambre?

e) ○ ¿Quieres comer algo también?   5) ¿Cuántos años tienes?

f) • Sí, entonces mejor no vamos al cine.   6) Si queremos ir, ¡tenemos prisa!

8. **Tener** is used in many expressions. From the preceding exercise, you can figure out what the following equivalents are. *

a) *to be hungry / thirsty*   _____

b) *to want to (do something)*   _____

c) *to be tired / sleepy*   _____

d) *to be ... years old*   _____

e) *to be in a hurry*   _____

Practice and Application

Verb—Present Indicative

9. What drinks should be offered? Number the sentences from 1–9 to create a dialogue. **

(   ) ● Claro, aquí lo tienes.

(   ) ○ Entonces, ¿por favor me das de piña?

(1) ● ¿Qué te ofrezco? Tengo cerveza, vino, licor...

(   ) ● Claro, te puedo dar jugo de piña, de melocotón...

(   ) ○ Primero prefiero algo fresco, porque hace mucho calor.

(   ) Es que soy alérgico al melocotón.

(   ) ○ Hombre, no hay ningún problema si eres tú quien lo bebe.

(   ) ¿Tienes algún jugo?

(   ) ¿Te importa si yo bebo jugo de melocotón?

el melocotón –
the peach
la piña – *the pineapple*

10. Folk sayings are not dependent on time. Some of these well-known sayings have English equivalents, while others do not. Find the correct verbs! **

a) A caballo regalado no se le __mira__ el diente.
Don't look a gift horse in the mouth.

b) Quien _____, _____.
He who pays the piper calls the tune.

c) Todos los ríos _____ al mar.
All rivers flow to the sea.

d) No _____ rico quien más _____, sino quien menos _____.
He is not richer who has more, but who needs less.

e) Cuando el río _____, agua _____.
When the river makes noise, it has water in it. (Where there's smoke, there's fire.)

f) Los niños y los borrachos _____ la verdad.
Children and drunks speak the truth.

g) Se _____ lo que se _____.
One does what one can.

h) La esperanza _____ al último.
Hope dies last.

i) Antes _____ un mentiroso que un cojo.
A liar trips before a cripple.

j) Una sonrisa no _____ nada pero _____ mucho.
A smile costs nothing, but it's worth a lot.

cae
cuesta
dicen
es
hace
lleva
manda
~~mira~~
muere
paga
puede
quiere
suena
tiene
vale
van

116

11. Many people think weddings are romantic. Choose the appropriate verbs below. **

a) Las bodas (son)/tienen ocasiones rituales y por eso en ellas se ponen/guardan muchas costumbres y tradiciones. ¿Cuáles de estas sabes/conoces ?

b) Las novias llevan/llegan un vestido blanco porque ese color prepara/simboliza la pureza. Sin embargo, en China por ejemplo las novias salen/visten de rojo.

c) El anillo de boda tiene/hace que ser de oro porque es/pone el metal que dura/tarda más y el círculo presenta/representa la eternidad.

d) El arroz que los amigos arrojan/muestran a los novios cuando entran/salen de la iglesia es símbolo de la comida, la felicidad y los hijos que no deben/acaban faltarle a la pareja.

la ocasión – *the occasion*
guardar – *here: to observe, keep*
la pureza – *the purity*
el anillo de boda – *the wedding ring*
el círculo – *the circle*
durar – *to last, endure*
tardar – *to take a long time*
la eternidad – *the eternity*
arrojar – *to throw*
la pareja – *the couple*

12. Do you know anything about Spain's most famous writer? Fill in the blanks in this short biography of Cervantes with the indicated verbs in the present tense. ***

a) La vida de este escritor __está__ llena de aventuras. **b)** A los 22 años _____ a Italia y dos años más tarde _____ como soldado en la famosa batalla de Lepanto, donde lo _____ en la mano izquierda, que desde entonces le _____ sin movimiento. **c)** _____ algunos años más en guerras, _____ tomado preso y _____ en la cárcel durante cinco años.

d) Al fin se _____ su rescate y _____ volver a Madrid.

e) Ahí _____ varios pequeños empleos, _____ y _____ sus primeras obras, que no _____ mucho éxito. **f)** En 1605 se _____ la primera parte del *Quijote*, pero Cervantes nunca _____ de tener dificultades económicas.

g) Al año siguiente de terminar su obra principal, _____ pobre y muy enfermo.

a) estar
b) irse, participar, herir (3ª pl.), quedar
c) pasar, ser, permanecer
d) conseguir, poder
e) ocupar, casarse, escribir, tener
f) publicar, dejar
g) morir

la batalla – *the battle*
herir – *to injure*
el movimiento – *the movement*
tomar preso – *to take prisoner*
la cárcel – *the prison, jail*
el rescate – *the ransom*

The Past

Llegué temprano para ver el apartamento. ①

Ya **había buscado** por toda la ciudad, pero sin éxito. ②

El edificio **estaba** en una calle tranquila. ③

"A ver," pensé. "Quizá por fin **he tenido** suerte y hoy es mi día." ④

Spanish has both simple and compound past tenses. Be patient until you have developed a feel for these tenses and their use!

1. I arrived early to see the apartment. 2. I had been searching all over town, but with no success. 3. The building was on a quiet street. 4. "Let's see," I thought. "Maybe I've finally been lucky, and today is my day."

The past tenses are used in Spanish to distinguish various shades of meaning that English often renders in different ways. Here is an overview of the various past tenses:

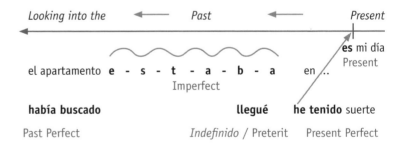

Looking into the ← *Past* ← *Present*

es mi día
Present

el apartamento **e - s - t - a - b - a** en ...
Imperfect

había buscado   **llegué**   **he tenido** suerte

Past Perfect   *Indefinido* / Preterit   Present Perfect

The Present Perfect

¿**Has terminado**
el proyecto?
①

No, esta semana
hemos tenido mucho
trabajo.
②

Por eso no **ha sido**
posible terminar todo.
③

1. Have you finished the project? 2. No, we've had a lot of work this week.
3. That's why it hasn't been possible to finish everything.

> The present perfect
> is used for actions
> or events that are in
> some way connected
> with the present.

> ▶ **Types of Verbs,**
> **Auxiliary Verbs,**
> p. 103

> ▶ **Past Participle,**
> p. 187

Formation

The present perfect is formed with the present tense of **haber** and the past
participle. The corresponding forms of the auxiliary verb always directly
precede the past participle. The participle ends in **-o**, regardless of the
number or gender of the subject.

(yo)	he	trabaja**o**
(tú)	has	teni**do**
(él / ella / usted)	ha	discuti**do**
(nosotros / -as)	hemos	escri**to**
(vosotros / -as)	habéis	pues**to**
(ellos / ellas / ustedes)	han	hech**o**

> Spanish has only one
> auxiliary verb for
> the present perfect.
> **He llegado y he**
> **comido** (*I have come*
> *and I have eaten*).

Basic Meaning:

What action has taken place within a space of time not yet expired or at
an indefinite time in any way connected with the present?

he terminado

earlier, previously — *now*

By using the present perfect, the speaker establishes a connection with
the present.

Use

> Luis **ha llamado** hace unos minutos y Juan ha **llamado** hoy también.

▪ The present perfect is used for actions or events that took place in the recent past or within a space of time not yet expired (such as **hoy**).

> Este año **he tenido** suerte, aunque todavía no **he ganado** en la lotería.

▪ – actions or events that began in the past but are continuing in the present (or within a space of time not yet expired).

> **Han visto** el parque Grau, ¿verdad?

▪ – actions or events whose effects extend into the present.

In Spanish, there are two simple past indicative tenses: the imperfect and the *indefinido*, or preterit. They are not interchangeable.

▶ **Indefinido**, p. 126

▶ **Present Perfect and Indefinido**, p. 130

The present perfect is used with the following statements of time:

– **hoy**	**Hoy** he recibido una carta de Inés.
– **hace un rato / un momento**	**Hace un rato** la he leído.
– **este / -a** + time expression	Ha viajado mucho **este año**.
– **ya, todavía no**	**Ya** ha estado en muchos países.
– **alguna vez, hasta ahora**	**Alguna vez** quiero viajar como ella.
– **nunca (hasta ahora)**	Yo no he ido **nunca** en barco.
– **una vez, muchas / varias veces**	Ella ha ido **varias veces**.

The Imperfect

> Cuando **era** niño, **vivía** en un pueblo pequeño que **estaba** cerca de la playa.

The imperfect describes situations or circumstances in the past or designates customary or habitual past actions.

When I was a child, I lived in a small village that was near the beach.

Formation

1. Regular Forms

The formation of the imperfect is quite simple. For the regular verbs, there are two groups of endings, one for verbs ending in **-ar** and the other for verbs ending in **-er** and **-ir**.

	trabaj**ar**	aprend**er**	escrib**ir**
(yo)	trabaj**aba**	aprend**ía**	escrib**ía**
(tú)	trabaj**abas**	aprend**ías**	escrib**ías**
(él / ella / usted)	trabaj**aba**	aprend**ía**	escrib**ía**
(nosotros / -as)	trabaj**ábamos**	aprend**íamos**	escrib**íamos**
(vosotros / -as)	trabaj**abais**	aprend**íais**	escrib**íais**
(ellos / ellas / ustedes)	trabaj**aban**	aprend**ían**	escrib**ían**

1. The first and third person singular forms are identical. The context usually reveals who the subject is.
2. The imperfect of **hay** is **había**.

2. Irregular Forms

	ser	**ir**	**ver**
(yo)	era	iba	veía
(tú)	eras	ibas	veías
(él / ella / usted)	era	iba	veía
(nosotros / -as)	éramos	íbamos	veíamos
(vosotros / -as)	erais	ibais	veíais
(ellos / ellas / ustedes)	eran	iban	veían

The imperfect has only three irregular verbs!

Basic Meaning:

What was it like in those days? What happened when (something took place)?

vivía en un pueblo

earlier, previously ← ———————————— → *now*

The imperfect does not express a connection with the present, nor does it say anything about the beginning, end, or successful completion of an action.

> ### Use
>
> Todos los días **comía** con mis padres y después **charlábamos**.
>
> ▪ Customary or habitual past actions are expressed in the imperfect.
>
> Silvia **era** una mujer muy guapa y **tenía** unos ojos muy expresivos.
>
> ▪ – descriptions.
>
> Pedro **estaba** enfermo; le **dolía** el estómago.
>
> ▪ – circumstances.
>
> No oí el teléfono porque **estaba** con los niños en el jardín.
> Yo **tendía** la ropa y ellos **jugaban** a la pelota.
> En eso **estábamos** cuando llamó mi hermano.
>
> ▪ – situations or processes that existed in the past and can form the background for a newly beginning action or a newly occurring event.
>
> **Quería** poner la mesa porque **íbamos** a tener visitas.
>
> ▪ – intentions in the past.
>
> ● ¿Qué **deseaba**?   ○ **Quería** una blusa talla 38.
>
> ▪ – certain polite expressions.

tender la ropa –
to hang out the clothes

The imperfect is often used in the following statements of time:

– **antes**	**Antes** había aquí una casa amarilla.
– **(en aquel) entonces**	En **aquel entonces** había poca gente.
– **todos los días**	El abuelo nos visitaba **todos los días**.
– **con frecuencia**	**Con frecuencia** íbamos con él a la playa.
– **normalmente**	**Normalmente**, pescábamos con él.
– **de niño / -a, joven**	**De niño**, me encantaba pescar.

1. Before a fashion show, the air is full of tension. Using the appropriate verbs, fill in the blanks in these minidialogues. *

hemos cosido – he puesto – has visto –
ha dicho – ha empezado – ha guardado – ha habido – ha traído –
~~habéis terminado~~ – han salido

coser – *to sew (on)*
equivocado – *here: wrong*
descalzo / -a – *barefooted*
lápiz labial – *lipstick*
el muestrario – *the sample folder*
guardar – *to put away*
el maletín – *the briefcase*
¡A callar! – *Be quiet!*
el desfile – *the fashion show*
la pasarela – *the runway*

a) • Chicas, ¿ya __habéis terminado__ la chaqueta?

   ○ No, todavía no le _____ los botones...

b) • Parece que aquí _____ una confusión.

   ¡La zapatería _____ estos zapatos en el color equivocado!

   ○ No importa, por suerte la modelo _____ que prefiere ir

   descalza, con este vestido se ve muy bien.

c) □ Vanessa, ¿ _____ mi lápiz labial? No sé dónde lo _____ .

d) • ¿Alguien _____ los muestrarios? ¡No están en el maletín!

e) ○ Chicos, ¡a callar todos! Ya _____ el desfile.

   • Sí, ya _____ Patricio y Didac con los primeros trajes a la

   pasarela...

> The present perfect of **hay** is **ha habido**.

2. Below are the sentences Maribel wrote in her diary about New Year's Eve. Put the verbs given on the right in the present perfect. *

a) Este año la fiesta de Año Nuevo __ha tocado__ en casa. **b)** _____

toda la familia y, contándonos a todos, _____ veintinuno.

c) Claro que _____ un poco apretados, pero nos lo _____

súper bien. **d)** La cena _____ riquísima y luego Guillermo, como

siempre, _____ muchísimos chistes. **e)** Lo _____ tan

bien, que al final, ¡todos nosotros _____ de la risa!

f) Después de cenar, los más jóvenes _____ a la playa para

seguir la fiesta y nosotros, los mayores, _____ en casa

charlando hasta las 5 de la mañana. **g)** Sí, la reunión _____ muy

agradable: puedo decir que el año _____ muy bien.

a) tocar
b) venir, ser
c) estar, pasar
d) estar, contar
e) hacer, llorar
f) irse, quedarse
g) resultar, empezar

apretado – *squashed together*
el chiste – *the joke*
llorar de risa – *to laugh till you cry*

Practice and Application

3. Some Puerto Ricans are really enthusiastic about the gloomy weather in Scotland. Change the order of the sentences to create a telephone conversation. *

guay – *awesome, brilliant (teen slang)*
envuelto – *here: enveloped, surrounded*

(   ) ● ¡Qué guay! ¿Entonces han visto todos esos castillos antiguos envueltos en niebla?

(   ) ○ Sí, sí. Ha sido realmente muy romántico, algo totalmente diferente.

(   ) ○ Pues... No, pero ha hecho frío y también ha habido un poco de niebla. ¡Nos ha gustado mucho!

(1) ● Hola Carmencita, ¿ya has vuelto? ¿Qué tal lo han pasado?

(   ) ○ Estupendamente. Hemos viajado por toda la isla.

(   ) ● ¡Qué bien! ¿Y ha llovido como en todas las películas sobre Escocia?

4. Underline only the present perfect forms in Exercise 3 and write down the nine infinitives in the same order used in the dialogue. *

volver, _____

_____

5. Today Diego made a decision that was a big surprise to his wife. Fill in the verbs: present or present perfect? **

la sorpresa – *the surprise*
fuera – *outside (here: the home)*
llevar las tareas domésticas – *to keep house, do the housework*
quedar encantado / -a – *to be delighted*

a) Normalmente, cuando yo _llego_ *(llegar)* a casa, me _____ *(esperar)* mucho trabajo. ¡Pero hoy me _____ *(encontrar)* una sorpresa! **b)** Siempre soy yo quien _____ *(cocinar)*, pero esta noche, ¡Diego _____ *(preparar)* unos espaguetis estupendos y lo mejor: ¡_____ *(limpiar)* la cocina!

c) Me _____ *(decir)* que _____ *(leer)* un libro que le _____ *(abrir)* los ojos y que ahora _____ *(saber)* qué difícil _____ *(ser)* la vida de las mujeres que no sólo _____ *(trabajar)* fuera, sino que además _____ *(llevar)* solas las tareas domésticas. **d)** Así que _____ *(decidir)* cambiar y _____ *(querer)* participar más en los trabajos de casa... **e)** Yo _____ *(quedar)* encantada, claro, ¡y le _____ *(dar)* un gran beso!

6. Are you familiar with the Before-and-After Show? Put the verbs in **bold** in the imperfect. *

Antes, Rosita...

a) _estaba_____ muy gorda, ahora **está** muy delgada.

b) _____ un peinado muy anticuado, ahora **lleva** uno moderno.

c) No _____ nada de la moda, ahora **sabe** muchísimo.

d) No _____ ejercicio, ahora **hace** aeróbicos todos los días.

e) _____ tiempo para sus amigos, ahora sólo lo **tiene** para ser bonita.

7. Today you cooked the way your grandmother used to cook. Fill in the verbs. Present perfect or imperfect? *

a) Hoy ___he hecho___ la sopa como la ____hacía____ la abuela.

b) _____ los tomates porque ella los _____ también.

c) _____ la ensalada exactamente como ella la _____.

d) ¡Y me _____ todo igual a como le _____ a ella!

hacer

pelar

preparar

salir

pelar – *to peel*
salir + dative – *to turn out*

8. This short novel tells what it was like for parents whose children had left the nest. How had life changed for Conchita and Emilio? Put the verbs listed on the right in the imperfect. **

a) Así _____ a estar solos los dos, como cuando _____ recién casados. **b)** Su vida ahora no _____ tantos sobresaltos.

c) Emilio _____ dedicarse a sus libros, por las tardes _____ a sus amigos y no _____. **d)** Conchita _____ por las mañanas en la tienda y por las tardes _____ las cosas de casa.

e) Todos los días _____ alguno de los hijos. **f)** A veces _____ Loli de Badajoz, otras veces Miguel. **g)** Los dos _____ por sus padres y los _____ con frecuencia. **h)** Cuando _____ todos juntos a la mesa, los padres _____ orgullosos de verlos tan adultos. **i)** Y cuando _____ solos tampoco lo _____ mal, pero sí los _____ de menos.

a) volver, estar
b) tener
c) poder, ver, aburrirse
d) trabajar, hacer
e) llamar
f) ser
g) preocuparse, visitar
h) sentarse, sentirse
i) estar, pasar, echar

el sobresalto – *here: something unexpected*
preocuparse – *to worry (about)*
echar de menos – *to miss*

The Indefinido

The *indefinido* is the main narrative tense in Spanish. It is used to express events, actions, and states that have been definitely completed.

① ¿**Estuviste** ayer en el partido de fútbol?

② Sí, ¡**fue** el mejor de mi vida!

③ ¡**Ganamos** 2 a 1!

1. Were you at the soccer game yesterday? 2. Yes, it was the best of my life!
3. We won 2 to 1!

Formation

1. Regular Forms

1. Pay attention to the stress! Compare **trabajo** (first person singular, present) and **trabajó** (third person singular, *indefinido*).
2. For verbs ending in **-ar** and **-ir**, the first person plural form is identical to that for the present. The context will make it clear which tense is meant.

▶ Present, Verb Groups with Vowel Change, p. 108

	trabaj**ar**	aprend**er**	escrib**ir**
(yo)	trabaj**é**	aprend**í**	escrib**í**
(tú)	trabaj**aste**	aprend**iste**	escrib**iste**
(él / ella / usted)	trabaj**ó**	aprend**ió**	escrib**ió**
(nosotros / -as)	trabaj**amos**	aprend**imos**	escrib**imos**
(vosotros / -as)	trabaj**asteis**	aprend**isteis**	escrib**isteis**
(ellos / ellas / ustedes)	trabaj**aron**	aprend**ieron**	escrib**ieron**

2. Irregular Vowel Changes in the Third Person

Verbs ending in **-ir** that undergo a change in the stem vowel in the present (**e ▶ i, e ▶ ie, o ▶ ue**), are irregular in the *indefinido* only in the third persons singular and plural, where they exhibit an **i** or a **u**.

	e ▶ i **seguir**	**e ▶ ie** **preferir**	**o ▶ ue** **dormir**
(yo)	segu**í**	prefer**í**	dorm**í**
(tú)	seguiste	preferiste	dormiste
(él / ella / usted)	s**i**guió	pref**i**rió	d**u**rmió
(nosotros / -as)	seguimos	preferimos	dormimos
(vosotros / -as)	seguisteis	preferisteis	dormisteis
(ellos / ellas / ustedes)	s**i**guieron	pref**i**rieron	d**u**rmieron

In addition, this group includes:

corregir	*to correct*	elegir	*to choose, elect*
medir	*to measure*	pedir	*to order, ask for*
reír	*to laugh*	repetir	*to repeat*
servir	*to serve*	divertirse	*to have fun*
sentir	*to feel*	mentir	*to lie*
		morir	*to die*

3. Irregular Groups

Some verbs have an irregular stem in the *indefinido*. The endings correspond to those of regular verbs ending in **-er** / **-ir** with the exceptions of the first and third persons singular, which in addition are stressed on the next-to-last syllable.

	poder	hacer	decir
(yo)	pude	hice	dije
(tú)	pudiste	hiciste	dijiste
(él/ella/usted)	pudo	hizo	dijo
(nosotros/-as)	pudimos	hicimos	dijimos
(vosotros/-as)	pudisteis	hicisteis	dijisteis
(ellos/ellas/ustedes)	pudieron	hicieron	dijeron

1. Since all irregular verbs have the same endings, all you have to do is memorize the first person singular, and then the rest is easy.
2. The third person singular **hizo**, for the sake of pronunciation, is spelled with a **z**.

Verbs that end in an irregular stem with **-j** lose the **i** of the ending in the third person plural: **-jieron ▶ -jeron**.

You can learn the irregular *indefinido* stems more easily if you divide the verbs into the following groups:

tener:	**tuve**			decir:	**dije**
estar:	**estuve**	v	j	traer:	**traje**
andar:	**anduve**			traducir:	**traduje**
		irregular *indefinido* stems			
querer:	**quise**			poder:	**pude**
hacer:	**hice**	i	u	poner:	**puse**
venir:	**vine**			saber:	**supe**

1. The *indefinido* of **hay** belongs to the **u** group: **hubo**.
2. Related verbs are conjugated exactly the same way as the main verb: **proponer**, **suponer** like **poner**; **mantener**, **entretener** like **tener**, etc.

4. Irregular Verbs

1. **Ser** and **ir** have the same forms in the *indefinido*.
2. Note: **fui = yo, fue = él/ella/usted**.
3. **Dio** and **vio** are stressed on the **-o**, but carry no written accent because they are monosyllabic.

Only these verbs cannot be assigned to any group:

	ser/ir	dar	ver
(yo)	fui	di	vi
(tú)	fuiste	diste	viste
(él/ella/usted)	fue	dio	vio
(nosotros/-as)	fuimos	dimos	vimos
(vosotros/-as)	fuisteis	disteis	visteis
(ellos/ellas/ustedes)	fueron	dieron	vieron

5. Orthographic Changes in the *Indefinido*

In some verbs, the spelling changes before the ending **-é** of the first person singular in order to preserve the pronunciation:

c ▶ qu before **é**
mar**car**:   mar**qué**, marcaste, marcó, marcamos, marcasteis, marcaron
g ▶ gu before **é**
pa**gar**:   pa**gué**, pagaste, pagó, pagamos, pagasteis, pagaron
z ▶ c before **é**
empe**zar**: empe**cé**, empezaste, empezó, empezamos, empezasteis, empezaron

The letter combinations **ze** and **zi** do not exist (except in names).

With **oír** and verbs ending in **-eer**, **-aer**, and **-uir**, the unstressed **i** between the vowels in the third persons singular and plural is replaced by **y**.

oír ▶ oyó, oyeron
oír: oí, oíste, o**y**ó, oímos, oísteis, o**y**eron
-eer ▶ -eyó, -eyeron
leer: leí, leíste, le**y**ó, leímos, leísteis, le**y**eron
-aer ▶ -ayó, -ayeron
caer: caí, caíste, ca**y**ó, caímos, caísteis, ca**y**eron
-uir ▶ -uyó, -uyeron
constr**uir**: construí, construiste, constru**y**ó, construimos, construisteis, constru**y**eron

Traer does not belong to this group, but is written with a **j** in all persons: **traje, trajeron**.

Basic Meaning:

What happened (then)? Or How was it in the end?

Fui al estadio.   **Vi** el partido.   **Me gustó** mucho.

earlier, previously   *now*

The *indefinido* is used to express definitely completed past action. Unlike the present perfect, it is not connected with the present.

Use

Recibí una carta de mi hermana. Toda su vida **soñó** con ese viaje.

- The *indefinido* expresses concrete actions or events that the speaker regards as completed and not connected with the present.

En 2001 **visitamos** tres veces la fábrica.

- – sets a limit to repeated actions that have been completed.

Fue una fiesta estupenda. La música **me pareció** buenísima.

- – overall impressions or overall assessments.

Abrí la puerta y **vi** una luz. De repente **escuché** la voz de Manuel.

- – actions / events that occur suddenly or in sequence, and result in the course of the narrative and / or the framework of the action.

• Luis **cambió** de trabajo.   ○ ¡Por fin **encontró** algo mejor!

- – frequently, verbs whose meaning is the turning point, beginning, or end of an action.

The *indefinido* often is used with the following statements of time:

– **ayer, anoche**	¿Llamaste **ayer** al banco?
– **el/la** + time expression + **pasado/-a**	**La semana pasada** fui al cine.
– **en** + year / season	Sebastián nació **en 1995.**
– **de … a, desde … hasta**	Estuve en Quito **de mayo a junio.**
– **hace** + number + time expression	**Hace unos días** vi la película.
– **el otro día**	**El otro día** me encontré a Juan.
– **de pronto, de repente**	**De pronto**, noté que estabas ahí.

The *Indefinido* and Other Tenses

If the time of day at which an action occurred is stated with the word "today" and is past, then the *indefinido* is used.

It is useful to memorize the time expressions with which the present perfect, the imperfect, or the *indefinido* commonly are used. But even then the rules are not absolute. The use of these tenses depends more on what the speaker wants to express, on how he / she wants to depict what has taken place.

1. Present Perfect or *Indefinido*?

- ¡Por fin **hemos hecho** la presentación! ¿Qué les parece?
- Bien. Esta semana **hemos trabajado** duro, pero **ha valido** la pena.

The present perfect places emphasis on the connection to the present or refers to a space of time that has not yet expired.

In some countries in LA, the use of the present perfect and the *indefinido* is different. For example, in Mexico the present perfect is used much less than in Spain.

- Por fin **hicimos** la presentación. **Quedó** bien, ¿no?
- Sí, toda la semana **trabajamos** muy duro, pero **valió** la pena.

The *indefinido* tells us that something has been completed or refers to a space of time that is definitely in the past.

2. *Indefinido* or Imperfect?

Background: Imperfect   Action: *Indefinido*

Estaba en el coche   cuando **escuché** la noticia.

earlier, previously   *now*

The imperfect generally is used to depict circumstances, states of being, situations, or backgrounds. The action is recounted in the *indefinido*.

The choice of one tense or another allows the speaker to depict the occurrence in the way he / she wishes, for example, as one of the following:

– habit.	En verano **iba** todos los días a nadar.
– completed, repeated action.	En verano **fui** tres veces a nadar.
– description.	En Mallorca **hacía** mal tiempo.
– habit.	En Mallorca **hizo** mal tiempo.
– habit.	Todos los sábados **salíamos** a bailar.
– repeated action at a completed stage.	Todos los sábados **salimos** a bailar.
– description or background depiction.	Cuando salimos, **empezaba** a llover.
– onset of an action.	Cuando salimos, **empezó** a llover.
– description or repetition.	El curso **terminaba** en noviembre.
– end of an action.	El curso **terminó** en noviembre.

Basically, these are the guidelines: imperfect = background, description, repetition; *indefinido* = action, completed stage, overall evaluation.

The reaction, too, is different:
1. • **Estaba** mal.
   ○ ¿Sí? ¿Qué tenías?
2. • **Estuve** mal.
   ○ ¿Cuándo?

Shades of Meaning in Some Verbs

The combination of certain verbs with the *indefinido* or imperfect can express differences in meaning.

No **conocías** a Pepe, ¿verdad? ¿Cuándo **conociste** a Pepe?	**conocer**	+ imperfect + indefinido	to know to become acquainted
José ya **sabía** el resultado. José **sabía** tener paciencia. El jueves José **supo** el resultado.	**saber**	+ imperfect + indefinido	to know, to know how to to learn
Teníamos mucha sed. Después de las empanadas, **tuvimos** mucha sed.	**tener**	+ imperfect + indefinido	to have, be to get, become

la paciencia – *the patience*

The Past Perfect

① Marvin nunca **había visto** nieve hasta que llegó a Estados Unidos.

② Antes nunca **había viajado** a ese país, siempre había vivido en el Caribe.

▶ Past Participle,
p. 187

---

1. *Marvin had never seen snow before he came to the United States.*
2. *He had never traveled to that country before; he had always lived in the Caribbean.*

Formation

The past perfect, or pluperfect, is formed with the imperfect of **haber** and the past participle. The corresponding forms of the auxiliary verb always directly precede the past participle; they are never separated. The participle ends in **-o**, regardless of the number or gender of the subject.

(yo)	**había**	trabaja**do**
(tú)	**habías**	teni**do**
(él / ella / usted)	**había**	discuti**do**
(nosotros / -as)	**habíamos**	escri**to**
(vosotros / -as)	**habíais**	pues**to**
(ellos / ellas / ustedes)	**habían**	hec**ho**

Basic Meaning:

What happened before another action? Or
What preceded another state of being?

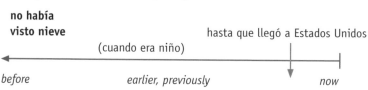

**no había
visto nieve** hasta que llegó a Estados Unidos

(cuando era niño)

before   *earlier, previously*   *now*

The past perfect expresses an action that took place before another action or before another state of being in the past.

1. Match the verbs on the right with the subjects on the left. *

a) yo: ~~repetí~~, _____

b) tú: _____

c) él/ella/usted: _____

d) nosotros/-as: _____

e) vosotros/-as: _____

f) ellos/ellas/ustedes: _____

~~repetí~~ dio
fue hicimos
escribiste dijeron
empecé pusisteis
viste recordamos
siguió estuvisteis
pidieron tuve
comimos tomaste
limpiasteis pudieron

2. Are you familiar with the cartoonist Guillermo Mordillo? Write down the infinitives of the verbs in red in this short biography. **

a) Guillermo Mordillo nació en 1932 en Buenos Aires, hijo de españoles que llegaron a Argentina como inmigrantes. **b)** Mordillo realizó sus primeros trabajos a los 18 años y pronto fundó con unos amigos un estudio de dibujos animados. **c)** De los 23 a los 28 años estuvo en Perú y se dedicó a la publicidad, pero después decidió volver al dibujo y se fue a los EEUU y más tarde, en 1963, a París. **d)** Pronto empezó a trabajar para diferentes periódicos y revistas. **e)** Poco a poco se hizo famoso y en los años que siguieron recibió muchos premios y publicó muchos libros. **f)** En 1980 se mudó a Mallorca, donde sigue dibujando.

fundar – *to found*
un estudio – *a studio*
los dibujos animados –
the cartoons
la publicidad –
the advertising
el dibujo – *the drawing*
hacerse famoso –
to become famous

a) <u>nacer</u>____, _____, b) _____, _____,

c) _____, _____, _____, _____, d) _____,

e) _____, _____, _____, _____, f) _____

3. Match the two columns to find out who these famous people were. *

a) Isabel la Católica fue la reina que

b) Cristóbal Colón fue un marino italiano

c) Salvador Dalí fue un pintor famoso que

d) Miguel de Cervantes fue un autor clásico

e) Francisco Franco fue un dictador que

1. que escribió el "Quijote".

2. gobernó España por 40 años.

3. financió a Cristóbal Colón.

4. tuvo un estilo muy original.

5. que descubrió América.

Practice and Application

Indefinido and Other Tenses

4. Two friends are discussing an interesting trip. Put the verbs below in the *indefinido*. **

a) ir
b) viajar, ser
c) conocer
d) visitar, ver
e) vivir
f) pasar
g) volar, quedarse, ahorrarse, pagar

a) • Hola, Carlos, ¿adónde _____ en las vacaciones?

b) ○ _____ con Alex a México. ¡ _____ un viaje precioso!

c) • ¡Qué suerte! Y, ¿qué _____ ustedes del país?

d) ○ _____ el D.F., naturalmente. Es una ciudad increíble.

   Y también _____ la zona de Yucatán.

e) • En Yucatán y Centroamérica _____ los mayas, ¿verdad?

f) ○ Sí. Alex y yo _____ varios días en esa región.

   • ¡Qué interesante! ¿Y el precio, qué tal?

g) ○ Bien, porque _____ con una oferta de "último minuto", y

   además, en la Ciudad de México _____ con unos amigos…

   Así _____ el hotel y casi no _____ nada.

   • ¡Qué bien! ¡Qué viaje! Me gustaría poder hacerlo también.

5. A murder mystery! Assign the verbs to the correct tense categories. **

asesinar – *to murder*
el primo – *the cousin*
odiar – *to hate*
el ambiente – *the atmosphere*
tenso – *tense*
el enemigo – *the enemy*

¿Quién asesinó a Eva Cruz Guerra? Antonio Guerra, su primo, la encontró el sábado por la mañana en el parque. "He pasado hoy por ahí, como cada mañana", dijo Antonio a este periódico. "Desde la última fiesta familiar no la había visto más. Bueno, pues como he dicho, iba por el parque… De repente, la vi en un banco: ¡Había muerto, qué horrible!" Le hemos preguntado si cree que ha habido algún posible motivo. "Bueno," respondió. "Su hermana Ana y ella siempre habían sido rivales, ¿sabe? Eva también trabajaba en el banco, pero Ana tenía un puesto más importante. Alguna vez las dos me hablaron de un jefe un poco raro, sí. Una vez me dijeron que él odiaba a las mujeres y que por eso el ambiente en el banco era muy tenso para ellas. Y luego… nuestro abuelo fue general y claro, en su vida ha hecho muchos enemigos. No sé, no sé. Realmente no sé quién ha sido."

a) *Indefinido*: asesinó _____

b) Imperfecto: _____

c) Perfecto: _____

d) Pluscuamperfecto: _____

6. Practice makes perfect! Fill in the blank areas of the table. *

		Indefinido	Imperfect	Perfect Perfect	Past Perfect	Infinitive
a)	1st sing.	vi	veía	he visto	había visto	ver
b)	2nd sing.			has sido		
c)	3rd sing.				había seguido	
d)	1st pl.		estábamos			
e)	2nd pl.					decir
f)	3rd pl.		tenían			
g)	1st sing.	puse				

7. Fill in the blanks in these minidialogues in the company cafeteria of a large firm. Which tense is right here: imperfect, *indefinido*, or present perfect?**

a) encontrar, estar

b) pensar, estar, trabajar, aprender, tener

c) hacer, hacer, salir, ir, conocer

a) • La semana pasada yo <u>encontré</u> un billete de 100 pesos.

  ○ ¿De verdad? ¿Dónde _____?

b) ■ Yo _____ que el Sr. Perea es el mejor candidato. _____

  dos años en París, donde _____ en una empresa. Así que

  _____ muy bien el francés y ya _____ experiencia

  en el extranjero.

c) • ¿Qué _____ este fin de semana, Julián?

  ○ Pues el sábado no _____ nada especial, pero ayer mi novia

  y yo _____ con unos amigos a cenar. _____ a un

  restaurante que no _____, ¡buenísimo!

8. Banking arrangements. What happened previously? Choose one of the verbs in each pair. ***

el extracto – the (bank) statement

cobrar – to deduct

doble – twice

a) (Tuve)/Había tenido que bloquear la tarjeta porque la perdí/había perdido.

b) Llamé/Había llamado al banco para preguntar por qué no me llegó/había llegado el dinero.

c) En el extracto nos cobraron/habían cobrado el teléfono doble, así que ayer fui/había ido a protestar.

Indefinido and Other Tenses

9. Match the halves of the sentences below. **

a) No fui a ver a Lucía

b) Le compramos un regalo al niño

c) Estábamos ya durmiendo

d) A Pepa le encantaban los perros

e) Un día, llegó un señor

f) Aprendí inglés en una academia

1) porque el martes fue su cumpleaños.

2) que quería ver al jefe con urgencia.

3) que no estaba lejos de mi casa.

4) porque sabía que no estaba en casa.

5) hasta que uno la mordió en la pierna.

6) cuando de repente oímos un ruido extraño.

10. Here you will learn something about the history of Puerto Rico. Choose the appropriate past tense form. ***

la tribu – *the tribe*
el/la indígena – *the native*
el levantamiento – *the uprising*
la defensa – *the defense, resistance*
la viruela – *smallpox*
sufrir – *to suffer*
el dominio – *the control*

a) Cuando Colón llegaba / llegó en 1493, vivían / vivieron allí 60 mil indígenas, sobre todo de las tribus arawak y taínas, que eran / fueron gente pacífica.

b) Los españoles conquistaban / conquistaron la isla y desde entonces obligaban / obligaron a los indígenas a trabajar como esclavos.

c) Pronto los indígenas dejaban / dejaron de creer que los blancos eran / fueron dioses e iniciaban / iniciaron un levantamiento, pero sin éxito.

d) Además, muchos indígenas morían / murieron porque no tenían / tuvieron defensas contra las nuevas enfermedades que traían / trajeron los conquistadores, por ejemplo la viruela.

e) Por su situación estratégica, entre 1508 y 1797 Puerto Rico sufría / sufrió muchos ataques de piratas ingleses y holandeses que llegaban / llegaron frecuentemente hasta el Caribe.

f) Durante el siglo XIX había / hubo varios intentos de independencia.

g) La economía de Puerto Rico dependía / dependió de la agricultura.

h) En 1898 España perdía / perdió el dominio de la isla en una guerra contra los Estados Unidos, y en 1917 Puerto Rico se convertía / convirtió en Estado Asociado de la Unión Americana.

11. A well-known fairy tale. Now you are faced with a choice: present perfect, imperfect, *indefinido*, or past perfect?

a) Hace mucho, <u>vivía</u> (vivir) en el bosque una familia que _____ (tener) dos hijos. **b)** El niño _____ (llamarse) Hansel y la niña, Gretel. **c)** Un día el padre _____ (mandar) a los niños a buscar leña, pero como el bosque _____ (ser) muy grande y oscuro, los pequeños _____ (perderse). **d)** – ¡No hay problema! – _____ (decir) Hansel, y rápidamente _____ (subirse) a un árbol para mirar. **e)** _____ (Descubrir) que cerca _____ (hay) una casa, y entonces los niños _____ (caminar) hasta allí. **f)** Cuando _____ (llegar), _____ (ver) que _____ (ser) la casa más maravillosa que nunca _____ (imaginarse): ¡toda de chocolate! **g)** – ¡Mmh, qué rica casa! – _____ (decir) los niños y _____ (empezar) a comérsela, porque no _____ (comer) en todo el día y _____ (estar) muy hambrientos. **h)** Pero de repente alguien, a quien ellos no _____ (ver) antes, _____ (llegar) volando en una escoba. **i)** _____ (Tratarse) de la dueña de la casa, que lamentablemente _____ (ser) una bruja mala, aunque ellos todavía no lo _____ (saber). **j)** Los _____ (saludar) amablemente y los _____ (invitar). **k)** Los niños _____ (ponerse) contentos y _____ (aceptar) la invitación. **l)** Ya en la casa, los dos _____ (cenar) y luego _____ (dormirse) soñando con el rico pastel que la señora les _____ (dar) antes. **m)** Pero al día siguiente, todo _____ (cambiar): Hansel _____ (despertar) en una jaula y desde ese momento, Gretel _____ (tener) que trabajar y trabajar. **n)** ¿Cómo _____ (terminar) la historia? Seguramente todos ustedes _____ (leer) alguna vez este cuento tan famoso.

la leña – *the firewood*
perderse – *to lose one's way*
imaginarse – *to imagine*
comérsela – *to eat it up*
hambriento / -a – *hungry*
la escoba – *the broom*
la bruja – *the witch*
ponerse contento – *to be happy*
dormirse – *to go to sleep*
soñar – *to dream*
la jaula – *the cage*

The Future

① Vas a ser muy feliz …

② Tendrás mucho éxito en la vida…

③ A los 40 años ya te habrás casado… ¿Quieres saber más?

④ Depende. ¿Cuánto me costará?

In addition to the "correct" future form of the verbs, Spanish also commonly uses the verbal phrase (periphrasis) **ir + a +** infinitive for the notion of action in the future.

1. You're going to be very happy … 2. You'll have a lot of success in life … 3. By the age of 40 you will already have married … Do you want to know more? 4. It depends. How much will it cost me?

When stating a time with reference to the future, you have various options in Spanish for expressing future actions or intentions.

▶ **Verbal Periphrasis,** p. 191

The future is used in colloquial speech more frequently in Spain than in LA.

Mañana **voy** al cine. *I'm going to the movies tomorrow.*	present
Mañana **voy a ir** al cine. *I'm going to go to the movies tomorrow.*	present of **ir + a** + infinitive
Mañana **iré** al cine. *I will go to the movies tomorrow.*	future
Mañana a esta hora ya **habré visto** la película. *By this time tomorrow I will have already seen the film.*	future perfect

Simple Future

The future tense is used to express future actions.

① Llegaremos en el avión que viene a las 8 de la mañana de Berlín.

② Lo siento, pero a esa hora no podré ir al aeropuerto a buscaros.

1. We will arrive at 8 in the morning on the plane from Berlin.
2. I'm sorry, but at that time I will not be able to go to the airport to pick you up.

Formation

1. Regular Forms

The formation of the future tense is not difficult. All the conjugational groups have the same endings, which are directly attached to the infinitive.

	trabajar	aprender	escribir
(yo)	trabajar**é**	aprender**é**	escribir**é**
(tú)	trabajar**ás**	aprender**ás**	escribir**ás**
(él / ella / usted)	trabajar**á**	aprender**á**	escribir**á**
(nosotros / -as)	trabajar**emos**	aprender**emos**	escribir**emos**
(vosotros / -as)	trabajar**éis**	aprender**éis**	escribir**éis**
(ellos / ellas / ustedes)	trabajar**án**	aprender**án**	escribir**án**

2. Irregular Forms with Shortened Stem

Some verbs have an irregular shortened stem, to which the endings are attached.

caber	**cabr-**	-é
decir	**dir-**	-ás
hacer	**har-**	-á
querer	**querr-**	-emos
poder	**podr-**	-éis
saber	**sabr-**	-án

1. Since all forms of the future tense have the same endings, all you have to do is memorize the first person singular.
2. The future of **hay** is **habrá**.
3. **Proponer, suponer,** etc. are conjugated the same way as **poner.**

3. Irregular Forms with -d- in the Stem

In some verbs, the final vowel of the infinitive is replaced by a **d.** The endings are attached to this new stem.

poner	**pondr-**	-é
salir	**saldr-**	-ás
tener	**tendr-**	-á
valer	**valdr-**	-emos
venir	**vendr-**	-éis
		-án

Future

Basic Meaning:

What will take place?

Llegaremos a Boston. Pronto **estaremos** ahí.

now ——————————— later

In Spanish, unlike English, future verb forms can also express something that is probable or supposed.

▶ **Open Conditional Sentence**, p. 233

English uses words such as *likely* or *probably* to indicate conjecture or supposition.

Pero, ¡serás tonto! – *Man, you must be really stupid!*
¡Si lo sabré yo! – *I know it only too well!*

▶ **Present Subjunctive**, p. 159

Use

¡Qué ilusión! Mañana a esta hora **estaremos** en la playa.

The future is used to refer to future events, situations, and states of being.

Si no tienes experiencia, no **conseguirás** trabajo.

– consequences of an action or a situation that the speaker regards as highly likely.

Tocan a la puerta. ¿Quién **será** a esta hora?

– suppositions.

Raúl no **tendrá** dinero, pero es el chico que me gusta.

– admissions or concessions.

Hoy no **saldrás**, ¡y basta! Me **ayudarás** en casa.

– commands or prohibitions.

Pero, **¡serás** tonto, Jorge! ¿Cómo le has prestado dinero a tu hermana? Nunca paga, ¡si lo **sabré** yo!

– certain expressions reflecting exaggeration or astonishment.

If dependent clauses with **cuando** (*when*), **en cuanto** (*as soon as*), **hasta que** (*until*), or **mientras** (*while*) are introduced, and if their action is in the future, the future tense is replaced by the present subjunctive.

- Cuando **llegue**, te llamaré enseguida.
- Bueno. Me quedaré despierta hasta que **llames**.
- *When I **arrive**, I'll call you at once.*
- *Fine. I'll stay awake until you call.*

The Future Perfect

¡Esta novela es fascinante! ¿Quién **habrá sido** el asesino?

▶ **Past Participle**,
p. 187

This novel is fascinating. Who is likely to have been the murderer?

Formation

The future perfect is formed with the future tense of **haber** and the past participle. The corresponding forms of the auxiliary verb always directly precede the past participle; they are never separated. The participle ends in **-o** and is invariable.

(yo)	**habré**	trabaja**do**
(tú)	**habrás**	teni**do**
(él / ella / usted)	**habrá**	discuti**do**
(nosotros / -as)	**habremos**	escri**to**
(vosotros / -as)	**habréis**	pues**to**
(ellos / ellas / ustedes)	**habrán**	hech**o**

Basic Meaning:

What probably has happened?

Ya **habremos llegado** mañana a esta hora.

now — later

Use

Mañana a las 8 ya **habremos terminado**.

The future perfect is used for actions or states of being that will have been completed in the future before another future event or another future action.

Juan no está en la fiesta. ¿No lo **habrán invitado**?

– suppositions about something that probably has already taken place.

Pero, ¿se **habrá visto** cosa igual? ¿Quién **habrá diseñado** eso?

– certain fixed expressions of astonishment.

¿Se habrá visto cosa igual? – Have you ever seen anything like it?

The Conditional

Yo en tu lugar **me pondría** *ropa más abrigada.* ①

No, mamá, ¡entonces **me vería** *como tú!* ②

¡Imagínate lo que **habrían dicho** *mis amigos!* ③

The conditional indicative tense is generally translated by the English *would*.

1. If I were you, I would wear warmer clothing. 2. No, Mom, then I would look like you!
3. Imagine what my friends would have said!

The conditional is a mood of the verb. It is used by the speaker to say that the action indicated could happen or could have happened. There are only two tenses in the conditional: the simple conditional (*condicional simple*) and the conditional perfect (*condicional perfecto*).

▶ **Mood, p. 105**

The Simple Conditional

*¿**Podría** decirme a qué hora llega el tren de Zamora, por favor?*

Could you tell me what time the train from Zamora arrives, please?

1. Note: The endings of the conditional correspond to those of the imperfect tense of verbs ending in **-er / -ir**. They are attached to the infinitive.
2. The first and third person singular forms are identical. The context will make it clear who the subject is.

Formation

1. Regular Forms

In the conditional, all the conjugational groups have the same endings, which are attached directly to the infinitive.

	trabajar	aprender	escribir
(yo)	trabajaría	aprendería	escribiría
(tú)	trabajarías	aprenderías	escribirías
(él / ella / usted)	trabajaría	aprendería	escribiría
(nosotros / -as)	trabajaríamos	aprenderíamos	escribiríamos
(vosotros / -as)	trabajaríais	aprenderíais	escribiríais
(ellos / ellas / ustedes)	trabajarían	aprenderían	escribirían

2. Irregular Forms with a Shortened Stem

The following verbs have an irregular shortened stem, to which the endings of the conditional are attached.

caber	**cabr-**	-ía
decir	**dir-**	-ías
hacer	**har-**	-ía
querer	**querr-**	-íamos
poder	**podr-**	-íais
saber	**sabr-**	-ían

1. The irregular verb stems of the conditional correspond to those of the future.
2. In place of **querría**, the form **quisiera** is commonly used.

3. Irregular Forms with -d- in the Stem

In some verbs, the final vowel of the infinitive is replaced by a **d**. The endings for the conditional are attached to this new stem.

poner	**pondr-**	-ía
salir	**saldr-**	-ías
tener	**tendr-**	-ía
valer	**valdr-**	-íamos
venir	**vendr-**	-íais
		-ían

1. Be sure to memorize the first person singular.
2. The simple conditional of **hay** is **habría**.

Use

Aquí **podríamos** poner una lámpara, ¿no crees? Así **habría** más luz.

- The conditional is used for events that could happen now or later under certain conditions.

¿**Sería** tan amable de ayudarme? ¿Qué hotel me **recomendaría**?

- – polite requests and questions.

- Yo **diría** que ese es el rey en persona, pero me **gustaría** saberlo.
- ○ Yo en tu lugar no lo **molestaría**. **Deberías** dejarlo en paz.

- – politely expressed opinions, wishes, and suggestions, as well as obligations that one should fulfill.

Si hiciera frío, **podríamos** nadar en la piscina cubierta.

- – consequences of an improbable or unfulfillable condition.

The translation of the Spanish conditional into English depends on the context. For example, **Podríamos hacer algo** (We *could* do something), **Yo diría que sí** (I *would* say so), **Deberías dejarlo** (You *ought* to give it up).

▶ **Contrary-to-fact Conditional Clause**, p. 233

> **Serían** las nueve de la noche cuando llamó tu hermano.
>
> ■ – conjectures about an event or an action in the past.
>
> El primer día de clase, nos presentaron a los muchachos que **bailarían** con nosotras durante todo el curso.
>
> ■ – events that, viewed from the past, still lie in the future.
>
> ¡Qué raro! Rosalba dijo que **vendría** a buscarme y no llega.
> (Dijo: "**Vendré** a buscarte.")
>
> ■ – statements in indirect discourse, if the introductory verb is in the past and the verb of the direct discourse is in the future.

▶ **Indirect Discourse**, p. 235

In colloquial speech, the construction **iba a** + infinitive is also frequently used to express a past intention: **Dijo que iba a venir a buscarme.**

The Conditional Perfect

Yo en tu lugar **habría gastado** menos dinero.

①

De haber sabido, me **habría quedado** en casa.

②

1. *If I were you I would have spent less money.*
2. *If I had known that, I would have stayed home.*

Formation

▶ **Past Participle**, p. 187

The conditional perfect is formed with the simple conditional of **haber** and the past participle. The corresponding forms of the auxiliary verb always directly precede the participle; they are never separated. The past participle ends in **-o**, regardless of the number or gender of the subject.

(yo)	**habría**	trabajad**o**
(tú)	**habrías**	tenid**o**
(él / ella / usted)	**habría**	discutid**o**
(nosotros / -as)	**habríamos**	escrit**o**
(vosotros / -as)	**habríais**	puest**o**
(ellos / ellas / ustedes)	**habrían**	hech**o**

Use

Habríamos utilizado la piscina cubierta en caso de haber hecho frío.

The English equivalent is usually *would have*, as in *we would have used*.

■ The conditional perfect is used for actions, events, or states of being that could have occurred in the past, if a condition had been fulfilled.

▶ **Contrary-to-fact Conditional Clause**, p. 233

Te **habría llamado** antes, pero no pude. Lo siento.

■ – events that did not occur or were missed in the past.

In the first two examples, you can also use **hubiera** instead of **habría** in colloquial speech.

Vamos al restaurante. Carlos dijo que a las nueve ya habrían **terminado** el trabajo y que estarían allí.
(Dijo: "A las nueve ya **habremos terminado** y estaremos allí.")

■ – statements in indirect discourse, if the introductory verb is in the past and the corresponding direct discourse contains a verb in the future perfect.

▶ **Indirect Discourse**, p. 235

The simple conditional and conditional perfect often are used together with the following expressions:

– de + infinitive	● **De** tener dinero, ¿te comprarías una casa?
– (yo) en tu lugar	○ **Yo en tu lugar** lo pensaría.
– en ese caso	● ¿Qué harías tú **en ese caso**?
– yo que tú	○ **Yo que tú**, lo habría consultado con un experto.

yo en tu lugar = yo que tú

Practice and Application

Conditional

1. Use the verbs given on the left to fill in the blanks below. *

haré
~~hará~~
iremos
pasaremos
Saldremos
traerá

a) Mañana _haré_ buen tiempo.

b) Raúl y yo _____ de excursión.

c) _____ temprano de casa.

d) Yo _____ una rica tortilla de arroz.

e) Él _____ el vino y el pan.

pasarlo a gusto – *to spend time pleasantly*

f) Seguramente lo _____ muy a gusto.

2. The day after tomorrow, the two of them will have their outing behind them. Provide information about what they will have done. *

~~habrá pasado~~
Habrá sido
habré vuelto
nos habremos
relajado

a) Pasado mañana el fin de semana ya _habrá pasado_ .

b) Raúl y yo _____ en el campo.

c) Yo _____ bastante tarde a casa.

d) _____ un bonito domingo.

3. You can see into the future, and you know what Pepe and his parrot will do tomorrow. Use the future tense. *

estar todavía dormido – *to be still asleep*
la impresora – *the printer*

a) Pepe, tú _saldrás_ *(salir)* de casa como siempre.

b) A esa hora Lorito _____ *(estar)* todavía dormido.

c) Tú _____ *(ir)* al trabajo.

d) Los colegas te _____ *(pedir)* ayuda para un proyecto urgente y

tú _____ *(hacer)* unas gráficas para ellos.

e) Al sacarlas de la impresora _____ *(tener)* un pequeño accidente.

f) Un compañero te _____ *(llevar)* al médico y luego a casa.

g) Lorito _____ *(alegrarse)* mucho de verte.

h) _____ *(Saludarte)* y te _____ *(decir)* las 10 palabras que

sabe.

4. By tomorrow evening at 10, Pepe and Lorito will have done all that.
Put the verbs from Exercise 3 in the future perfect tense. **

Mañana a las diez...

a)   _habrás salido_   e)   _____

b)   _____   f)   _____

c)   _____   g)   _____

d)   _____   h)   _____

5. Which statements go together? Make the correct matches. **

a)   ¿Qué harán en las vacaciones?   1)   No sé si querrá comer.

b)   Esta inversión crecerá en   2)   ¡Te juro que no volverá a
     un 10%.   pasar!

c)   Susana no se siente nada bien.   3)   Realmente se la recomiendo.

d)   El presidente es muy joven, ¿no?   4)   ¿No la habrás dejado en el
                                               coche?

e)   ¿Por qué no se podrá confiar   5)   Me imagino que iremos a la
     en ti?   playa.

f)   No sé dónde habré puesto   6)   Sí, tendrá a lo mucho 50 años.
     la llave.

la inversión –
the investment
a lo mucho – *at the
most*
confiar – *to trust*
jurar – *to swear*

el taller – *the workshop,
studio*
la artesanía –
the (handi)crafts
el recuerdo – *here: the
souvenir, memento*
asomarse – *to lean out*
el barranco –
the gully, ravine
colgante – *hanging*
el borde – *the edge*
la vega –
the fertile lowland
el mirador –
the watchtower
la fachada – *the façade*

6. What will we do in Sorbas, a village in the province of Almería? Follow
the suggestions of the tourist guide, numbering the sentences below
from 1 to 7. ***

a)   (   ) Finalmente, visitaremos un taller de artesanía donde ustedes
           podrán ver el trabajo de los artesanos y comprar algún recuerdo.

b)   (   ) Desde allí nos asomaremos al barranco y podremos apreciar las
           casas colgantes, construidas al borde de enormes rocas.

c)   (   ) Pasearemos por el barrio histórico y veremos las casas señoriales.

d)   (   ) También disfrutaremos del maravilloso panorama de la vega.

e)   (1) • Señores, esta tarde visitaremos el pueblo de Sorbas.

f)   (   ) Les contaré la historia de las familias que vivieron en ellas y
           siguiendo por las calles estrechas llegaremos hasta un mirador.

g)   (   ) Son privadas, pero admiraremos sus bonitas fachadas.

Future and Conditional

7. A conversation about the difficult economic situation. Put the verbs in **bold** in the simple conditional. *

a) • La situación económica es difícil. ¿Es bueno **guardar** dinero en casa?

○ No, yo no _guardaría_ dinero en casa.

b) • ¿Es mejor **poner** los ahorros el en banco?

○ Sí, los expertos dicen que ellos los _____ en el banco.

c) • ¿Es recomendable **gastar** mucho?

○ No creo. Tú seguramente no _____ mucho, ¿verdad?

d) • ¿Es un buen momento para **comprar** una casa?

○ Sí. De ser posible, nosotros la _____ .

e) • ¿Es buena idea **tener** dos trabajos?

○ ¡No! ¡Yo definitivamente no _____ dos trabajos!

8. Many useful expressions are formed with the conditional. Match the sentences with the appropriate explanations. **

a) ¿Me podría dar la hora?   1) request for advice

b) Me encantaría, pero ese día no puedo.   2) polite request

c) Deberían arreglar las cosas.   3) question in a department store

d) ¿Le gustaría ver la carta de vinos?   4) inquiry about the time of day

e) Yo diría que es mejor esperar un poco.   5) advice (obligation)

f) ¿Te importaría cerrar la ventana?   6) offer in a restaurant

g) ¿Tendría ese pantalón en otro color?   7) personal opinion

h) ¿Tú qué harías en mi lugar?   8) polite refusal of an invitation

arreglar – *here: to put in order*

te importaría – *would it matter to you*

9. Now underline the forms of the conditional and write down the eight infinitives. *

poder, _____

_____

10. Intercultural knowledge. Fill in the blanks with the appropriate verbs. **

a) Al tomar un taxi en España o Latinoamérica, _me sentaría_ en el asiento de atrás.

b) En invitaciones formales, _____ siempre hasta la última migaja.

c) En un restaurante, _____ un asiento libre en una mesa ocupada.

d) En un bar con amigos, _____ la cuenta entre todos.

e) De tener los zapatos sucios, los _____ a la entrada de la casa de mis amigos.

f) De ser mujer, si un español me saluda con "¡Hola, guapa!", _____ que quiere ligar.

g) Si he quedado con alguien en un bar, no _____ necesariamente a la hora en punto y _____ algo para leer.

h) Al despedirse mis amigos por primera vez, les _____ otro licor.

dejaría
me comería
llegaría
pensaría
ofrecería
pagaríamos
llevaría
me sentaría
ocuparía

el asiento – *the seat*
la migaja – *the crumb*
ligar – *to make advances, flirt*

11. Is this behavior interculturally correct? Write (C) for *correcto* and (I) for *incorrecto*. **

a) (C)   c) ( )   e) ( )   g) ( )
b) ( )   d) ( )   f) ( )   h) ( )

12. Hindsight is always 20/20! Put the verbs given below in the conditional perfect. ***

a) Yo que tú _habría pagado_ *(pagar)* menos por esta casa. ¡Ese precio es una barbaridad!

b) El camino que tomaron es muy largo, _____ *(poder)* tomar otro mejor.

c) Pero Paco, ¿por qué olvidaste el factor económico? Yo en tu lugar lo _____ *(tener)* en cuenta.

d) De haber sabido las consecuencias, nosotros nunca le _____ *(decir)* toda la verdad a Juliana.

una barbaridad – *here: a fortune*
tener en cuenta – *to take into account*

Affirmative Imperative

The Imperative

Anda, hijo, **ponte** los flotadores y **no te quedes** todo el tiempo en el agua, ¿eh? ①

¡**No te preocupes** tanto, mujer! **Relájate** un poco también. ②

> The imperative is used to give direct commands, ordering someone to do or not to do something.

▶ **Mood**, p. 105

1. Come on, son, put on your water wings and don't stay in the water all the time, okay?
2. Hey, don't worry so much! Relax a little too.

Unlike English, Spanish has one grammatical form for things one should do (affirmative imperative) and another for things one should not do (negative imperative).

The Affirmative Imperative

¡**Oiga**, camarero! **Traiga** la cuenta, por favor.

Excuse me, waiter! Bring the check, please.

Formation

1. Regular Forms

> The imperative of **ustedes** (or **vosotros**), in colloquial speech, is often replaced with the infinitive or with **a** + infinitive: **Niños, ¡venir a la mesa! ¡A comer!**

In forming the imperative, two groups of endings are used: one for verbs ending in **-ar** and one for verbs ending in **-er** and **-ir**.

	trabajar	aprender	escribir
(tú)	trabaja	aprende	escribe
(usted)	trabaje	aprenda	escriba
(nosotros/-as)	trabajemos	aprendamos	escribamos
(vosotros/-as)	trabajad	aprended	escribid
(ustedes)	trabajen	aprendan	escriban

The second person singular imperative (**tú**) and the third person singular present are identical in form.

The second person plural (**vosotros / -as**) is formed by replacing the final **-r** of the infinitive with **d**.

The forms of **usted**, **nosotros**, **ustedes** correspond to those of the present subjunctive. They differ from the present indicative forms only in that they have a vowel change: In the endings of the imperative, verbs ending in **-ar** have an **e**, while verbs ending in **-er** / **-ir** have an **a**.

> In LA, the forms for **vosotros** are not used.

> ▶ **Present Subjunctive**, p. 159

2. Verb Groups with a Change in the Stressed Forms

> ¡**Juega** un poco con tu imaginación! **Piensa** en una playa tranquila...

> ▶ **Present Indicative, Verb Groups,** p. 108 ff

Use a little imagination! Think of a quiet beach ...

In these groups, the stem changes only when it is stressed.

o ▶ ue	e ▶ ie	í	ú
volar	pensar	enviar	continuar
vuela	piensa	envía	continúa
vuele	piense	envíe	continúe
volemos	pensemos	enviemos	continuemos
volad	pensad	enviad	continuad
vuelen	piensen	envíen	continúen

> Verbs ending in **-ir** that belong to the (**ue**) and (**ie**) groups have an **i** or a **u** in the **nosotros / -as** form of the imperative: **sentir** – **sintamos**, **dormir** – **durmamos**.

3. *Oír* and Other Verb Groups

For these verb groups and for **oír**, the following applies: The forms for the second person singular (**tú**) and the second person plural (**vosotros / -as**) are regular. The other persons are derived from the first person present indicative.

> These forms are always derived from the first person present: pedir: **pido** ▶ **pida**, **pidamos**, **pidan**; traer: **traigo** ▶ **traiga**, **traigamos**, **traigan**, etc.

e ▶ i	zc	ig	
pedir	conocer	traer	oír
pide	conoce	trae	oye
pida	conozca	traiga	oiga
pidamos	conozcamos	traigamos	oigamos
pedid	conoced	traed	oíd
pidan	conozcan	traigan	oigan

Affirmative Imperative

▶ **Present Indicative, Verbs Groups, and Irregular Verbs,** p. 108 ff

4. Irregular Forms

These verbs exhibit irregular forms.

poner	hacer	salir	tener	venir
pon	haz	sal	ten	ven
ponga	haga	salga	tenga	venga
pongamos	hagamos	salgamos	tengamos	vengamos
poned	haced	salid	tened	venid
pongan	hagan	salgan	tengan	venga

decir	ver	dar	ser	estar	ir
di	ve	da	sé	está	ve
diga	vea	dé	sea	esté	vaya
digamos	veamos	demos	seamos	estemos	vayamos
decid	ved	dad	sed	estad	id
digan	vean	den	sean	estén	vayan

1. The forms **dé** and **sé** have a written accent, to distinguish them from the preposition **de** and the pronoun **se**.
2. **Vayamos** is often replaced with **vamos**.

5. Orthographic Changes

Where necessary, the spelling has to be adapted.

▶ **Orthographic Change in the Present,** p. 109

averiguar – to ascertain

Esco**ja** el menú, por favor.	-ger, -gir:	g ▶ j before a
Convenzamos al jefe.	-cer, -cir:	c ▶ z before a
¡Síganme!	-guir:	gu ▶ g before a
Mar**que** el número.	-car:	c ▶ qu before e
Pa**guen** en la caja.	-gar:	g ▶ gu before e
Empe**cemos** ya.	-zar:	z ▶ c before e
Averi**güen** bien los datos.	-guar:	gu ▶ gü before e

▶ **Object and Reflexive Pronouns,** p. 75 ff

6. Position of the Object Pronouns in the Affirmative Imperative

① ¿Me pongo el vestido negro?

② Sí, **pón**<u>telo</u>. Es muy sexy.

1. Shall I put on the black dress? 2. Yes, put it on. It's very sexy.

Object and reflexive pronouns must be attached to the affirmative imperative. If a sentence contains several pronouns, then the reflexive and / or dative pronouns come <u>before</u> the accusative pronoun, as here: pónga**sela**, cómpra**melo**.

1. The original stress is retained by means of the written accent: **pó**ntelo.
2. If **nos** is attached to the imperative of **ustedes**, a double -n results: **dí**gan<u>nos</u>.

¡Lava**os** los dientes y acost**aos**! ¡Es muy tarde ya!

If the reflexive pronoun **os** is attached to the **vosotros** form, then the **-d** is omitted (acosta<u>d</u> + **os** ▸ acost**aos**).

¡Lavémo**nos** los dientes y acostémo**nos**! ¡Es muy tarde ya!

If the reflexive pronoun **nos** is attached to the **vosotros** form, then the **-s** is omitted (acostemo<u>s</u> + **nos** ▸ acostémo**nos**).

Idos is an exception, but it is rarely used. **!**

1. If the infinitive is used instead of the imperative of **vosotros**, then **os** is directly attached: ¡Lava<u>ros</u> los dientes!
2. **Vayámonos** often is replaced with **vámonos**.

The Negative Imperative

Por favor, niños, ahora no **me molesten** y **no hagan** ruido, ¿vale?

Please, children, don't bother me now and don't make any noise, okay?

Formation

In the negative imperative, all forms of verbs ending in **-ar** have an **e** in the endings, and all forms of verbs ending in **-er** and **-ir** have an **a** in the endings.

The forms of the negative imperative correspond to the present tense forms of the subjunctive.

▸ **Present Subjunctive**, p. 159

	trabajar	aprender	escribir
(tú)	no trabaj**es**	no aprend**as**	no escrib**as**
(usted)	no trabaj**e**	no aprend**a**	no escrib**a**
(nosotros / -as)	no trabaj**emos**	no aprend**amos**	no escrib**amos**
(vosotros / -as)	no trabaj**éis**	no aprend**áis**	no escrib**áis**
(ustedes)	no trabaj**en**	no aprend**an**	no escrib**an**

The irregular verbs are derived from the form for **usted** and follow the patterns of the verb groups of the affirmative imperative, as below:

ser ▸ no seas, no sea, no seamos, no seáis, no sean
pensar ▸ no pienses, no piense, no pensemos, no penséis, no piensen
oír ▸ no oigas, no oiga, no oigamos, no oigáis, no oigan

Esa es mi chaqueta, ¡no **te la** lleves! ¡No **te la** pongas!

In the negative imperative, the object and reflexive pronouns are not attached. They directly precede the verb, still retaining this sequence: reflexive and / or dative pronoun <u>before</u> accusative pronoun.

▸ **Object and Reflexive Pronouns**, p. 75 ff

asombrarse –
to be amazed
batir – *to beat,*
whisk (eggs)
añadir – *to add*

Use

Pasa y **siéntate**. No te **asombres** por el desorden en mi oficina.

The imperative is used for demands, requests, and orders ...

Bata los huevos y **añádalos** a las patatas.

– instructions and recipes ...

No **llamen** ahora, **llamen** mañana. **Tengan** un poco de paciencia.

– advice and suggestions.

Common turns of speech and phrases of civility with the imperative:

¡Oiga!	*Excuse me!*
¡Dígame!	*Hello?* (on the phone)
Tenga.	*Here you are.*
¡Déjalo, no te preocupes!	*Forget it, don't worry about it!*
No te molestes.	*Don't go to any trouble.*
¡Anda, no me digas!	*Go on, you don't say!*
¡Cuenta, cuenta!	*Come on, out with it!*

Many Ways of Expressing Requests or Demands

Demands, orders, or instructions are not expressed in Spanish by means of the imperative exclusively; there are other ways as well:

By using **vamos a +** infinitive, the speaker includes himself / herself.

– infinitive or **a** + infinitive	Niños, **¡venir** a la mesa! ¡A **comer!**
– **vamos a** + infinitive	**Vamos a tomar** una cerveza.
– **por qué no** + interrogative sentence	**¿Por qué no** hacemos una pausa?
– **poder** + infinitive	**¿Puedes venir** un momento?
– **querer** + infinitive	**¿Quieres ayudarme**, por favor?
– verb of wishing + subjunctive	**Quiero que vengas**, por favor.
– impersonal expression + subjunctive	**Es importante que no faltes.**
– present tense	Ahora mismo **me dices** lo que pasa.
– simple future	**Vendrás** a casa ahora mismo.

1. Write the verbs on the appropriate lines. **

a) tú: _____

b) usted: repita, _____

c) nosotros / -as: _____

d) vosotros / -as: _____

e) ustedes: _____

repita   den
hagamos   poned
ven   escribe
baile   hablemos
seguid   oigan
id   sea   tomen
sal   recuerde

2. Who could have said this to whom? Match the sentences. **

1. un cliente a la camarera – 2. una madre a su hijo –
3. la jefa a su secretaria – 4. un enamorado a su novia –
5. un fotógrafo a la modelo

a) ( ) Ponte un poco más adelante y sube el brazo un poco. Así,
quédate así, ¡perfecto!

b) ( ) Corrija por favor la carta y démela enseguida para firmarla. Ah, y
mándela hoy mismo, por favor.

c) ( ) ¡No hagas tanto desorden en tu habitación, Julito! Vamos, ¡haz
la cama y pon la ropa en el armario!

d) (1) Muéstrenos el menú del día, por favor. Ah, y tráiganos también
una botella de agua mineral sin gas.

e) ( ) Anda, ya no te enfades conmigo... Mírame a los ojos y dame un
beso, ¡mi amor!

adelante – *here: forward*
enfadarse – *to get angry*

3. Now underline all the imperative forms used in the previous exercise,
and write down the fifteen infinitives. *

ponerse, _____

_____

_____

_____

Imperative

4. Which form is used, polite or familiar? You decide; write **tú** or **usted** in the parentheses. **

a) ¡Tráemelo! (_tú_) e) Siéntese. (____)

b) Mejor ponte una corbata. (____) f) Pero oye... (____)

c) ¡Ayúdenos! (____) g) Escúchame. (____)

d) Dígame. (____) h) ¡Váyase! (____)

5. We looked around town and found a lot of signs. Complete them by using the imperative of **usted**. **

pisar – *to step on*
el césped – *the grass, lawn*
tirar – *here: pull*
empujar – *here: push*
la basura – *the trash, garbage*

a) En el parque: No _pise_____ (pisar) el césped.

b) En un teléfono público: _____ (introducir) una moneda.

c) En una puerta: _____ (Tirar) – _____ (Empujar).

d) Frente al hospital: No _____ (hacer) ruido, por favor.

e) En la calle: _____ (Poner) la basura aquí.

f) Frente a un edificio: No _____ (aparcar) frente a esta puerta.

6. You would like to pass on these instructions to two friends, whom you naturally address with the familiar pronoun. Use the forms for **ustedes**. **

a) No _pisen_____ (pisar) el césped. d) No _____ (hacer) ruido.

b) _____ (introducir) una moneda. e) _____ (Poner) la basura aquí.

c) _____ (Tirar) – _____ (Empujar). f) No _____ (aparcar) ahí.

7. Practice makes perfect! Fill in the missing information in the table. *

	infinitive	tú	usted	nosotros/-as	vosotros/-as	ustedes
a)	empezar	empieza	empiece	empecemos	empezad	empiecen
b)		vende				
c)					subid	
d)	ir					
e)			diga			

8. Elsa, quite excited, is giving instructions, because she has planned a Sunday outing with the family. Fill in the blanks with the imperative forms of the verbs provided. ***

a) ¡Vamos, niños, <u>dejen</u> *(dejar)* de dormir, _____ *(levantarse)*!

b) Cariño, _____ *(ayudarme)*, _____ *(subir)* estas cosas al coche.

c) Hombre, ¡no _____ *(quejarse)* tanto! _____ *(Acomodarlo)* _____ a tu manera, siempre ha cabido todo en el maletero.

d) Niños, ¡_____ *(hacer)* las camas y _____ *(poner)* un poco de orden antes de irnos! ¡*(Ponerse)* _____ el bañador debajo de la ropa!

e) Bueno, por fin. Ahora, ¡_____ *(irse)* todos a la playa!

cariño – *darling*
acomodar – *to find a place for*
caber – *to fit*
el maletero – *the trunk*

9. So you like to contradict? Then turn these imperatives around. **

a) ¡No te acerques! <u>¡Acércate!</u>

b) ¡No te vayas! _____

c) ¡No me lo diga! _____

d) ¡Ponéoslas! _____

e) ¡Ríanse! _____

f) ¡Hazlo! _____

acercarse – *to come closer*
reírse – *to laugh; to laugh at*

10. Your advice is always in demand. Form the imperatives and replace the underlined words with the appropriate object pronouns. ***

a) • ¿Servimos vino con la paella?   ○ Sí, <u>servidlo</u>. *(vosotros)*

b) • ¿Sigo una dieta vegetariana?   ○ Claro, _____. *(tú)*

c) • ¿Leemos esta novela?   ○ Bueno, _____. *(nosotros)*

d) • ¿Le pido la loza a Santa Claus?   ○ Claro, _____. *(tú)*

e) • ¿Le compro un coche a mi hijo?   ○ No, _____. *(usted)*

f) • ¿Le traemos el catálogo al jefe?   ○ No, _____. *(vosotros)*

g) • ¿Me pongo estos pendientes?   ○ Sí, _____. *(tú)*

h) • ¿Terminamos este ejercicio?   ○ Sí, _____. *(nosotros)*

▶ **Object Pronouns**, p. 75 ff

los pendientes – *the earrings*

The Subjunctive

By using the subjunctive, someone expresses what is going in his / her heart or mind, including wishes, intentions, emotions, and doubts.

Overview

el taco – *Mexican specialty: filled tortilla*

• ¡Ojalá **estén** buenos los tacos! *I hope the tacos are good!*	present
○ Qué bueno que los **hayas preparado**. *How nice that you've made them.*	present perfect
Y **quisiera** probar la salsa, por favor... *And I'd like to try the salsa, please ...*	imperfect
¡Huy! ¡Me **hubieras dicho** que era tan picante! *Oops! You should have told me that it was so spicy!*	past perfect

The English subjunctive, unlike the Spanish, is rarely used. In Spanish, the subjunctive is essential for discussing hypothetical or potential events and subjective reactions.

In contrast to the indicative, the subjunctive refers to desires, emotions, doubts, possibility, or other future intentions. These may be realized or not.

With a few exceptions, the subjunctive occurs only in dependent clauses. Many are introduced by the conjunction **que** (*that*) and have a different subject than the main clause. If the main clause and the dependent clause have the same subject, the infinitive often is used:

Infinitive	Subjunctive
Quiero quedarme en casa.	**Quiero que** te quedes en casa.
I want to stay home.	*I want **you** to stay home.*
= *I am staying home.*	

▶ **Independent and Dependent Clauses**, p. 232

The subjunctive also is used in adverbial, relative, and conditional clauses. Usually the main clause contains a so-called subjunctive trigger, that is, a term that requires the subjunctive.

Present

Es necesario que **pongas** mucha atención para que **entiendas** bien esto.

It is necessary for you to pay good attention, so that you understand this properly.

> The present subjunctive can refer to the present (**Quiero que termines** *ahora mismo*) or to the future (**Quiero que termines** *mañana*).

Formation

1. Regular Forms

The formation of the present subjunctive is based on the following paradigm:

	trabajar	aprender	escribir
(yo)	trabaje	aprenda	escriba
(tú)	trabajes	aprendas	escribas
(él / ella / usted)	trabaje	aprenda	escriba
(nosotros / -as)	trabajemos	aprendamos	escribamos
(vosotros / -as)	trabajéis	aprendáis	escribáis
(ellos / ellas / ustedes)	trabajen	aprendan	escriban

> The present subjunctive is derived from the imperative form for **usted**.

The forms of the present subjunctive differ from the present indicative forms only by the presence of a vowel change: The endings for the **-ar** verbs contain an **e**, while those for the **-er** / **-ir** verbs contain an **a**.

2. Verb Groups with a Change in the Stressed Forms

Verbs ending in **-ar** and **-er** and belonging to the groups (**ue**), (**ie**), (**í**), and (**ú**) retain these changes in the present subjunctive in the same persons as in the present indicative (that is, when the stem is stressed).

▶ **Present Indicative, Verb Groups,** p. 108 ff

o ▶ ue	e ▶ ie	í	ú
volver	pensar	enviar	continuar
vuelva	piense	envíe	continúe
vuelvas	pienses	envíes	continúes
vuelva	piense	envíe	continúe
volvamos	pensemos	enviemos	continuemos
volváis	penséis	enviéis	continuéis
vuelvan	piensen	envíen	continúen

> **Jugar (u ▶ ue)** and **oler (o ▶ hue-)** also belong to this group.

Verbs ending in **-ir** and belonging to the (**ue**) and (**ie**) groups exhibit vowel changes in the present subjunctive in the forms that are stressed on the stem. In addition, in the first and second person plural, the **o** becomes **u** and the **e** becomes **i**.

o ▶ ue	e ▶ ie
dormir	sentir
duerma	sienta
duermas	sientas
duerma	sienta
durmamos	sintamos
durmáis	sintáis
duerman	sientan

3. Additional Verb Groups

Most verbs that exhibit any irregularity in the first person retain it in all persons of the present subjunctive.

Always memorize the first person, and then the rest is easy.

infinitive	pres. ind. yo	present subjunctive
pedir	pido	pida, pidas, pida, pidamos, pidáis, pidan
conocer	conozco	conozca, conozcas, conozca, conozcamos, conozcáis, conozcan
hacer	hago	haga, hagas, haga, hagamos, hagáis, hagan
oír	oigo	oiga, oigas, oiga, oigamos, oigáis, oigan
traer	traigo	traiga, ...
construir	construyo	construya, ...
poner	pongo	ponga, ...
tener	tengo	tenga, ...
decir	digo	diga, ...

4. Irregular Forms

1. The impersonal **hay** takes the form **haya**.
2. The monosyllabic **des** and **deis** have no written accent. **Dé** has one, in order to distinguish it from the preposition **de**.

ver	dar	ser	estar	ir	saber
vea	dé	sea	esté	vaya	sepa
veas	des	seas	estés	vayas	sepas
vea	dé	sea	esté	vaya	sepa
veamos	demos	seamos	estemos	vayamos	sepamos
veáis	deis	seáis	estéis	vayáis	sepáis
vean	den	sean	estén	vayan	sepan

5. Orthographic Changes

Where necessary, the spelling must be adapted.

Quiero que esco**j**áis un regalo.	**-ger, -gir:**	g ▶ j before **a**
Es importante que me conven**z**as.	**-cer, -cir:**	c ▶ z before **a**
No nos gusta que nos si**g**an.	**-guir:**	gu ▶ g before **a**
Espero que no te equivo**qu**es.	**-car:**	c ▶ qu before **e**
¡Ojalá los chicos lle**gu**en pronto!	**-gar:**	g ▶ gu before **e**
Tal vez empe**c**emos otro proyecto.	**-zar:**	z ▶ c before **e**
Es necesario que averi**gü**emos bien.	**-guar:**	gu ▶ gü before **e**

> If the spelling of the verbs changes in the imperative, this remains true for the subjunctive as well.

> ▶ **Imperative**, p. 152

> **Caber** (*to fit*) has the form **quepa** in the present subjunctive.

averiguar –
to investigate

Use

> No es problema que **vayamos** de excursión aunque **esté** nublado.

It's not a problem to go on an outing, even if it's cloudy.

Usually the present subjunctive is found in a dependent clause, whose main clause contains a subjunctive trigger in the present, present perfect, simple future, or imperative.

1. When <u>must</u> the subjunctive be used?

In these cases, you have no alternative:

- ● **¡Que** les **vaya** bien!
  ○ Gracias. Y ahora ... ¡**Vivan** las vacaciones! ¡**Muera** el estrés!

  – in expressions that express a wish in general. They may be introduced by **¡Que ...!** (*May ...*) or **¡Ojalá!** (*I hope*).

  Madre: Ven, Nidia. > *Hija:* ¿Qué? > *Madre:* ¡**Que vengas**!

  – in colloquial speech, when a demand that has not yet been met is repeated.

  Sírvase con ensalada. Para la receta de la salsa, **véase** la página 20.

  – in formal instructions, by way of exception with **-se** attached.

> 1. Generally, no object and reflexive pronouns are attached to the subjunctive.
> 2. When introducing a wish, **¡Que ...!** bears no written accent.

Memorize the major subjunctive triggers in their basic meanings!

Hija, ven aquí **para que** te diga algo... ¿No puedes ordenar tu cuarto **sin que** yo te lo pida, **en lugar de que** estés todo el día oyendo música? ¡Hoy no sales **antes de que** ordenes un poco!

– in dependent clauses after certain conjunctions such as **para que** (*in order that*), **sin que** (*without*), **antes / después (de) que** (*before / after*), and **en vez / lugar de que** (*instead of*), **a menos que** (*unless*), **en (el) caso (de) que** (*in case that*), **con tal (de) que** (*provided that*).

Quiero que hagan una lista de clientes. El jefe **ha pedido que** se la demos pronto, ¡así que no **les aconsejo** que lo dejen para mañana!

– in dependent clauses introduced by **que**, after verbs of causing, including verbs expressing wishes, commands, requests, permission, advice, intention, suggestions, hope, necessity, demands, etc.

1. When **esperar** means *to expect*, the indicative follows: Espero que no faltará nada.
2. Both **permitir** and **prohibir** can be followed by the infinitive: **Te prohíbo que digas** nada. = Te **prohíbo decir** nada.

querer	*to want, wish*	esperar	*to hope*
desear	*to wish*	pedir	*to ask, ask for*
preferir	*to prefer*	ordenar	*to order*
permitir	*to permit*	prohibir	*to prohibit, forbid*
conseguir	*to obtain, get*	hacer	*to make*
proponer	*to suggest*	rogar	*to request, ask*
exigir	*to demand*	insistir	*to insist*
aconsejar	*to advise*	recomendar	*to recommend*
evitar	*to avoid*	impedir	*to prevent*
necesitar	*to need*	más vale	*it is better*

Me alegra que por fin tengamos un día libre, pero no me **gusta que** tengamos todo el trabajo de casa. **Siento** que no podamos salir.

▶ **Verbs with the Dative**, p. 215

– in dependent clauses introduced by **que**, after expressions of feeling or emotion, such as pleasure, displeasure, joy, sorrow, anxiety, anger, fear, indifference, regret, amazement.

If you're fairly sure that the fear will be realized, the indicative can be used after **temer**: Temo que Jorge no vendrá.

gustar	*to like*	molestar	*to bother*
encantar	*to love, like very much*	preocupar	*to worry*
		estar harto/-a	*to be fed up*
fastidiar	*to annoy*	enfadar	*to make angry*
alegrar	*to make happy*	importar	*to be important, matter*
dar igual	*to be all the same*		
odiar	*to hate*	detestar	*to detest*
sentir	*to regret*	temer	*to fear*
sorprender	*to surprise*	quejarse (de)	*to complain*

Es bueno que descanses, no **es urgente que** me ayudes ahora.

– usually after the impersonal construction **es / está** + adjective / noun + **que**, which frequently expresses an assessment, but sometimes a possibility or a probability as well.

es posible / imposible que	*it is possible / impossible that*
es fácil / difícil que	*it is likely / unlikely that*
es bueno / malo que	*it is good / bad that*
es mejor / peor que	*it is better / worse that*
es maravilloso / horrible que	*it is wonderful / terrible that*
es necesario / útil que	*it is necessary / useful that*
es normal / raro que	*it is normal / strange that*
es lógico / ilógico que	*it is logical / illogical that*
es una suerte / un problema que	*it is lucky / a problem that*
es una pena / lástima que	*it is too bad / a pity that*
es una tontería / una locura que	*it is foolish / insane that*
estar bien / mal que	*to be good / bad that*

¡**Parece mentira que** la hija de Raúl ya tenga 18 años! **Puede ser que** sea tan guapa como él, pero **dudo que** sea tan arrogante.

– in dependent clauses introduced by **que**, after expressions of doubt or uncertainty, such as **dudar** (*to doubt*), **puede (ser)** (*it may be*), **parece mentira** (*it is incredible*).

Que yo sepa, vamos a ser ocho personas. **El hecho de que** venga Juan es una gran sorpresa, ¿no?

– in dependent clauses introduced by **que** that precede the main clause (*insofar as*), and after **El hecho de que** (*The fact that*).

Yo te buscaré **dondequiera que** estés.

– in relative clauses with **quienquiera**, **cualquiera**, **dondequiera**, and **comoquiera** (*whoever, whichever, wherever, however*).

Vayas adonde vayas, lleva tu tarjeta de crédito.

– in formulas of repetition that signify an open choice (*no matter who / what / where*, etc.) and in which the same verb is doubled in the subjunctive and linked by a relative pronoun or adverb.

Also after the construction ¡**Qué** + adjective / noun + **que ...!** with many of these examples, when they do not refer to the past:
¡**Qué lástima que** no vengas **a la fiesta!**

After expressions of certainty, such as **es verdad / cierto**, etc., the indicative follows (see below).

If these expressions are negated, the speaker can express certainty by using the indicative, as here:
No dudo que vendrá.

Memorize the fixed expressions in the subjunctive, such as **como sea** (*no matter how*), **quien sea** (*no matter who*), **como quieras** (*as you wish*), **pase lo que pase** (*come what may*).

2. When Is There a Choice between Subjunctive and Indicative?

In these cases you need to choose between the subjunctive and the indicative, depending on what you would like to express:

> ! The indicative is always used with **a lo mejor** (*maybe, perhaps*): **A lo mejor tienes razón.**

Indicative	Subjunctive
high probability	*rather unlikely*
Tal vez tienes razón.	**Tal vez tengas** razón.
Quizá será mejor esperar.	**Quizá sea** mejor esperar.

- in main clauses after expressions of probability such as **quizá**, **tal vez**, **acaso**, **probablemente**, or **posiblemente**.

affirmative = *certainty*	negative = *uncertainty*
Veo que tienes fiebre.	**No veo que tengas** fiebre.
Creo que hay que ir al doctor.	**No creo que haya** que ir al doctor.
He dicho que será lo mejor.	**No digo que sea** lo mejor.
Es que sólo **es** una gripe.	**No es que** sólo **sea** una gripe.

- in dependent clauses introduced with **que**, after expressions of belief, opinion, physical or mental perception, or telling, and in impersonal sentences using **es** / **está** + adjective / noun + **que** that indicate certainty.

> 1. Note the position of the **no**, and compare: **No creo que venga**. **Creo que no viene.**
> 2. With words such as **dudar** it is just the opposite: if they are negated, the indicative (= certainty) follows.

> If the verbs with * express causation, the subjunctive is used: **El jefe dice que vayas a su oficina.**

creer	*to believe*	pensar	*to think*
parecer	*to seem / think (judgment)*	estar seguro/-a	*to be sure*
		ver	*to see*
darse cuenta	*to realize*	notar	*to notice*
suponer	*to suppose*	explicar*	*to explain*
decir*	*to say*	es verdad	*it is true*
es (cierto)	*it is true*	es seguro	*it is definite*
es(tá) correcto	*it is correct*	es evidente	*it is obvious*
está demostrado	*it is proven*		

With these expressions there is a subtle difference in meaning, which deviates from the rule: If you want to present the contents of the dependent clause as an objective declarative statement and the main clause only as a comment on it, then you use the indicative, even if the verb of believing is negated:

Paco **no cree que fumas**.	= You smoke (declarative statement), but Paco doesn't believe it.
Paco **no cree que fumes**.	= Whether you smoke or not is unknown to the speaker as well.

fact (known)	imagination / wish (unknown)
Mi novia es una mujer **que tiene** muchos intereses. Nos vemos **cuando podemos**.	Busco una novia **que tenga** muchos intereses. Nos veremos **cuando podamos**.

– in relative clauses. With the indicative we describe something known or something that actually exists. With the subjunctive we define more precisely what we imagine or wish, and we may not know whether the wish can be realized.

fact (known)	future (possible / unknown)
Mientras más insistes, menos me **convences**.	**Mientras más insistas, menos** me **convencerás**.

– in comparisons, with **mientras más / menos** or **cuanto antes / más / menos**, which in English mean *the more ..., the more ....*

fact / habit	future (possible / unknown)
Llamo a mi novia **cuando llego**. Siempre es tarde **hasta que termino** el trabajo. **Mientras preparo** la cena, escucho la radio.	● Llámame **cuando llegues**. ○ Pero será tarde **hasta que termine** el trabajo. **Mientras prepares** tú la cena, no me importa la hora.

– in adverbial clauses with **cuando** (*when*), **hasta que** (*until*), **mientras** (*while / as long as*), **cada vez que** (*each / every time that*), **en cuanto** (*as soon as*), **después (de) que** (*after*), **tan pronto como** (*as soon as*), etc.

dependent clause = new information	known information / possibility
Aunque es tarde, he venido. ≈ *Although it's late, I've come.*	**Aunque sea** tarde, he venido. *Even if it is/might be late, I've come.*
Aunque está lloviendo, hay que salir con el perro. ≈ *Although it's raining, somebody has to take the dog out.*	**Aunque llueva,** hay que salir con el perro. *Even if it rains/might rain, somebody has to take the dog out.*

– in clauses with **aunque** (*although*) and **a pesar de que** (*although*). In the indicative, the content of the dependent clause is an objective statement or a piece of new information. In the subjunctive, it is assumed that the listener already knows the information in the dependent clause, or the information is presented as a possibility (as in the second example).

If a relative clause states that something or someone does not exist, then the subjunctive is always used: **No hay nada que me guste.**

1. **Mientras** + indicative is translated as *while*; **mientras** + subjunctive is rendered as *as long as*.
2. In adverbial clauses with **antes (de) que**, the subjunctive is always used, since they always refer to something in the future: **Ven antes de que oscurezca.**

Subjunctive

1. Connect the two columns so as to express nothing but good wishes. **

a) ¡Buenas noches!   1. Vete despacio y que llegues
                                                  bien.

b) ¿Estás enfermo? ¡Pobrecito!   2. ¡Que duermas bien!

c) Está lloviendo mucho.   3. ¡Pero que aproveche!

d) ¡Que tengan un buen viaje!   4. ¡Que te acuerdes de todo!

e) Yo ya he comido, gracias.   5. Pues que te mejores.

f) ¡Que tengas suerte en el examen! 6. ¡Que les vaya muy bien!

2. Today there is a protest. Underline the subjunctive forms as well as the words that trigger them. **

a) construir

b) _____

c) _____

d) _____

e) _____

f) _____

g) _____

h) _____

a) Los padres de familia necesitan que se construyan más escuelas.

b) Los jóvenes dudan que todos puedan encontrar trabajo.

c) Los conductores piden que sea más fácil aparcar en las ciudades.

d) Mucha gente teme que aumente la contaminación.

e) Las mujeres no piensan que las empresas les paguen bien.

f) Para las amas de casa, es hora de que bajen los precios.

g) Es necesario que los ciudadanos digan sus opiniones.

h) Es natural que vaya tanta gente hoy a las protestas.

3. In the margin next to Exercise 2, write the infinitives of the verbs in the subjunctive. **

a) mandar, tardar
b) poner, responder
c) reenviar
d) ser, escribir

el chiste – *the joke*
de mal gusto –
in bad taste
descargar – *to unload*
el correo – *here: e-mail*
el asunto – *here: the
subject*
reenviar – *to forward*

4. Ruth tells us what she likes and dislikes about e-mails. Only the verbs in the present subjunctive are missing; write them in the blanks. **

a) Me molesta que la gente me _mande_ chistes de mal gusto o presentaciones que _____ mucho en descargarse.

b) No me gusta que la gente no _____ claramente el asunto o que _____ un correo mío sin referirse a él.

c) Odio que alguien me _____ algo con media página de direcciones.

d) En el trabajo me gusta que los mensajes _____ cortos, pero en la vida privada me encanta que mis amigos me _____ correos largos.

5. Practice makes perfect! Fill in the missing information in the table. **

	infinitive	yo	tú	él/ella/usted	nosotros/nosotras	vosotros/vosotras	ellos/ellas/ustedes
a)	viajar	viaje	viajes	viaje	viajemos	viajéis	viajen
b)	volar	vuele	vueles	vuele	volemos	voléis	vuelen
c)	conocer	conozca	conozcas	conozca	conozcamos	conozcáis	conozcan
d)	estar	esté	estés	esté	estemos	estéis	estén
e)	ir	vaya	vayas	vaya	vayamos	vayáis	vayan
f)	quedarse	me quede	te quedes	se quede	nos quedemos	os quedéis	se queden
g)	volver	vuelva	vuelvas	vuelva	volvamos	volváis	vuelvan

6. Recently quite a lot has been said on the subject of women vs. men. Fill in the verbs below: infinitive or present subjunctive? **

a) Según algunos expertos, la mujer quiere _comunicarse_ porque es un ser social. **b)** Quiere que su compañero la _____ sin que le _____ soluciones. **c)** Los hombres desean _____ problemas prácticos de una manera racional y necesitan _____ menos. **d)** Para una mujer es posible _____ varias cosas a la vez, pero un hombre pide que "ella" no lo _____ ni lo _____ cuando está haciendo una cosa. **e)** Es que un hombre necesita silencio para que _____ concentrarse. **f)** Los expertos les recomiendan a las parejas que _____ las diferencias y les aconsejan que _____ sobre ellas para que _____ cómo funciona la otra persona.

a) comunicarse
b) escuchar, ofrecer
c) solucionar, hablar
d) hacer, distraer, interrumpir
e) poder
f) aceptar, hablar, saber

el ser – *the being*
a la vez – *at the same time, simultaneously*
interrumpir – *to interrupt*

7. People have different tastes! Match the two columns. **

a) Busco coches que
b) La casa donde vivo me gusta
c) El hotel adonde vayamos
d) Por favor, invita sólo a personas
e) He preparado un plato sin carne

1. porque tiene jardín.
2. que no fumen, ¿eh?
3. corran a 240 km por hora.
4. para los que sean vegetarianos.
5. tiene que tener piscina.

Practice and Application

8. Two dialogues heard at a shopping center have gotten mixed up. Straighten things out by numbering the utterances below from 1 to 8. **

sentar bien – *to fit / to suit*
el segundero – *the second hand*
luminoso – *luminous*
adorar – *to adore*

a) (   ) • Comoquiera que te vistas, te ves guapísima, ¡mi amor! No hay nada que no te siente maravillosamente.

b) (   )   Aquí está este, que tiene un segundero luminoso, pero es uno de los que no están en oferta. ¿No le importa que no esté rebajado?

c) (1) ■ Buenos días. Necesito un reloj que **tenga** segundero.

d) (   ) ○ Bueno… ¿Crees que esta blusa rosa que está aquí me queda bien?

e) (   ) ○ ¡Uff! ¡Mientras más me adoras, menos me ayudas a comprar algo que realmente me quede!

f) (   ) □ Muy bien. Veré si tengo alguno que sea como usted lo quiere…

g) (   ) • Mi vida, vamos adonde tú quieras. Cómprate todo lo que te guste.

h) (   ) ■ ¡Me encanta, es muy moderno! Cueste lo que cueste, me lo llevo.

9. Complete these minidialogues by using the present subjunctive of the verbs provided. **

a) esperar, volver
b) comprender, explicar, darse
c) terminar, poder, acabar, empezar
d) estar, ser, estar, salir, ser

exigir – *to demand*
darse cuenta – *here: to realize*
acabar – *to finish*
la tesina – *the dissertation*
embarazada – *pregnant*
salir bien – *here: to go well*

a) • Mario, esta noche llegaré tarde, no es necesario que me esperes ___.

○ No te preocupes, no cenaré hasta que tú _____ a casa.

b) • El jefe nos exige constantemente, sin que _____ nuestra situación.

○ Pues es necesario que nosotros se la _____. Hablaremos con él hasta que _____ cuenta.

c) • Toño, cuando _____ tus estudios, ¿qué vas a hacer?

○ Bueno… Espero que _____ terminar en un mes. Y cuando _____ mi tesina, es necesario que _____ a trabajar.

d) • ¡Huy, Juana! ¡Qué bueno que _____ embarazada! ¿Prefieres que _____ niño o niña?

○ Para mí, lo único importante es que el bebé _____ sano. Mientras todo _____ bien, me da lo mismo lo que _____.

10. Three young women, María (*M*), Ana (*A*), and Pilar (*P*) are discussing the effect of fairy tales on children. Mark the appropriate verb forms. **

M: a) ¿Creen que a todos los niños les (gustan)/ gusten los cuentos?

A: b) Yo supongo que la mayoría de los niños los leen / lean .

M: c) Para mí, es bueno que se conservan / conserven estas tradiciones.

P: d) Pues yo pienso que los cuentos son / sean anticuados. Hacen que los niños adquieren / adquieran una visión muy simple del mundo.

A: e) Es que los niños necesitan que les explican / expliquen las cosas de una manera fácil y simple.

P: f) Quizá tienes / tengas razón, pero temo que los cuentos aumentan / aumenten los miedos de los pequeños con todos esos monstruos, brujas, lobos...

A: g) Al contrario. En los cuentos, es un hecho que los buenos siempre ganan / ganen , y eso permite que los chicos se identifican / se identifiquen con ellos y desarrollan / desarrollen confianza en sí mismos.

P: h) Pero, ¿no les molesta que los cuentos son / sean brutales?

A: i) Bueno, aunque algunos parecen / parezcan brutales, yo creo los niños no se dan / den cuenta. Ellos no ven que los personajes sufren / sufran ...

M: j) Más bien, yo pienso que la impresión que dejan / dejen los cuentos es que son / sean algo maravilloso y además, ¡es tan agradable que toda la familia está / esté junta para leer cuentos! Los psicólogos insisten en que es importante que hay / haya recuerdos así, recuerdos agradables que duran / duren toda la vida.

P: k) No sé... A lo mejor tienen / tengan razón. Yo supongo que algún día voy / vaya a tener hijos... Pero cuando los tengo / tenga , no creo que les leo / lea cuentos. Seguro preferiré que jugamos / juguemos con la computadora...

> Just be patient! Give yourself plenty of time to develop a feel for the subjunctive.

conservar – *to preserve, conserve*
adquirir (ie) – *here: to acquire, get*
el miedo – *the fear*
ganar – *here: to win*
la bruja – *the witch*
el lobo – *the wolf*
desarrollar – *to develop*
la confianza en sí mismo – *the self-confidence*
sufrir – *to suffer*
más bien – *rather*

169

Subjunctive

11. Guillermo has come to the U.S. as an exchange student. A friend tells him what awaits him. Fill in the verbs, and choose between the present indicative and the subjunctive. ***

a) llegar, ir, haber
b) citar, ser
c) retrasarse,
   perder, llamar
d) llegar, planear
e) existir, seguir
f) estar, ser, venir
g) ser
h) cumplir, hacer
i) haber, tirar,
   recordar
j) hacer
k) interrumpir,
   querer, terminar
l) perder, hablan,
   estar
m) mirar, parecer
n) gustar, ser

esperar – to expect
citar – to arrange,
to meet
de veras – really
perder– here: to miss
a largo plazo –
in the long term
de hecho – in fact
el peatón –
the pedestrian
cumplir – here: to
obey, follow
el horario – here: the
garbage pickup times
tirar – here: to throw
away
perder el hilo – to lose
the thread
recién – LA only,
not until
¡Ojo! – Careful! Watch
out!

a) Cuando __llegas__ a Alemania, normalmente esperas que _____ a haber diferencias culturales, pero luego, ¡no puedes creer que _____ tantas! **b)** Por ejemplo, cuando un alemán te _____ a una hora, ¡es importante que tú _____ de veras puntualísimo! **c)** Claro que es posible que el tren _____ o que tú _____ el bus, y en ese caso no hay problema mientras _____ para avisar. **d)** Un alemán se disculpa aunque sólo _____ diez minutos tarde a una cita porque ellos consideran necesario que todo se _____ a largo plazo. **e)** Aquí me sorpende siempre que _____ tantas reglas y me parece increíble que toda la gente las _____. **f)** Por ejemplo, de hecho una persona espera el semáforo de peatones cuando _____ en rojo, aunque _____ las doce de la noche y no _____ ningún coche. **g)** No creo que eso _____ posible en Colombia, ¿no? **h)** Aquí a la gente le preocupa que todos _____ con las reglas, quieren que tú _____ bien las cosas. **i)** Por eso, si olvidas los horarios que _____ para que la gente _____ las botellas de vidrio a los contenedores, ya habrá alguien que te los _____. **j)** No te ofendas cuando lo _____, porque lo hace con buena intención. **k)** Otra cosa: a los alemanes no les gusta que nadie los _____. Cuando _____ decir algo, siempre esperan hasta que la otra persona _____ de hablar. **l)** Me parece que _____ el hilo si los interrumpen mientras _____ ... quizá es porque en alemán el verbo _____ al final y recién entonces entienden la frase. **m)** ¡Ah, y ojo con chicas alemanas! Les molesta que los hombres las _____ de un modo insistente que les _____ "machista". **n)** Bueno, ¡tranquilo! No es ningún problema que te _____ las chicas, mientras _____ amable y respetuoso ...

Present Perfect Subjunctive

¡Espero que **se hayan divertido** en las vacaciones!
①

¡Sí, mucho! Ven cuando hayas **terminado** tu trabajo y te mostramos las fotos.
②

The present perfect subjunctive describes a completed action in the past (for example, **Espero que <u>se hayan divertido</u>**) or also in the future (**Ven cuando <u>hayas terminado</u>**).

---

1. I hope you've had a good time on vacation!
2. Yes, come by when you've finished your work, and we'll show you the photos.

Formation

▶ **Past Participle**, p. 187

The present perfect subjunctive is formed with the present subjunctive of **haber** and the past participle. The corresponding forms of the auxiliary verb always directly precede the past participle; they are never separated. The participle always ends in **-o**.

(yo)	**haya**	trabaj**o**
(tú)	**hayas**	teni**do**
(él / ella / usted)	**haya**	discuti**do**
(nosotros / -as)	**hayamos**	escrit**o**
(vosotros / -as)	**hayáis**	puest**o**
(ellos / ellas / ustedes)	**hayan**	hech**o**

▶ **Use of the Present Subjunctive**, p. 161 ff

Use

The present perfect subjunctive follows the same rules as the present subjunctive; that is, it usually is found in a dependent clause whose main clause exhibits a subjunctive trigger in the present, imperative, present perfect, or simple future. The difference is that the event or the action in the dependent clause is already completed or is said to have taken place at a certain time. Examples:

¡**Ojalá** los chicos **hayan llegado** bien!
No sé nada de Ana, **a menos que** hoy me **haya enviado** un e-mail.
Convendrá que mañana a esta hora ya **hayamos salido** de casa.
Me encanta que me **hayas traído** flores.
Ha sido mejor que no les **hayas dado** dinero a los niños.
¡Bravo! ¡**Parece mentira que** **hayan dejado** la cocina tan limpia!
¡**Quienquiera que** **haya dicho** eso es un genio!
Quizá Manolo **haya tenido** algún problema y por eso no ha llegado.
Podemos ir a tomar algo juntos **cuando hayas vuelto** de tu viaje.
Mueva la salsa **hasta que se hayan mezclado** todos los ingredientes.
No conozco a **nadie que** **haya estado** en Tierra del Fuego.

Imperfect Subjunctive

Las niñas siempre querían que **viviéramos** en el campo.

①

Su sueño era que **tuviéramos** animales: un caballo, una vaca y un gato.

②

The imperfect subjunctive usually is used in dependent clauses when the subjunctive trigger is in the past or in the conditional.

---

1. *The girls have always wanted us to live in the country.*
2. *It was their dream to have animals: a horse, a cow, and a cat.*

▶ **Use of the Present Subjunctive**, p. 161 ff

▶ *Indefinido* **(Preterit)**, p. 126

The use of the imperfect subjunctive generally depends on the tense of the subjunctive trigger. The action described by the imperfect subjunctive can, from the speaker's point of view, refer to the present (**Es como si ahora él <u>fuera</u> invisible**), to the future (**Me pidió que <u>volviera</u> mañana**), or to the past (**Hizo que <u>viniera</u> anoche**).

Formation

The imperfect subjunctive is derived from the third person plural of the *indefinido*. By separating the ending **-ron**, you obtain the stem of the imperfect subjunctive. This applies to both the regular and the irregular verbs.

Learn both forms, so that you can recognize them when you read and hear Spanish. When speaking, it is sufficient to give preference to the form ending in **-ra**.

Spanish has two interchangeable forms for the imperfect subjunctive. One ends in **-ra**, the other in **-se**. Despite regional differences, the **-ra** forms are now more common.

1. Regular Forms

To the new stem, attach the endings as follows:

Ending with **-ra:**			
	trabaj**ar**	aprend**er**	escrib**ir**
indefinido, third pers. pl.	trabaj**aron**	aprend**ieron**	escrib**ieron**
(yo)	trabaj**ara**	aprend**iera**	escrib**iera**
(tú)	trabaj**aras**	aprend**ieras**	escrib**ieras**
(él / ella / usted)	trabaj**ara**	aprend**iera**	escrib**iera**
(nosotros / -as)	trabaj**áramos**	aprend**iéramos**	escrib**iéramos**
(vosotros / -as)	trabaj**arais**	aprend**ierais**	escrib**ierais**
(ellos / ellas / ustedes)	trabaj**aran**	aprend**ieran**	escrib**ieran**
Ending with -se:			
(yo)	trabaj**ase**	aprend**iese**	escrib**iese**
(tú)	trabaj**ases**	aprend**ieses**	escrib**ieses**
(él / ella / usted)	trabaj**ase**	aprend**iese**	escrib**iese**
(nosotros / -as)	trabaj**ásemos**	aprend**iésemos**	escrib**iésemos**
(vosotros / -as)	trabaj**aseis**	aprend**ieseis**	escrib**ieseis**
(ellos / ellas / ustedes)	trabaj**asen**	aprend**iesen**	escrib**iesen**

> Please note: All forms of the imperfect subjunctive are stressed on the stem!

2. Irregular Forms

All the irregularities that affect the *indefinido* apply also to the imperfect subjunctive.

infinitive	*indef., third pers. pl.*	*imperfect subjunctive*
ir = ser	**fue**ron	fuera, fueras, fuera, fuéramos, fuerais, fueran
dar	**die**ron	diera, dieras, diera, diéramos, dierais, dieran
ver	**vie**ron	viera, vieras, viera, viéramos, vierais, vieran
decir	**dije**ron	dijera, dijeras, dijera, ...
dormir	**durmie**ron	durmiera, durmieras, durmiera, ...
estar	**estuvie**ron	estuviera, estuvieras, estuviera, ...
hacer	**hicie**ron	hiciera, hicieras, hiciera, ...
leer	**leye**ron	leyera, leyeras, leyera, ...
poner	**pusie**ron	pusiera, pusieras, pusiera, ...
seguir	**siguie**ron	siguiera, siguieras, siguiera, ...
tener	**tuvie**ron	tuviera, tuvieras, tuviera, ...
traer	**traje**ron	trajera, trajeras, trajera, ...

> The impersonal **hay** has the form **hubiera**.

Imperfect Subjunctive

Use

▶ **Use of the Present Subjunctive**, p. 161 ff

The use of the imperfect subjunctive follows, with few exceptions, the same rules as those for the use of the present subjunctive. Usually it is found in a dependent clause that has a different subject than the main clause and whose action occurs at the same time as or later than that of the main clause.

!

Quisiera has become independently established as a phrase of civility (more formal than **quería**), as in **Quisiera hablar con usted** (*I would like to speak with you*) or **Quisiera por favor una cita para mañana** (*I'd like an appointment for tomorrow, please*).

If **Quisiera** is followed by a dependent clause with a different subject, then the verb is in the imperfect subjunctive: **Quisiera que llamaras tú.**

▶ **Conditional Clauses**, p. 232

canoso / -a – *gray-haired*

El jefe **quería que** lo informara de **lo que** pasara en la oficina.
¡**Fue increíble que** no hubiera nadie en la montaña!
Mi abuelo nunca **había creído que** nosotros tocáramos la trompeta.
Nos gustaría que usted nos explicara cómo funciona este aparato.
Yo nunca te **habría pedido que** hicieras algo así.

▌ The imperfect subjunctive is used in the dependent clause if the main clause contains an expression of causation, emotion, uncertainty, etc. in the imperfect, *indefinido*, past perfect, simple conditional, or conditional perfect.

Lalo me mostró los regalos de Navidad **sin que** lo supiera mamá.
Decidí buscar a Juan en Madrid **hasta que** lo encontrara.
Cuando tuviera hijos, Marta pensaba hablarles en inglés **para que** lo aprendieran muy bien.
Teresa no conocía a **nadie que** viviera en Tierra del Fuego.

▌ – if a subjunctive trigger (such as conjunctions, relative pronouns, etc.) or a repetition formula occurs in a context of the past.

¡Óscar, bailas **como si** fueras un elefante! Anda, haz un esfuerzo, ¡baila **como si** quisiéramos ganar el campeonato dentro de un mes!

▌ – after **como si** (*as if*), when the irreal or impossible comparison in the dependent clause refers to the present or to the future.

Si mi padre tuviera pelo, estaría completamente canoso.

▌ – in a conditional clause, if it has to do with a condition that is inapplicable, improbable, or difficult to fulfill.

¡**Ojalá** me llamara Ricardo! ¡**Si tan sólo** estuviera con él!
¡**Quién** pudiera volar! Pero **aunque** pudiera, sé que él no me quiere.

▌ – in expressions of wishing with **ojalá**, etc., and clauses with **aunque**, if the speaker wants to say that the fulfillment of the wish and / or the possibility is very unlikely or impossible.

Past Perfect Subjunctive

¡Qué bonito regalo! ¡Pero no os **hubierais molestado**!

What a lovely gift! But you shouldn't have gone to such trouble!

Formation

The past perfect subjunctive is formed with the imperfect subjunctive of
haber and the past participle. The corresponding forms of the auxiliary
verb always directly precede the past participle; they are never separated.
The participle always ends in **-o**.

(yo)	**hubiera**	/ **hubiese**	trabajad**o**
(tú)	**hubieras**	/ **hubieses**	teni**do**
(él / ella / usted)	**hubiera**	/ **hubiese**	discuti**do**
(nosotros / -as)	**hubiéramos**	/ **hubiésemos**	escrit**o**
(vosotros / -as)	**hubierais**	/ **hubieseis**	puest**o**
(ellos / ellas / ustedes)	**hubieran**	/ **hubiesen**	hech**o**

▶ **Past Participle**,
p. 187

Use

The past perfect subjunctive follows the same rules as the imperfect
subjunctive. The event or the action in the dependent clause, however,
is already completed.

Oh, ¡**no me imaginaba que** tú hubieras escrito un libro!
Luis siempre me esperaba **hasta que** hubiera terminado mi trabajo.
Me encantó que hubieras traído el postre para todos.
Habría sido una lástima que no hubiéramos ido al concierto.

▋ The past perfect subjunctive is used in a dependent clause, when
the main clause contains an expression of causation, emotion,
uncertainty, etc. in the imperfect, *indefinido*, past perfect, simple
conditional, or conditional perfect and the action or event in the
dependent clause has already taken place.

Lalo me mostró los regalos de Navidad **sin que** le hubiera dicho
nada a mamá, por supuesto.
Decidí quedarme en Madrid **hasta que** hubiera encontrado a Juan.
Teresa no conocía a **nadie que** hubiera estado en Tierra del Fuego.

▋ – when a subjunctive trigger (such as a conjunction, relative
pronoun, etc.) occurs in the context of the past.

> ¡Uff, Gerardo hace **como si** no nos **hubiera visto**! ¡Qué pesado!

■ – after **como si** (*as if*), when the irreal or impossible comparison in the dependent clause refers to the past.

> **Si** te **hubieras casado** con Pepe, no habrías venido a Europa.

■ – in a conditional clause, when it has to do with an unfulfilled condition in the past.

> • **¡Ojalá** Carlos no **se hubiera ido**!
> ○ Pero **aunque** no lo **hubiera hecho**, no serían felices juntos.

■ – in expressions of wishing with **ojalá** and clauses with **aunque**, when the wish was not fulfilled or the action did not take place.

> Si te hubieras casado con Pepe, no **hubieras venido** a Europa.
> En caso de haber hecho calor, **hubiéramos utilizado** la piscina.
> Te **hubiera llamado** antes, pero no pude. Lo siento.

■ In colloquial speech, the past perfect subjunctive commonly substitutes for the conditional perfect. It expresses unfulfilled conditions and unrealized consequences and circumstances.

Sequence of Tenses in Main Clause and Subordinate Clause with the Subjunctive

In expressions of causation, because of their meaning, you will be unlikely to find anterior action in the dependent clause.

The action of the dependent clause can occur at the same time as that of the main clause (simultaneous) or after it (posterior), or it can be completed before that of the main clause (anterior). The present and imperfect tenses of the subjunctive express simultaneity or posteriority, while the present perfect and the past perfect refer to anteriority. The most common combinations are as follows:

! Sometimes there are exceptions, with the context being the determining factor. For example: **Mi madre <u>vino</u> ayer para que yo <u>pueda</u> irme mañana al hospital.** (*My mother came yesterday so that I can go into the hospital tomorrow.*)

Main clause in indicative		Dependent clause in subjunctive		
These are the so-called tenses of the present:				
Present	**Espero ...**			
Pres. Perf.	**Me ha molestado ...**	**que** lea	la carta.	Present
Future	**Temerán ...**	**que** haya leído		Pres. perf.
Imperative	**Procura ...**			
These are the so-called tenses of the past:				
Imperfect	**Esperaba ...**			
Indefinido	**Me molestó ...**	**que** leyera / leyese	la carta.	Imperf.
Past perf.	**Había temido ...**	**que** hubiera leído		Past perf.
Simp. cond.	**Nos gustaría ...**	hubiese		
Cond. perf.	**Nos habría gustado**			

1. Today is the last day of vacation, and many vacationers are returning home. Put the verbs provided in the present perfect subjunctive. **

a) Es probable que __haya habido__ *(haber)* atascos en las carreteras.

b) Espero que no _____ *(ocurrir)* muchos accidentes.

c) Ojalá que no _____ *(llover)* mucho en el Mar del Norte, donde ha estado mi vecina.

d) Su perro está con los abuelos, a menos que ella ya lo _____ *(recoger)*.

e) Podemos ver sus fotos cuando las _____ *(revelar)*.

f) ¡Parece mentira que las vacaciones _____ *(pasar)* tan pronto!

el atasco – *the traffic jam*
ocurrir – *to happen*
recoger – *to pick up*
revelar – *to develop*

2. Practice makes perfect! First, write the third person plural form of the *indefinido* of the verbs provided, and then derive the imperfect subjunctive of the person indicated from that form.

a) third pers. pl. *indef.*: ___fueron,_____

   imperf. subjunctive, yo: ___fuera,_____

a) ser, pedir, tener

b) third pers. pl. *indef.*: _____

   imperf. subjunctive, tú: _____

b) enterarse, leer, decir

c) third pers. pl. *indef.*: _____

   imperf. subjunctive, usted: _____

c) conocer, poner, beber

d) third pers. pl. *indef.*: _____

   imperf. subjunctive, nosotros: _____

d) hacer, trabajar, divertirse

e) third pers. pl. *indef.*: _____

   imperf. subjunctive, vosotros: _____

e) ver, acostarse, seguir

f) third pers. pl. *indef.*: _____

   imperf. subjunctive, ustedes: _____

f) consultar, dar, oír

Practice and Application

Subjunctive

3. The new generation of retirees is quite active! Complete this e-mail from Don Jorge to his friend by using the imperfect subjunctive. ******

Hola, Joaquín,

a) Ya pasó un mes desde que dejé el trabajo, y yo no pensaba que

<u>hubiera</u> *(haber)* tanto que hacer como jubilado. **b)** Tampoco temía

que _____ *(aburrise)* sin que _____ *(tener)* que ir a la

oficina. **c)** Pero por ejemplo, no habría imaginado que _____

(poder) aprender algo completamente nuevo: Ahora voy a un curso de

informática. **d)** Antes era imposible que _____ *(dedicarse)* a la

música y era una lástima que casi no _____ *(tocar)* la guitarra,

que me gusta mucho. **e)** Ah, y además, no era frecuente que

_____ *(hacer)* deporte, pero ahora salgo a caminar regularmente.

f) Aunque cada año me lo _____ *(proponer)* ... Claro, quizá me

_____ *(faltar)* la disciplina, pero ahora definitivamente me es

más fácil organizarme, ¡y me siento como si _____ *(ser)* mucho

más joven! **g)** Y tú, ¿cómo estás? Ojalá no _____ *(estar)* tan

lejos, podríamos vernos más seguido ahora que tengo tiempo. **h)** Me

gustaría que Rita y tú _____ *(venir)* a Oviedo pronto, ¿qué les

parece? **i)** Quisiera que me _____ *(decir)* cuándo les conviene,

¿a lo mejor para las Fiestas?

el jubilado – *the retiree, retired person*

salir a caminar – *to go for a walk, take a walk*

4. Connect the halves to form meaningful sentences. *******

a) Sería fantástico que ustedes   1. que pusiéramos la radio?
b) Señorita, le agradecería que   2. si fuera usted tan amable.
c) Nos interesaría su oferta   3. nos visitaran en verano.
d) ¿Te gustaría que   4. no felicitaras a tu madrina.
e) ¿Les molestaría   5. me enviara el formulario por fax.

f) Quisiera hablar con la Sra. Soto,   6. te fuera a buscar al gimnasio?
g) Me parecería mal que tú   7. que ayudaran un poco en casa.
h) Yo les pediría a mis hijos   8. si usted nos diera un buen precio.

el gimnasio – *the gym(nasium), fitness center*
la madrina – *the godmother*

5. What do Spanish periodicals publish during the so-called "summer slump" when nothing happens? In the following article, underline the forms of the imperfect subjunctive, as well as their triggers. ✱✱✱

a) Aquí nadie le dio importancia al hecho de que unas revistas de moda publicaran fotos de unas ministras españolas. **b)** Pero en España, fue un escándalo que las políticas hicieran de modelos.

c) Poco antes había sido un gran avance que hubiera, por primera vez, tantas mujeres en el gobierno. **d)** Por eso, a algunas personas les pareció pésima idea que estas revistas presentaran su lado "vanidoso".

e) Temieron que estas fotos fomentaran clichés sobre las mujeres en general. **f)** Otros criticaron que estas ministras, aunque fueran socialistas, llevaran ropa muy cara en las fotos. **g)** Les molestó que no mostraran más sensibilidad hacia la gente pobre. **h)** Pero también hubo personas a quienes les gustó que las ministras posaran para las revistas. **i)** Para ellas fue agradable que las fotos y las entrevistas dejaran ver el lado humano de estas mujeres.

el avance – *the advance, progress*
el gobierno –
the government
vanidoso/-a – *vain, conceited*
fomentar – *to promote*
el cliché – *the cliché*
la entrevista –
the interview

a) _publicar_____

b) _____

c) _____

d) _____

e) _____

f) _____ ,

_____

6. In the margin, write down the infinitives of the verbs in the subjunctive. ✱✱

g) _____

h) _____

7. In a large firm, a great many things are discussed during the lunch break. In these dialogues, choose the correct form. ✱✱✱

i) _____

a) • Mi mujer no quiere que yo (trabaje)/ trabajara tanto.
  ○ Pues antes mi marido no quería que yo trabaje / trabajara fuera de casa, pero ha cambiado de opinión.

fuera – *outside*

b) • Me parece excelente que vosotros queráis / quisierais aplicar el nuevo programa de inmediato.
  ○ Fue muy útil que tú nos lo expliques / explicaras tan claramente.

c) • ¿Y tus padres no querían que Tomás y tú vivan / vivieran juntos?
  ○ Bueno, no era fácil que mis padres a su edad cambien / cambiaran sus ideas, pero ahora claro que aceptan que vivamos / viviéramos juntos.

d) • Hace ya varios días el nuevo jefe me llamó y me dijo que vaya / fuera a verlo, pero no he tenido la oportunidad.
  ○ ¿Desea usted que yo se lo presente / presentara ? Si quiere que vayamos / fuéramos después de la comida, por mí no hay problema.

Practice and Application

8. Professionally, José is in a difficult situation. Could things be different, perhaps? Follow his train of thought by numbering the sentences below from 1 to 8. **

eficiente – *efficient*
rendir – *here: to accomplish, achieve*
el puesto – *the position, job*
vacío/-a – *empty*

a) ( ) Si tuviera menos estrés, podría trabajar mejor.

b) ( ) Si fuera súper eficiente, me cambiarían de puesto.

c) ( ) Si pudiera trabajar mejor, rendiría más.

d) ( ) Si mi escritorio estuviera más vacío, encontraría todo más rápido.

e) (1) Si me cambiaran de puesto, ya no tendría la misma jefa.

f) ( ) Si mi jefa no fuera tan caótica, yo tendría menos estrés.

g) ( ) Si encontrara todo más rápido, sería súper eficiente.

h) ( ) Si rindiera más, mi escritorio estaría más vacío.

9. Complete this excerpt from a short story by putting the verbs in the indicative or the subjunctive. ***

a) Gloria estaba cansada de que su trabajo nunca _____ *(terminar)*. **b)** Después de la oficina, era normal que ella _____ *(limpiar)* la casa e _____ *(hacer)* la comida. **c)** Aunque Pedro,

desempleado/-a – *unemployed*
eficiente – *here: successful*
solicitar – *to request*
el canal (de TV) – *the television channel*

su marido, _____ *(estar)* desempleado, no pensaba que un hombre _____ *(tener)* que ayudar en la casa y se iba todo el día con sus amigos. **d)** Gloria no creía que esa forma de buscar trabajo _____ *(ser)* eficiente. **e)** En su opinión, habría sido mejor que Pedro _____ *(solicitar)* ayuda a la oficina de empleo. **f)** Pero él opinaba que los trabajos que te _____ *(ofrecer, 3. Pl.)* allí _____ *(ser)* malos y _____ *(estar)* mal pagados. **g)** Para Gloria, no estaba demostrado que siempre _____ *(ser)* así. **h)** A ella no le gustaba que él no le _____ *(pedir)* su opinión y decidió decírselo esa misma noche, cuando él _____ *(llegar)*. **i)** Pero cuando Pedro _____ *(llegar)*, todo fue como siempre, sin que _____ *(darse)* cuenta del estado de su mujer. **j)** Encendió la tele y bebió una cerveza mientras _____ *(cambiar)* canales. **k)** Y Gloria lo dejó que _____ *(descansar)*, y, otra vez, no dijo nada.

10. Do you remember the famous fairy tale about Little Red Riding Hood? Here are a few comments on it. Fill in the blanks by using the past perfect subjunctive of the verbs provided. ***

a) ¡Pobre Caperucita! ¡Ojalá le _____ (hacer) caso

a su madre! **b)** Si Caperucita no _____ (hablar)

con el lobo, no le habría pasado nada. **c)** Claro que ella nunca

_____ (imaginarse) que el lobo quería comérsela.

d) A pesar de lo que le _____ (decir) su mamá,

Caperucita fue muy amable con el lobo. **e)** Y él se comió a la abuela y

luego, con su gorro de dormir, esperó hasta que _____

(llegar) la niña. **f)** A ella le sorprendió que la abuela ya

_____ (abrir) la puerta antes de que llegara ella...

g) Y bien: Si este cuento lo _____ (escribir) un autor

mexicano, el malo habría sido quizá un coyote y no un lobo.

hacer caso –
to pay attention, obey

11. Translate the missing parts. ***

a) Pero, ¡por favor! Me tratas _____ tonto.
But please! You treat me as if I were stupid.

b) Mis padres _____ devolverles el dinero.
My parents were afraid that I couldn't give the money back to them.

c) _____ lo _____, yo me voy a comprar una moto.
Whatever you may say, I'm going to buy myself a motorcycle.

d) ¡Ojalá _____ a tiempo todavía!
I hope you were still able to leave on time!

e) No me gustó nada que _____.
I didn't like it at all that my sister had put on my shoes.

f) Hijos, envíenme un mensaje _____.
Children, send me a message when you've reached home.

g) Es mejor que _____ de otro modo.
It's better that we do things differently.

h) Nos habría gustado que _____
con nosotros.
We would have liked you to stay with us.

Unconjugated Forms of the Verb

¿**Ser** o no **ser**? Esa es la cuestión...

①

¡Psst! Me has **distraído**, ¡y esta es una escena importantísima!

③

Oye, Lola, me estoy **aburriendo**...

②

1. To be or not to be? That is the question ... 2. Listen, Lola, I'm bored ...
3. Shhhh! You've distracted me, and this is an extremely important scene!

Overview

Unconjugated verb forms cannot form an independent sentence. Their endings tell us nothing about person, number, verb tense, or the attitude of the speaker toward the statement.

▶ **Verb Forms**, p. 104

Isabel quiere **vivir** en un pueblo tranquilo. *Isabel wants to live in a quiet village.*	Infinitive
Siempre ha **vivido** en una ciudad. *She has always lived in a city.*	Past participle
Ahora anda muy **sonriente**... *Now she goes around smiling ...*	Adjectival present participle
porque está **construyendo** una casa aquí. *because she is building a house here.*	Present participle

The Infinitive

The infinitive is the basic form of the verb, as it is listed in the dictionary.

Me gusta **leer** el periódico antes de ir al trabajo.

I like to read the newspaper before going to work.

In the infinitive, Spanish verbs have these endings: **-ar**, **-er**, or **-ir**. These endings determine the conjugational groups to which they belong. Reflexive verbs are recognizable by the pronoun **-se**, which is directly attached to the infinitive.

▶ **Reflexive Verbs**, p. 216

trabaj**ar**	com**er**	viv**ir**

Use

1. As a Noun

¡Tu constante **cambiar** de idea me enerva!

■ When used as nouns, infinitives can be accompanied by determiners, adjectives, or prepositional complements.

El **poder** no elimina los **deberes** ni los **quehaceres**.

■ Only a few infinitives have become "real nouns" and also have a plural form. They all are masculine.

el amanecer	*the dawn, daybreak*	el pesar	*the sorrow, grief*
el atardecer	*the evening, dusk*	el placer	*the pleasure*
el deber	*the duty*	el poder	*the power*
el haber	*the credit*	el quehacer	*the task, work*
el parecer	*the opinion*	el ser	*the being*

Comer antes de **dormir** no es bueno.
Necesitas **dar** tiempo para **digerir** los alimentos.

■ In a sentence, the infinitive can take on the functions of a noun: for example, it can be a subject or an object, or it can follow prepositions such as **antes de**, **después de**, **por**, **para**, etc.

▶ **The Noun as Part of a Sentence**, p. 16

Prefiero no **discutir** más. No es necesario **seguir** con este tema.

■ The infinitive frequently follows **ser** + adjective or verbs expressing emotion such as **preferir**, **gustar**, etc. No preposition intervenes between this construction and the infinitive. If the infinitive is negated, it is directly preceded by **no**.

Sentences with **ser** + adjective + infinitive render generally valid pronouncements.

2. As a Verb

Es mejor **darle** al niño con regularidad pequeñas porciones.

■ As a verb, the infinitive can have direct or indirect objects and be accompanied by an adverb or an adverbial expression.

▶ **Modal Verbs**, p. 104

● ¿Sabes **usar** este programa de computadora? Lo deberías **aprender**.
○ Es que mi padre no me deja **usar** su computadora.

■ The infinitive directly follows the modal verbs, such as **deber** (*to have to, must*), **dejar** (*to let*), **poder** (*to be able, can*), **saber** (*to know how to, can*), **querer** (*to want, wish*), **tener que** (*to have to, must*), and **hay que** (*you need to, it is necessary to*).

No preposition is used between a modal verb and an infinitive!

Unconjugated Forms of the Verb

Overview

▶ **Placement of Object Pronouns**, p. 80

▶ **Verbal Periphrasis**, p. 191

In infinitive constructions, the object pronouns can either precede the verb unit or be attached to it. Compare **Voy a decirte** / **Te voy a decir** una cosa.

Note: The present of **acabar de** + infinitive corresponds to the English present perfect (**acabo de ver** = I *have just* seen); the imperfect corresponds to the English past perfect (**acababa de ver** = I *had just* seen).

▶ **The Imperative**, p. 150

The modal verb is conjugated in the corresponding person, as below:

	querer + infinitive		**tener que** + infinitive	
(yo)	quiero	trabajar	tengo	que ver
(tú)	quieres	comer	tienes	que llegar
(él, ella, usted)	quiere	dormir	tiene	que leer
(nosotros/-as)	queremos	salir	tenemos	que llamar
(vosotros/-as)	queréis	tener	tenéis	que volver
(ellos, ellas, ustedes)	quieren	terminar	tienen	que irse

Voy a decirte una cosa.

▌ The infinitive is found in frequently used constructions, the so-called verbal periphrases. The most important of them are as follows:

	to be going to **ir a** + infinitive		*to have just* **acabar de** + infinitive	
(yo)	voy	a trabajar	acabo	de ver
(tú)	vas	a comer	acabas	de llegar
(él, ella, usted)	va	a dormir	acaba	de leer
(nosotros/-as)	vamos	a salir	acabamos	de llamar
(vosotros/-as)	vais	a tener	acabáis	de volver
(ellos, ellas, ustedes)	van	a terminar	acaban	de irse

Todos estamos trabajando, ¿y tú qué haces? **Dormir. ¡A trabajar!**

▌ The infinitive takes the place of a sentence in the indicative mood or substitutes, with or without the preposition **a**, for an imperative.

Vi al ladrón entrar al banco. = Vi al ladrón, que entraba al banco.

▌ After verbs of perceiving, it can shorten a relative clause that refers to the direct object of the main clause.

De no llegar Juan (= Si Juan no llega), perderemos el tren.

▌ Together with certain prepositions, it forms shorter alternative constructions that are used instead of dependent clauses.

Esta receta es muy **fácil de hacer**. = Es muy fácil hacer esta receta.

▌ It is found after certain adjectives + preposition, for example, after **fácil/difícil/capaz de** or **bueno/malo/útil para**.

Use of Infinitive Constructions to Replace Dependent Clauses

Instead of certain adverbial clauses, you can use an infinitive construction.

Al bajarse del tren (= Cuando se bajó del tren), reconocí a Inés enseguida. *When she got off the train, I recognized Inés at once.*

– **al** + infinitive indicates a point in time (*when, on*).

Antes de probar tu receta (= Antes de que probara tu receta), las berenjenas no me gustaban. *Before trying (= Before I tried) your recipe, I did not like eggplant.*

– **antes de** + infinitive indicates the second action in a sequence (*before*).

No conseguirás nada **con gritar** (= gritando / aunque grites). *You will achieve nothing by shouting (= if / even if you shout).*

– **con** + infinitive expresses manner or an objection *(by; if, even if)*.

De recibir noticias (= Si recibo noticias), te llamo. *If I get news, I'll call you.*

– **de** + infinitive indicates a condition (*if*).

Se quedan aquí **hasta terminar** (= hasta que terminen) los deberes. *You'll stay here until you finish the chores.*

– **hasta** + infinitive indicates a time limit (*until*).

Después de comer (= Después de que comamos) todos, ¿irás al cine? *After we all eat, will you go to the movies?*

– **después de** + infinitive indicates the first action in a series (*after*).

Nada más haber entregado (= En cuanto haya entregado) el último examen, me voy de vacaciones. *As soon as I have turned in the last exam, I'm going away on vacation.*

– **nada más** + infinitive indicates a time in the future (*as soon as*).

Por ahorrar (= Porque quería ahorrar), al final pagué más dinero. *Because I wanted to save, in the end I paid more money.*

– **por** + infinitive expresses a reason or justification (*because*).

In this way you can replace verbs in various tenses and moods, determining their meaning (and often their subject as well) from the context.

▶ Past Participle
p. 187

The Participle

② ¿Has **visto** el periódico?

Julia, ¿por qué estás tan **sonriente**?

①

Hay un cartoon muy **divertido**.

③

Spanish has two types of present participle, adjectival and verbal, and a past participle.

1. Julia, why are you smiling? 2. Have you seen the newspaper?
3. There's a very amusing cartoon.

The Adjectival Present Participle

In Spanish, the forms of the adjectival present participle function primarily as nouns and adjectives, whereas the English present participle (-*ing* form) functions both as an adjective and as part of the verb.

Spanish has an adjectival present participle that is limited in use. It ends in **-ente** and in most cases has become established as a noun or as an adjective. It is roughly equivalent to the English –*ing* form and can readily be expanded to form a relative clause, as here:

un **caminante** = una persona **que camina**
un niño **sonriente** = un niño **que sonríe**

Examples of nouns:

el/la asistente	*assistant*	el incidente	*incident*
el/la caminante	*walker*	el/la inmigrante	*immigrant*
el/la cantante	*singer*	el/la oyente	*listener*
el/la delincuente	*delinquent*	el/la presidente	*president*
el/la descendiente	*descendent*	el/la sobreviviente	*survivor*
el/la estudiante	*student*	el solvente	*solvent*
el/la fabricante	*manufacturer*	la variante	*variant*
el/la hablante	*speaker*	el/la vigilante	*guard*

Examples of adjectives:

angustiante	*nightmarish*	influyente	*influential*
brillante	*brilliant*	obediente	*obedient*
competente	*competent*	procedente	*coming, arriving*
corriente	*current*	protestante	*Protestant*
creciente	*growing*	perteneciente	*belonging*
estimulante	*stimulating*	referente	*regarding*
exigente	*demanding*	repelente	*repellent*
imponente	*imposing*	residente	*resident*
interesante	*interesting*	sonriente	*smiling*

The Past Participle

Formation

1. Regular Forms

Verbs ending in **-ar** add the ending **-ado** to the stem of the infinitive, while verbs ending in **-er** / **-ir** add the ending **-ido**.

via**jar** ▸ viaj**ado**	cono**cer** ▸ cono**cido**	vi**vir** ▸ viv**ido**

> The past participle is used as a verb or as an adjective.

2. Irregular Forms

The most important verbs with an irregular past participle are:

abrir	*to open*	▸ ab**ierto**	poner	*to put*	▸	**puesto**
cubrir	*to cover*	▸ cub**ierto**	resolver	*to solve, resolve*	▸	res**uelto**
morir	*to die*	▸ **muerto**	volver	*to return*	▸	**vuelto**
escribir	*to write*	▸ escri**to**	romper	*to break*	▸	ro**to**
ver	*to see*	▸ vis**to**	freír	*to fry*	▸	fri**to**
decir	*to say*	▸ **dicho**	hacer	*to make, do*	▸	**hecho**

> Related verbs exhibit the same irregularities. **Descubrir** resembles cubrir (des**cubierto**), devolver, **volver** (de**vuelto**), etc.

Some nouns are derived from these participles, including **la cubierta** (*the cover; the deck*), **el / la muerto / -a** (*the dead person*), **el puesto** (*the place, position*), **la vuelta** (*the change [money]*), **el escrito** (*the writing*), **la vista** (*the view, sight*), **el dicho** (*the saying*), and **el hecho** (*the fact*).

Use

1. As a Verb (invariable)

The past participle is used along with the auxiliary verb **haber** to form the compound tenses and forms. In this function, it is invariable and always ends in **-o**.

> In some regions of LA, people use **el vuelto** instead of **la vuelta** for *change* (coins or money returned in exchange).

Participle

Here is an overview of the compound tenses and forms:

He comprado un libro excelente.	– present perfect indicative
Había empezado la escuela.	– past perfect indicative
Manana **habrá terminado** todo.	– future perfect indicative
¿Tú qué **habrías hecho**?	– conditional perfect
Dudo que Laura **haya llamado**.	– present perfect subjunctive
Hubiera sido agradable, pero...	– past perfect subjunctive
No creo **haber invitado** a Pepe.	– perfect infinitive
Es bonito **haber sido invitado**.	– perfect passive infinitive
Habiendo dicho esto, se fue.	– perfect participle

2. As a Variable Form

1. Compare **He <u>cocido</u> las papas** (*I have boiled the potatoes*) and **Son papas <u>cocidas</u>** (*They are boiled potatoes*).
2. A very few forms of the past participle are used as nouns, such as **el / la discapacitado / -a** (*the handicapped person*)

▶ **Passive**, p. 240

Queridos niños, ¿quieren las papas **fritas** o **cocidas**?

As in English, the past participle can be used as an adjective. Then Spanish requires that it agrees in number and gender with the noun it modifies.

Uff, ¿qué hacemos? ¡Nuestro vuelo a La Paz **ha sido cancelado**!

The auxiliary verb **ser** + past participle forms the passive.

¿Por qué están todas las puertas **abiertas**?

The auxiliary verb **estar** + part participle expresses the result of an action.

Note the English meanings of these verbs.

Lalo **está acostado** en la cama.	estar acostado / -a	*to be lying down*
¡Por fin! El bebé **está dormido**.	estar dormido / -a	*to be asleep*
¿Ya **estás levantada**?	estar levantado / -a	*to be up*
Estamos sentados en la terraza.	estar sentado / -a	*to be seated*

¿Dónde han puesto las cartas ya **firmadas** (= que ya están firmadas)?
Una vez hecho (una vez que hagamos) el resumen, podemos irnos.

The past participle can shorten a relative clause or an adverbial clause.

▶ **Verbal Periphrasis**, p. 191

Deja apagadas las luces, ¿eh?

In certain verb combinations, it forms so-called periphrases.

The Present Participle

¿Qué estás haciendo?

Sigo **escuchando** mi nuevo CD.

① ②

1. What are you doing? 2. I'm continuing to listen to my new CD.

> The present participle describes an action that is in progress. It is used primarily to form the progressive and is always invariable.

Formation

1. Regular Forms

To the stem of the infinitive, add the ending **-ando** to **-ar** verbs and the ending **-iendo** for **-er** / **-ir** verbs.

viaj**ar** ▶ viaj**ando**	conoc**er** ▶ conoc**iendo**	viv**ir** ▶ viv**iendo**

2. Irregular Forms

preferir *(ie)*	▶	prefiriendo	sentir *(ie)* ▶ sintiendo
pedir *(i)*	▶	pidiendo	reír *(i)* ▶ riendo
venir *(g, ie)*	▶	viniendo	decir *(g + i)* ▶ diciendo

Verbs ending in **-ir** that undergo the vowel change **e ▶ ie** or **e ▶ i** in the present have an **i** in the present participle.

▶ **Verb Groups, Present**, p. 108

dormir *(ue)*	▶	durmiendo	morir *(ue)* ▶ muriendo
poder *(ue)*	▶	pudiendo	

Verbs ending in **-ir** that undergo the vowel change **o ▶ ue** in the present have a **u** in the present participle.

leer	▶	leyendo	creer ▶ creyendo
traer *(ig)*	▶	trayendo	oír *(g, y)* ▶ oyendo

If the verb stem ends in a vowel, the **i** between vowels changes to **y**.

> Ir, too, has a **y**:
> ir ▶ yendo.

Use

Ahora que **estoy esperando** un bebé, mi madre ha estado **llamándome** con más frecuencia.

▶ **Verbal Periphrasis**, p. 191

The verbal present participle forms various periphrases. The most important is the progressive form with **estar** or **seguir** + present participle. It is used to describe actions in the process of taking place or continuing.

The auxiliary verb is conjugated in the appropriate person, as below:

	to be doing **estar** + pres. part.		to continue doing **seguir** + pres. part.	
(yo)	estoy	trabajando	sigo	viendo
(tú)	estás	comiendo	sigues	comiendo
(él, ella, usted)	está	durmiendo	sigue	leyendo
(nosotros/-as)	estamos	saliendo	seguimos	hablando
(vosotros/-as)	estáis	teniendo	seguís	haciendo
(ellos, ellas, ustedes)	están	terminando	siguen	relajándose

Use of the Present Participle to Replace Dependent Clauses

In place of some adverbial clauses, you can use a construction containing the verbal present participle (*gerundio*).

Recordándote (= Cuando te recordaba), me emocionaba.
When I remembered you, I was very moved.

The present participle can express circumstances or a sequence (*When ... or ... and ...*).

> One description that has become an adjective is **hirviendo: agua hirviendo** (*boiling water*).

Dándose (= Porque se dio) cuenta de la situación, Nidia no dijo nada. *Since she was aware of the situation, Nidia said nothing.*

– an explanation or substantiation (*since / because ...*).

Aun diciéndomelo (= Aunque me lo digas) tú, ¡no me lo puedo creer! *Although you tell me so, I can't believe it!*

– an objection, frequently containing **aun** (*although / even though*).

> In colloquial speech, many directions are given this way: **La cafetería está subiendo por las escaleras. = Usted llega a la cafetería si sube por las escaleras.**

Vi a un miembro de la Cruz Roja **recogiendo dinero**.
I saw a member of the Red Cross (who was) collecting money.

– a description (replacing a relative clause).

Cuando me llamaste, vine **corriendo**.
When you called me, I came running.

– manner.

Volando (= Si vuelas) con esta línea aérea, será más barato.
If you fly with this airline, it will be cheaper.

– a condition.

Verbal Periphrasis

> **Estoy haciendo** esta dieta porque **acabo de leer** que es buenísima.

I'm following this diet because I have just read that it is very good.

A verbal periphrasis consists of a conjugated verb + an infinitive, past participle, or present participle. The meaning of the conjugated verb often differs from its meaning when it stands alone. Example:

volver	*to return*
volver a + infinitive	*to do (verb) again*

Some verbal periphrases are used with a certain preposition, while others are not.

Always memorize the preposition at the same time!

1. Verbal Periphrases with an Infinitive

Iba a llamarte, pero he cambiado de idea. **Voy a** enviarte un e-mail.
I was going to call you, but I changed my mind. I'm going to send you an e-mail.

- **ir a** + infinitive expresses a future action. This form is used especially for intentions in the near future. In the imperfect, it expresses an intention in the past.

In some regions of LA, **ir a** + infinitive is the preferred future form. The traditional future tense is used only in literary language.

Acabo de ver a Eva, ¡y me **acaba de decir** que se casa! *I've just seen Eva, and she has just told me that she's getting married!*

- **acabar de** + infinitive expresses the immediate past, that is, something that has just taken place.

Normalmente **acabamos de cenar** a las diez.
Normally we finish eating dinner at 10 o'clock.

- **acabar de** + infinitive, depending on the context, also means *to finish* or *to be through with*. In the *indefinido*, the construction has only this meaning.

!

When negated, **acabar de** means *to manage*, as here: **No acabo de entenderte.** (*I can't manage to understand you.*)

Después de la reunión, el jefe **acabó por aceptar** mis ideas.
After the meeting, the boss ended up accepting my ideas.

- **acabar por** + infinitive means *to finally ...*, *to end up ...* .

Verbal Periphrasis

Nos las arreglamos para organizar todo solos.
We managed to organize everything alone.

- **arreglárselas para** + infinitive means *to manage to ... .*

¡No **me atrevo a mirar!** *I don't dare to look!*

- **atreverse a** + infinitive means *to dare to ... .*

Con un poco de música siempre **consigo relajarme.**
With a little music, I always manage to relax.

- **conseguir / lograr** + infinitive (without a preposition) means
  someone manages to ... or succeeds in ... .

¡**Deja de hablar** todo el tiempo! *Stop talking all the time!*

- **dejar de** + infinitive means *to stop ... .*

Los llamé, pero entonces los niños **se echaron a correr.**
I called them, but then the children started to run.

- **echar(se) a** + infinitive means *to (suddenly) start to, begin to ... .*

¿A qué hora **empiezas a trabajar**?
What time do you start to work?

- **empezar / comenzar a** + infinitive means *to start to, to begin to ... .*

Todo el tiempo me **haces reír.**
You make me laugh all the time.

- **hacer** + infinitive (without a preposition) means *to make ... .*

¿Por qué **insistes en hacer** todo sola?
Why do you insist on doing everything alone?

- **insistir en** + infinitive means *to insist on ... .*

Intentaremos traducir esta frase.
We will try to translate this sentence.

- **intentar** + infinitive (with no preposition) means *to try to ... .*

Intentar and **tratar de** + infinitive have the same meaning, but no preposition is used between **intentar** and the infinitive!

Nunca **llegué a hacer** mi soñado viaje a Perú.
I never got to take my dream trip to Peru.

- **llegar a** + infinitive means *to go so far as ..., to get to ... .*

En las vacaciones **pienso ir** a Ecuador.
During vacation I plan to go to Ecuador.

- **pensar** + infinitive (with no preposition) means *to intend to...,
  to plan to ... .*

Ahora mismo **me pongo a preparar** la ensalada.
I'll start preparing the salad right now.

- **ponerse a** + infinitive means *to start (energetically / suddenly)
  to ... .*

¿**Han quedado en verlos** el fin de semana?
Did they agree to see you this weekend?

- **quedar en** + infinitive means *to agree (on) ... .*

Siento molestarte, pero te quiero preguntar una cosa.
I'm sorry to bother you, but I want to ask you something.

- **sentir** + infinitive means *to be sorry to ... .*

Después de comer **suelo echarme** una siesta.
After eating I'm in the habit of taking a nap.

- **soler** + infinitive means *to be in the habit of, to usually ... .*
  Soler (*ue*) is used only in the present or imperfect.

¿Por qué **has tardado** tanto **en llamar**?
Why did you take so long to call?

- **tardar en** + infinitive means *to take (a long) time to ... .*

Trata de hacerlo hoy mismo.
Try to do it today.

- **tratar de** + infinitive means *to try to ... .*

Un momento, ¡todavía no **he terminado de hablar**!
Just a moment, I haven't finished talking yet!

- **terminar de** + infinitive means *to finish ... .*

A ver, te lo **vuelvo a explicar**.
Let's see, I'll explain it to you again.

- **volver a** + infinitive means *to do ... again.*

> ! **Soler** (*ue*) never occurs alone; that is, it always is used with an infinitive.

> In Spain, **soler** is much more common in colloquial speech than in LA.

2. Verbal Periphrases with a Past Participle

The shades of meaning present in the following verbal periphrases are often difficult to translate. They all express a state of being as the result of an action, which often is to be found in the sentence's context.

In verbal periphrases, the past participle behaves like an adjective. With intransitive verbs, it agrees with the subject; with transitive verbs, it agrees with the direct object:

▶ **Types of Verbs**,
  p. 103

Laura anda muy **enamorada**.	intransitive
Laura tiene a **Juan** muy **enamorado**.	transitive

Mi amiga **andaba** un poco **deprimida**.

- **andar** + past participle describes a continuing action or a lasting state of being.

Simón **se fue deprimido** a casa de Sonia, pero **volvió** más **animado**.

- **ir(se) / venir / volver** + past participle describes the state or condition of the subject during the action of the verb.

Todos **quedaron** muy **satisfechos**.

- **quedar(se)** + past participle expresses a result.

Los niños **tienen prohibida** la televisión.

- **tener** + past participle expresses a state or condition as the result of an action.

Llevar + puesto is used only for clothing and means *to wear*: <u>Lleva puestas</u> unas botas.

Llevo hechas dos terceras partes de los deberes.

- **llevar** + past participle expresses how far one has come with the action thus far.

Mi amiga **lleva** dos horas conectada al internet.

- **llevar** + space of time + past participle expresses the length of an action or of a state of being.

¡**Deja** las luces **apagadas**!

- **dejar** + past participle expresses the consequences of an action.

Mi televisor **sigue roto**.

- **seguir** + past participle expresses that the action is still continuing or the state is still enduring.

3. Verbal Periphrases with a Present Participle

All verbal periphrases with a present participle describe the length or continuation of an action in its course. The precise shades of meaning depend on the main verb.

Estoy aprendiendo mucho. *I'm learning a lot.*

– **estar** + present participle is the progressive form and refers to action in progress.

Some verbs that express a state of being do not form the progressive; they include **estar**, **saber**, **recordar**, etc.

• ¿**Continúas teniendo** problemas con el internet?
○ Sí, los mensajes **siguen tardando** mucho.
• *Do you continue having problems with the Internet?*
○ *Yes, messages keep being delayed.*

seguir / continuar + present participle refers to continuing action.

Pero **voy aprendiendo** algunos trucos.
But I'm gradually learning some tricks.

– **ir** + present participle means *gradually* or *bit by bit*.

Ahora **ando / vengo leyendo** libros especializados.
I've been reading specialized books for some time now.

– **andar / venir** + present participle means *for some time*.

También mi hermano **empezó experimentando** con la guitarra … .
My brother also started out experimenting with the guitar … .

– **empezar** + present participle means *at the start*.

… y **acabó siendo** un experto con ella.
…and ended up being an expert with it.

– **acabar / terminar** + present participle means *in the end*.

Se pasa la vida arreglando aspiradoras.
He spends his life fixing vacuum cleaners.

– **pasarse** + time + present participle means *to spend the whole time … .*

In colloquial speech, **pasárselas** + present participle means *to spend the time …:*
Se las pasa arreglando computadoras.

Lleva ya varios años haciendo esto.
He has been doing this for several years now.

– **llevar** + time + present participle means *to do … for … .*

Practice and Application

Unconjugated Forms of the Verb

gust -   sab-
quit-   sal-
ten-   ped-
discut-   llor-
ca-   dorm-
llov-   escuch-
cant-   entend-

1. Write the complete infinitive forms of the verbs given on the left in the appropriate blanks below. *

a) **-ar:** gustar _____

b) **-er:** _____

c) **-ir:** _____

Watch out!
pedir = *to ask (for);
to order*
pedar = *to break
wind*

---

quitar – *to remove,
take away*
llorar – *to cry*
llover – *to rain*
caer – *to fall*

la maleta – *the suitcase*
hace calor – *it's hot*
cansado / -a – *tired*
gordo / -a – *fat*
gimnasio – *here:
fitness center, gym*

2. Complete the sentences below, using forms of **ir** + preposition. *

a) Tengo muchos libros y no sé cuándo los _voy a_____ leer.

b) Jesús, ¿ _____ ocupar el teléfono mucho tiempo? Es que espero una llamada ... .

c) ¡Pero, hijas, si ya mañana nos vamos a Bolivia! ¿A qué horas _____ hacer las maletas?

d) ¡Hace mucho calor! ¡Creo que _____ ducharme otra vez!

e) ¡Uff! Si estamos tan cansados, mejor _____ dormir.

f) Pepe dice que está muy gordo y por eso ahora _____ ir al gimnasio todos los días.

3. Match the statements with the appropriate reactions. *

a) ¿Quieres probar este helado? Es nuevo y está delicioso.   (3)

b) Pueden venir al cine con nosotros, si quieren.   ( )

c) Yo hago el postre. Sé hacer un flan muy bueno.   ( )

d) ¡Deja ya de trabajar, Jimena! Ya es muy tarde.   ( )

---

la grabadora –
the burner
la jarra – *the pitcher*
la esquina – *the corner*

e) Mira, acabamos de comprar esta nueva grabadora de DVD.   ( )

1. ¡Excelente! Entonces yo puedo preparar una jarra de té.

2. Bueno. ¿Vamos al bar de la esquina a tomar una cerveza?

3. No gracias, ahora prefiero tomar sólo un café ...

4. ¿Y ya saben usarla? Porque yo quiero hacer una copia de esta película ...

5. ¡Qué lástima! Tenemos que estudiar, hoy no podemos ir con ustedes.

4. Unneeded words have crept into some of the sentences below. Mark out the superfluous words.

a) Me gusta ~~de~~ hacer deporte.

b) Queremos a pedir una ensalada mixta para todos.

c) Tengo que estudiar este fin de semana.

d) ¡Huy, qué bonito regalo! La verdad es que no sé por qué decir.

e) Sonia, ¿puedo para hacer una llamada por tu móvil?

f) ¿Me dejas a llevarme el coche, papi?

g) Para ir al centro hay que tomar el autobús número 15.

5. Certain expressions are missing from this article about a Chilean tennis coach. Choose the correct expressions from those provided in the margin. **

a) Son las 11 de la noche y Antonio <u>acaba de terminar</u> su trabajo del día. **b)** "_____ solamente por las tardes", comenta. "Por las mañanas tengo tiempo para otras cosas: _____ _____ inglés, por ejemplo. **c)** Una de mis metas es _____ _____ bien, ya que _____ en este país".

d) A los 24 años, Antonio _____ solamente tenista profesional en su país y _____ como entrenador en un club en Estados Unidos. **e)** "_____ ambas actividades", dice, "si eres tenista, muy pronto tienes que _____ _____ en que a los 30 años ya eres prácticamente viejo.

f) Por eso _____ un campo afín. **g)** Como entrenador, no necesito _____ , es genial."

h) ¿Y sobre la idea de _____ en Chile? "No sé," suspira. **i)** "Cuando vives mucho tiempo fuera, _____ ni de aquí ni de allá. A veces sueño con volver, pero la vida me trata bien en Estados Unidos".

~~acaba de terminar~~
acabas por no ser
he decidido vivir
dejar de jugar
dejó de ser
empezó a trabajar
lograr hablarlo
he intentado
encontrar
Pienso combinar
ponerte a pensar
trato de aprender
Suelo trabajar
volver a vivir

la meta – *the goal*
el entrenador –
the coach, trainer
ambos / -as – *both*
afín – *here: related*
suspirar – *to sigh*
fuera – *away*

6. Patricia tells about her experiences on the Camino de Santiago. Mark the correct expression. ***

la limosna – *alms*
el albergue – *the hostel*
llevar a cabo – *to carry out*
por su lado – *for / on his part*
la peregrinación – *the pilgrimage*

a) En el año 2003, mi compañero Miguel y yo decidimos / pensamos a hacer el Camino de Santiago, aunque no teníamos ni un euro.

b) Nos pusimos a / Solimos pensar en diferentes posibilidades para financiarnos. **c)** "¿Tú te atreverías a / alegras con pedir limosna?", preguntó Miguel. **d)** "Yo sí", respondí. "Y creo que así haremos / conseguiremos reunir suficiente para lograr / volver a pagar los albergues y la comida". **e)** Y así fue que Miguel y yo quedamos en / dejamos de llevar a cabo el plan. **f)** Nos echamos a / Llegamos a caminar desde Bilbao y todos los días acabábamos de / nos las arreglábamos para conseguir de dos a cinco euros. **g)** Pero aparte del aspecto práctico, el Camino de Santiago llegó a / terminó de ser para los dos una experiencia espiritual muy profunda.

h) Solíamos / Íbamos a hablar poco mientras caminábamos; con frecuencia cada uno volvía de / se ponía a meditar por su lado.

i) La peregrinación nos hizo / volvió a pensar mucho en lo que realmente era importante y lo que no. **j)** Y claro, cuando por fin llegamos a Santiago, habíamos terminado de / llegado a conocernos súper bien... y al cabo de un año acabamos por / acabamos de casarnos.

esforzarse – *to make an effort*

a) _____
b) _____
c) _____
d) _____
e) _____
f) _____

7. In the margin, write the infinitive or present participle construction that can take the place of the dependent clause in **bold**. ***

a) **Cuando llegó** a la oficina, Martín vio el mensaje de inmediato.

b) **En cuanto aclare** la situación, te llamo.

c) **Aunque tiene** normalmente poca paciencia, el profesor nos ha explicado hoy todo muy bien.

d) Tenemos que esforzarnos **hasta que consigamos** resultados positivos.

e) Claro, ¡no encuentras nada **porque eres** tan desordenado!

f) **Antes de que nos vayamos**, quisiera hablar un momento con el jefe.

8. In the blanks in the minidialogues below, write the progressive form of the verbs provided on the right. *

a) • Perdón, ¿está Roberto?

   ○ Sí, pero no puede acercarse, __se está duchando__ .

b) • Quería hablar con la Sra. Fuentes, por favor.

   ○ En este momento _____ por otra línea.

c) • Hola, Sr. Paredes, quiero hablar con Paquita.

   ○ Hola, Manolo. Pues mira, llama más tarde porque justo ahora

   nosotros _____ .

d) • ¿Está Lina? Aquí habla Esteban.

   ○ No, Lina y Sara _____ en la Cordillera y

   vuelven el día 10. Pero yo le doy a Lina el recado.

e) • Oiga, ¿usted es el del anuncio? ¿_____ una casa?

   ○ No, yo _____ un piso. Supongo que se ha

   equivocado.

a) ducharse
b) hablar
c) cenar
d) esquiar
e) vender, alquilar

acercarse – *to get closer*
la línea – *the line*
el recado – *the message*
se ha equivocado –
*here: you have the
wrong number*

9. Using the numbers from 1 to 7, arrange the sentences of this little short story in the proper order. **

a) ( ) Así que, limpiándose las lágrimas, Esperanza se propuso empezar con ánimo esa nueva etapa de su vida.

b) (1) Cuando se murió su marido, Esperanza **estuvo llorando** durante semanas.

c) ( ) Y al final, se había pasado los días cuidando al marido enfermo.

d) ( ) "Y estoy segura de que, dondequiera que esté, se alegrará si ve que voy aprendiendo a vivir otra vez".

e) ( ) Pero después, poco a poco, se fue consolando.

f) ( ) "Él no va a volver a vivir, aun si yo sigo llorando", pensó.

g) ( ) Llevaba años dedicándose solamente a las tareas del hogar.

limpiarse – *here: to wipe
away*
la lágrima – *the tear*
el ánimo – *here: courage*
cuidar – *here: to take
care of*
dondequiera que esté –
wherever he may be
consolarse – *to console
oneself, take comfort*
aun si – *even if*
dedicarse a –
to devote oneself to

10. Now underline the present participle constructions in the short story above. **

Practice and Application

Unconjugated Forms of the Verb

11. Fill in the missing endings in these dialogues. **

a) • Quería comprar estos calendarios que están rebajad_os_ .

  ○ Claro que sí. ¿Los quiere envuelt____ para regalo?

envolver – here: to wrap
cansado / -a – here: exhausting, tiring
acalorado / -a – here: heated, angry
solucionar – to solve
distraído / -a – absent-minded

b) • ¡Uff! Este día ha sid____ muy cansad____. Hemos tenid____ muchas discusiones acalorad____, pero, por suerte, hemos solucionad____ la mayoría de los problemas.

c) • Oiga, señorita, esta palabra está mal escrit____. La ha puest____ usted con h.

  ○ Ay, ¡Perdón! Es que estaba distraíd____. ¡Me parece que he estad____ sentad____ ante la computadora demasiadas horas y ya no estoy concentrad____! Ya está, ya la he corregid____.

d) • Lo siento, señores, la farmacia todavía está cerrad____. Está abiert____ al público por la mañana de 8.30 a 14.30 de lunes a viernes.

12. Conversations during the noon break. Complete them with an infinitive, past participle, or present participle. **

jubilarse – to retire
el objetivo – the objective, aim
el plazo – the deadline
fijar – to set, fix
comerse – to eat up

a) Llevamos un mes _trabajando_ *(trabajar)* en este proyecto y ya hemos _____ *(obtener)* los primeros resultados.

b) • Su marido acaba de _____ *(jubilarse)*, ¿verdad, Sra. Villena? ¿Y qué está _____ *(hacer)* ahora con todo su tiempo libre?

  ○ Pues ahora anda _____ *(aprender)* idiomas y _____ *(leer)* mucho.

c) No sé cuándo estarán _____ *(terminar)* los planos para el nuevo edificio. Los ingenieros han tardado mucho en _____ *(organizarse)*.

d) _____ *(Trabajar)* muy duro, seguramente lograremos _____ *(conseguir)* los objetivos dentro del plazo _____ *(fijar)*.

e) Anoche, como no logramos _____ *(ponerse)* de acuerdo sobre el restaurante, acabamos _____ *(quedarse)* en casa y _____ *(comerse)* los restos de la nevera.

13. Read this article about the Sephardim, or Sephardic Jews, and complete the text, using the expressions provided.

a establecerse – acabó por ser – así llamados – Contando – era tolerada – fueron expulsados – ha cambiado – ha ido tomando – han ido – llevaron – manteniendo – prestadas – reconquistada – se fueron adaptando – siguen hablando – sigue siendo hablada – que tuvieron que salir – va a poder entender

a) Durante cientos de años, los judíos de todo el mundo <u>han ido</u>

de un país a otro. **b)** Pero, ¿sabía usted que muchos de los

descendientes de los judíos _____ de

España a fines de la Edad Media, los _____

"sefardíes", todavía _____ español?

c) En 1942, los judíos _____ porque, una vez

_____ España de manos de los moros, ninguna otra

religión, aparte de la católica, _____. **d)** _____

_____ entre los judíos y los árabes a muchas personas de

excelente preparación, ese paso en la historia de España _____

_____ una pérdida lamentable desde el punto de

vista cultural. **e)** Distintas circunstancias _____ a los

sefardíes _____ en países diferentes. **f)** Con el tiempo,

_____ a las culturas locales, por ejemplo en

Turquía, en los Balcanes, en el Norte de África y en otras regiones,

pero _____ intactos algunos rasgos de sus antiguas

tradiciones. **g)** La lengua que _____ en

casa se basa en el español de entonces, pero como toda lengua, con

los siglos_____. **h)** Por ejemplo, poco a poco

_____ palabras _____ de

los idiomas circundantes y así existen hoy algunas interesantes

diferencias regionales. **i)** Sin embargo, si usted habla español,

probablemente _____ a los sefardíes.

el descendiente – *the descendent*
los sefardíes – *the Sephardim*
expulsar – *to expel, drive out*
reconquistar – *to reconquer*
el moro – *the Moor*
el paso – *the step*
la pérdida – *the loss*
establecerse – *to settle*
mantener – *here: to keep, maintain*
el rasgo – *the characteristic, feature*
circundante – *surrounding*

ser, estar, hay

Special Verbs

Ser, estar, hay

> The English verb "to be" can be rendered in Spanish with **ser**, **estar**, or **hay**.

¡Cuidado! Ahí **hay** una vaca.
①

¿Dónde **está**?
②

Ahí, ¿la ves? **Es** una vaca negra.
③

1. Watch out! There's a cow over there. 2. Where is it? 3. There, do you see it? It's a black cow.

The verbs **ser**, **estar**, and **hay** are real "traps" for many language learners, because Spanish has two verbs that are the equivalent of "to be," plus the word **hay,** and they are not interchangeable. Give yourself plenty of time to develop a feeling for when to use which verb!
Luckily, there are some helpful rules.

Use of *ser*

> The verb **ser** is used to express "objective" information.

Este **es** mi hijo Jorgito.
①

¡Huy! **Es** un bebé lindísimo.
②

1. This is my son, Georgy. 2. Wow! He's a pretty baby!

Ser identifies and defines things and persons and assigns them to categories.

> Generally, **ser** is used before nouns.

- ¿Quién **es**? ▶ ○ **Soy** yo. **Soy** la profesora.
- ¡Oh! ¿Qué **es** esto? ▶ ○ **Son** chocolates, pero **son** míos.

– **Ser** + noun or pronoun is used to give more detailed information about persons or things.

Luis **es** mi tío. **Es** médico y es peruano. **Es** católico pero **es** liberal.

■ – to show nationality, occupation, religious or political affiliation, kinship, etc.

For temporary activities, use **estar** + de: <u>Está de médico en un proyecto.</u>

Magdalena **es** rubia y muy atractiva. Sus hermanos **son** muy alegres.
Este restaurante **es** excelente y no **es** demasiado caro.

■ – to describe characteristic states or conditions. The determining factor is not whether the property or quality is invariable or enduring, but whether it serves to place a person or thing (temporarily or inherently) in a group.

▶ **Adjectives**, p. 45

Because they are interpreted as defining, the following adjectives generally are used with **ser**:

feliz	*happy*	infeliz	*unhappy*
rico	*rich*	pobre	*poor*
responsable	*responsible*	irresponsable	*irresponsible*
culpable	*guilty*	inocente	*innocent*

Note:
to be … years old =
tener … años
to be … meters tall =
medir … metro(s)

• ¡**No es posible**! ¿**Es un hecho** que van a subir los precios?
○ ¡**Es verdad**! **Es necesario** leer el periódico.

■ – in many impersonal expressions with the structure **es** + adjective, followed by an infinitive or a dependent clause (such as **fácil/difícil**, **cierto**, **bueno/malo**, **importante**, **necesario**, **normal**, **(im)posible**, **(im)probable**, **(in)útil**, **(in)justo**, etc.) or with the structure **es** + noun **verdad**, **un hecho**, etc.)

Este bolso **es de** cuero, ¿verdad? ¿**Es de** Italia?
Este coche **es del** jefe.
Siéntete en casa, que **eres de** la familia.

■ – with the preposition **de**, to express origin, material, possession, or affiliation.

• ¿Esto **es para** mañana?
○ Sí. El vino **es para** la fiesta y las flores **son para** Marcia.

■ – with **para**, to show disposition, purpose, or recipient.

ser, estar, hay

¿Qué fecha **es** hoy? Hoy **es** el 20 de enero.
¡Qué pereza, ya no **es** domingo! **Es** hora de ir al trabajo.
¿**Son** las seis? ¡Ya **es** muy tarde! Ya casi **es** de noche.

▶ **Time Expressions**, p. 261

– to make statements about time: date, day of the week, hour, time of day (for example, with **tarde** (*late*), **temprano / pronto** (*early*), **de mañana / tarde / noche** (*in the morning / afternoon / evening*), **hora de** (*it's time to ...*), etc.).

▶ **Numbers**, p. 257

Somos cuatro, entonces **son** cuatro porciones.
¡Ya sé cuál **es** el resultado! Cinco y diez **son** quince.
● ¿Cuánto **es** en total, señor? ▶ ○ **Son** quinientos euros.

– for number, amount, results, and statement of a total sum.

El concierto **es** en el castillo. Va a **ser** en el salón rococó.

– to state the location of events, telling where they *take place*.

▶ **Past Participle**, p. 187

Cuzco **fue fundada** por los incas.

– together with the past participle, to construct the passive voice.

▶ **Passive**, p. 240

Use of *estar*

Estar is used to show location or position; to express accidental or temporary conditions and states; or to give subjective evaluations.

Huy ... no **estoy** nada bien ... ¿Dónde **estoy**?

①

Tranquila, **estás** en el hospital y **estás** recién operada.

②

1. Oh ... I'm not feeling well at all ... Where am I?
2. Take it easy, you're in the hospital and you've just had surgery.

¡Mis llaves no **están**!
● ¿**Está** Rodrigo? ▶ ○ No **está**, lo siento.

– **Estar** is used with certain subjects, to express presence or absence

Note: **Estar** is never used with the preposition **a** to express location! **Estar** is frequently used with **en** or other prepositions of place.

¿Dónde **está** el señor Pérez? ¿**Estará** mañana en la fábrica?

– to indicate place in the sense of *position* (*sit, stand, lie*, etc.), when the subject is specified, that is, in the following constructions:

El jefe **está** en la oficina.	– definite article + noun
Correos está cerca.	– names
¡Uff! ¿Dónde **está** ese libro?	– demonstrative determiner + noun
Mis cosas no **están** en su lugar.	– possessive determiner + noun
Todos estamos aquí.	– indefinite pronoun
	todo / -a / -os / -as

> If **todo** is preceded by the preposition **de**, then you should use **hay: Aquí <u>hay de todo</u>**.

- ¿Cómo **está** tu padre?
- Todavía **está** muy enfermo, aunque ya **está** fuera de peligro.

– **Estar** is used to express state of being or a changeable state.

> The stative passive falls into this category, since it expresses the result of an action.

Because the meaning always contains a comparison, the following adjectives are always used with **estar**:

lleno	*full*	vacío	*empty*
sano	*healthy*	enfermo	*sick*
vivo	*alive*	muerto	*dead*
contento	*happy, pleased*	harto	*full; fed up*
satisfecho	*satisfied*	insatisfecho	*dissatisfied*
ocupado	*busy*	preocupado	*worried*
maduro	*ripe, mature*	inmaduro	*unripe, immature*
solo	*alone*	acompañado	*accompanied*
completo	*complete*	roto	*broken*
permitido	*permitted*	prohibido	*forbidden*

▸ **Stative Passive**, p. 240

- ¿Por qué **estás de pie**? ¿No **estabas acostado**?

– to describe a position of the body, such **as estar de pie** (*to be standing up*), **estar sentado / -a** (*to be seated*), **estar acostado/-a** (*to be lying down*).

- Leticia **está de** camarera para ganar un poco de dinero.

– with the preposition **de**, to describe an occasional or temporary activity.

- ¿Vienes, Andrés? ▸ ○ **Está** bien, ya voy.

– with the adverbs **bien**, **mal**, **regular**, **mejor** and **peor**.

> **Bien / mal** are always used with **estar!**

ser, estar, hay

In this meaning,
estar + adjective
sometimes is rendered
as "to look," as here:
Estás muy guapa
(*You look very pretty*).

Por Dios, Fernando, ¡qué antipático **estás**!
¿Cómo? ¿Tu hija **está** casada ya?
He visto a Ángel, ¿te acuerdas de él? Pues **está** totalmente calvo.

– to say that someone exhibits a momentary, accidental, or striking
   behavior or appearance, or that a change has taken place.

Esta chaqueta **está** demasiado cara.

– to underscore a personal opinion or evaluation.

In evaluating food
and drink, always use
estar: La sopa <u>**está**</u>
deliciosa.

- Esta falda **me está** un poco **larga**, ¿no crees?
○ ¡Qué va! **Te está** muy **bien**, Sofia.

– with a dative pronoun + clothing + adjective or the adverbs
   bien / **mal**, in the sense of *to suit*.

¡Qué maravilla! ¡Por fin **estamos de vacaciones**!
Yo **estoy a favor** del viaje. Y ustedes, ¿**están de acuerdo** también?

– in numerous fixed expressions.

Such expressions include:

de viaje	*away, on a trip*	de buen humor	*in a good mood*
de visita	*visiting*	de vacaciones	*on vacation*
de paso	*passing through*	para bromas	*as a joke*
al principio	*at the start*	al teléfono	*on the telephone*
de acuerdo	*agreed*	en desacuerdo	*in disagreement*
al corriente	*up-to-date*	en contra	*opposed*
a favor	*in favor*	de mal humor	*in a bad mood*
en un lío	*in trouble*		

Estamos a diecinueve de marzo.
Estamos a dos grados bajo cero. ¡Qué frío! Ya **estamos en** invierno.

– in the first person plural with the preposition **a**, to give the date
   and temperature, and with **en** to indicate the season.

▶ **Present Participle**,
p. 189

Las gambas **están a** mitad de precio.

– with the preposition **a**, to name a variable price.

¡No hagas tanto ruido, que el bebé **está durmiendo**!

– together with the present participle in the progressive form.

1. Summary of Differences Between *ser* and *estar*

ser	estar
¿Quién **es** usted? – *identification (who it is)*	¡Mis llaves no **están**! – *(non)presence*
¿Qué **es** esto? **Es** un reloj. – *definition (what it is)* La clase **es** en el salón grande. – *exception: venue (where something specific takes place)*	El reloj **está** demasiado caro. – *evaluation, relative (comparing)* Ya **estamos** en Colombia. – *location (where someone specific is located)*
Luis **es** peruano, **es** mi tío. – *nationality, kinship, etc.*	¿Qué tal? ¿**Estás** bien? – *state / condition: health* El vaso **está** lleno. – *state / condition: temporary, relative* **Estamos** sentados a la sombra. – *state / condition: position of the body*
Tatiana **es** profesora. – *occupation*	Tatiana **está** de profesora. – *temporary activity*
Eres muy delgado. – *characteristic condition*	¡Qué delgado **estás**! – *noticeable characteristic, relative*
Magdalena **es** soltera. – *objective attribution*	Magdalena **está** soltera. – *temporary condition, relative*
Es de Juan / **de** cuero / **de** aquí. – *ownership, material, origin*	Me **está** un poco estrecho. – *with dative; for clothing*
Es para mañana / **para** ti. – *disposition, recipient*	
Es la una / lunes / de noche. – *time expression*	**Estamos** a 7 de septiembre. – *exception: specific statements of time, such as the date*
Son 10 euros, y la propina, **son** 11. – *sum, quantity, number, result*	El pescado **está** a 5 euros el kilo. – *variable price*
Es fácil / necesario / cierto. ***Es** + adjective / noun*	**Estamos** de viaje / de acuerdo. – *fixed expressions*
América **fue** descubierta en 1492. – *passive*	No todo **está** descubierto. – *stative passive*
	¿Por qué te **estás** riendo? – *progressive form*

> **!**
> Casado / -a con + person can be used only with **estar**:
> **Estoy casada con Alfredo desde hace 10 años.**

The differences in meaning expressed by **ser** and **estar** give rise to many plays on words and stylistic effects, as here: **¡Qué inteligente estás hoy!** This says that the person otherwise is not deemed to be intelligent; it is a pointed expression of irony.

2. Changes in Meaning of Some Adjectives with *ser* and *estar*

Some adjectives have different meanings, depending on whether they are used with **ser** or with **estar**.

Only with estar:
Está bien.
(*That's okay.*
That's right.)
Está mal.
(*That's not okay.*
That's not right.)

el tío / la tía –
in colloquial speech:
guy / babe

	ser	estar
bueno	*good-natured / of good quality* Juan **es** muy **bueno.** Este aparato **es bueno.**	*healthy / delicious / sexy* Ya **estoy bueno** y sin gripe. La langosta **está** muy **buena.** Eh tía, ¡qué **buena** que **estás!**
malo	*bad / of poor quality* Ese chico **es malo.** Este aparato **es malo.**	*ill / rotten, spoiled* Todavía **estoy malo.** El pescado **está malo.**
abierto	*open-minded* Mis amigos **son abiertos.**	*open* El banco ya **está abierto.**
aburrido	*boring* Ese libro **es aburrido.**	*bored, tired* Ya **estoy aburrido** de estudiar.
alegre	*lively* Esta música **es** muy **alegre.**	*tipsy* Con el vino **estamos alegres.**
atento	*considerate, thoughtful* **Es** usted muy **atento.**	*attentive* ¿**Están atentos** en clase?
callado	*quiet = taciturn, sedate* **Es** una persona **callada.**	*hushed, silent* La noche **estaba callada.**
cansado	*tiring* El camino **es cansado.**	*tired* ¡Qué **cansado estoy!**
cerrado	*reserved* **Es** un chico muy **cerrado.**	*closed* El banco **está cerrado.**
claro	*light* El color **es** muy **claro.**	*clear* ¿**Está** todo **claro?**
consciente	*aware* **Soy consciente** de todo.	*conscious* El enfermo no **está consciente.**
delicado	*delicate, touchy* El tema **es delicado.**	*frail, infirm* El enfermo **está delicado.**
despierto	*quick, sharp* Mónica **es** muy **despierta.**	*awake* El niño ya **está despierto.**
grave	*grave, weighty* El problema **es grave.**	*seriously ill* El abuelo ya no **está grave.**

joven	*young* A los 15 **eres** muy **joven**.	*young-looking, youthful* Mi abuela todavía **está joven**.
libre	*unattached* Me gusta **ser libre**.	*free, vacant* ¿**Está libre** ese asiento?
limpio	*clean* El hotel **es** muy **limpio**.	*well-cleaned* La habitación **está limpia**.
listo	*smart, clever* **Eres** muy **listo**, ¿verdad?	*ready* Ya nos vamos. ¿**Están listos**?
molesto	*annoying, pesky* Las moscas **son molestas**.	*annoyed* ¿Por qué **estás molesta**?
ordenado	*orderly (character)* Pepe **es** muy **ordenado**.	*straightened up, neat* El escritorio no **está ordenado**.
orgulloso	*arrogant, haughty* ¡No **seas orgulloso**!	*proud* **Estamos** muy **orgullosos** de ti.
rico	*rich, wealthy* Me gustaría **ser rico**.	*delicious* La sopa **está** muy **rica**.
seco	*curt, sharp* Marisa **es** un poco **seca**.	*dry, dried* La ropa no **está seca** todavía.
seguro	*safe, risk-free* Este negocio **es seguro**.	*certain, sure* No sé, no **estoy seguro**.
terco	*stubborn (by nature)* Juan **es** muy **terco**.	*defiant, bullheaded* El niño **está terco** con su idea.
tonto	*stupid* ¡No **seas tonto**!	*foolish, silly* Niño, ¡**estás tonto**!
sucio	*dirty = shady* Este negocio **es sucio**.	*dirty, messy* La cocina **está sucia**.
verde	*green* El nuevo sofá **es verde**.	*unripe* Los mangos **están verdes**.
viejo	*old* Mi abuela **es vieja**.	*aged, elderly in appearance* He visto a Pedro; **está viejo**.
vivo	*vivacious, lively* **Es** muy **viva** esta chica.	*alive* Mi padre ya no **está vivo**.

¡**Ya está**! is a shortened version of ¡**Ya está listo**! and means *It's ready now*!

ser, estar, hay

Hay and *estar*

Hay is an impersonal form of the verb **haber**. It is invariable.

① Hay todavía pastel de manzana?

② No, lo siento, ¡pastel de manzana ya no **hay**!

③ Pero aquí **está** el de fresas.

1. Is there still any apple cake?
2. No, I'm sorry, there's no more apple cake! 3. But here's the one with strawberries.

▶ **Types of Verbs**, p. 103

Only in exceptional cases is **ser** used with an expression of location. Generally you have to choose between **Aquí está** and **Aquí hay**.

Haber as a full verb is used only in the impersonal form **hay**. It serves to introduce a topic or to give the location of unspecified things or persons. Frequently **hay** can be translated as *there is, there are,* but it can also be rendered as *lie, sit, stand,* etc.

| ¡**Hay** novedades! | En la mesa **hay** una invitación. |
| *There is news!* | *An invitation is (lying) on the table.* |

In the present tense, the verb always has the special form **hay**; for all other tenses, the third person singular is used: **ha habido**, **había**, **hubo**, **habrá**, etc. These verbs can be followed by either singular or plural nouns.

Últimamente **ha habido** muchos nuevos libros.

Summary of Differences Between *hay* and *estar*

hay = indefinite subject	estar = definite subject
¿Dónde **hay un** hotel? – *with the indefinite article*	**El** Hotel Ritz **está** en el centro. – *with the definite article*
Hoteles buenos, sí **los hay**. – *object pronoun*	**Ana está** allí, **yo** estoy aquí. – *name / subject pronoun*
No **hay** hoteles aquí. – *without an article*	¿Dónde **está este** hotel? – *with a demonstrative determiner*
Hay dos pensiones. – *with quantities or numbers*	¿Dónde **está mi** hotel? – *with a possessive determiner*
Hay **muchos** hoteles. – *with an indefinite determiner / pronoun*	No **todos están** en el centro. – *exception:* **todo**

Hay que means *one must, you have to, it is necessary to:* **Hay que firmar aquí.**

1. Mark the correct verb. *

a) Cuba (es)/está/hay una isla que es/está/hay entre el Mar Caribe
y el Golfo de México. **b)** La capital de Cuba es/está/hay La Habana.
c) Desde hace algunos años es/está/hay un boom turístico en la
isla. **d)** Muchos turistas visitan por ejemplo la Playa de Varadero, que
no es/está/hay lejos de la capital. **e)** Esta playa es/está/hay famosa porque no sólo es/está/hay ahí 20 km de costa que disfrutar,
sino también es/está/hay ya una infraestructura hotelera adecuada.
f) Pero en La Habana misma también es/está/hay playas, y además, es/está/hay una ciudad fascinante. **g)** El centro histórico,
la Habana Vieja, es/está/hay Patrimonio de la Humanidad de la
UNESCO.

la isla – *the island*
desde hace – *for ...*
(length of time)
disfrutar – *to enjoy*
la infraestructura
hotelera – *the hotel
infrastructure*
mismo/-a – *here: itself*
el Patrimonio de la
Humanidad – *UNESCO
World Heritage site*

2. Match the questions (a–f) with the correct answers (1–6). *

a) (3) ¿Qué hay de comer? ¡Tengo hambre!

b) (   ) Mamá, ¡no sé dónde están mis libros! ¿Los has visto?

c) (   ) ¿De verdad está Shakira en el restaurante?
¿Cuál de esas chicas es?

d) (   ) ¡Huy! ¿Qué es ese ruido tan raro?

e) (   ) Hola, Gerardo, ¡qué milagro! ¿Desde cuándo estás aquí?

f) (   ) Oye, Rosario, ¿dónde está tu marido? ¿No viene hoy al bar?

de comer – *here: to eat*
¡Qué emoción! – *here:
How exciting!*
¡Qué milagro! – *I'm sur-
prised to see you!*
granizar – *to hail*
el granizo – *the hail*
el techo – *here: the roof*

1. Desde hace un mes. Estoy de profesor en una escuela de verano.

2. Es aquella rubia que está allí, ¿la ves? ¡Qué emoción, estar en el
mismo lugar que alguien tan famoso!

3. Arroz con pollo. Es una nueva receta, ¡y está riquísima!

4. No, está en la cama porque está muy cansado. Su trabajo es tan
estresante...

5. No, pero aquí al lado de la puerta hay unos. ¿Son esos?

6. Es que está granizando. Es el granizo que está cayendo sobre el techo.

Practice and Application

3. Fill in the correct verb: ¿**ser**, **estar**, or **hay**? *

a) • Oiga, camarero, ¿ _____ Rioja?

○ Sí, señores, aquí _____ . _____ un vino estupendo. _____

muy bueno, de verdad.

b) • Hola, María, ¿cómo _____? ¿Qué cuentas, chica?

desempleado / -a –
unemployed
perdido / -a – *here:*
confused
la oferta – *the bid*
el escritorio –
the desk
el suministrador –
the supplier

○ Bien, bien, pero ahora _____ desempleada y _____

buscando trabajo. Aquí cerca _____ una empresa donde buscan

secretarias, y como _____ secretaria de idiomas, pues ...

c) • Perdón, el Hotel Conquistador, ¿ _____ por aquí?

○ No, señorita, en este pueblo no _____ ningún hotel con ese

nombre. Pero _____ un hotel, _____ el Hotel Continental.

_____ en la Plaza de las Flores.

d) • ¡Qué raro! En esta fiesta todos _____ diferentes. Normalmente

Roberto _____ muy serio, pero hoy _____ muy

divertido. Y Juan Manuel, que normalmente _____ muy

simpático, ¡hoy _____ insoportable!

○ Debe _____ por el vino, ¿no crees?

e) • _____ que llenar este formulario. ¿A qué fecha _____

(nosotros)?

○ No _____ seguro, ¿qué día _____ hoy?

• _____ jueves, hombre, _____ más perdido que yo.

f) • Lolita, ¿dónde _____ las ofertas de la casa Muñoz?

○ _____ en su oficina, Sr. Pértegaz.

• ¿Cuántas _____ ?

○ Sólo _____ una oferta de la casa Muñoz. Pero también

_____ dos faxes de otro cliente. _____ en su escritorio.

• Muy bien. ¿ _____ también correspondencia del nuevo

suministrador?

○ Sí, señor, aquí _____ .

4. With whom and where are the people in Exercise 3 talking? Write the appropriate letters in the parentheses. *

1. (   ) Es un turista que está en la calle y habla con una persona del pueblo.

2. (   ) Son dos colegas, probablemente están en su lugar de trabajo.

3. (   ) Es un jefe y su secretaria. Están en la oficina.

4. (   ) Son unos amigos que están en una fiesta donde algunas personas están bebiendo bastante.

5. (a) Son unos clientes que están hablando con el camarero en un restaurante.

6. (   ) Son dos amigos que se encuentran, quizá están en una reunión.

5. Fill in the correct verb: **ser**, **estar**, **hay**, or **tener**. **

a) Las pequeñas manías que todos tenemos normalmente no __son__ un problema. **b)** Sin embargo, _____ personas que _____ manías exageradas. **c)** Por ejemplo, algunas _____ horas y horas frente a la computadora, otras _____ dependientes de su trabajo. **d)** _____ gente que sólo _____ contenta cuando _____ muchas cosas y por eso su manía _____ comprar y comprar. **e)** _____ personas que comen y comen y no se dan cuenta cuando en realidad ya _____ satisfechas.

f) Juan _____ un ejemplo de esto. **g)** _____ abogado y _____ 51 años. **h)** Podría _____ muy feliz porque _____ una familia muy agradable, pero lamentablemente su manía _____ ver la televisión y todo el tiempo _____ ahí, cambiando canales. **i)** Su mujer y sus hijos _____ intereses diferentes, y por eso no quieren _____ en casa los fines de semana. **j)** En consecuencia, Juan _____ muy solo; se _____ aislando cada vez más. **k)** Afortunadamente, _____ una terapia para él: con la ayuda adecuada, su problema _____ solución.

la manía – *here: quirk, peculiarity*
exagerado / -a – *exaggerated*
frente a – *in front of*
dependiente – *dependent*
darse cuenta – *to realize*

podría – *here: he could*
cambiar canales – *to channel-surf*
en consecuencia – *as a result*
aislarse – *to isolate oneself*
cada vez más – *more and more*

Practice and Application

Special Verbs

6. In a firm. Mark the correct verb. ***

capacitado / -a – *here: qualified*
la competencia – *the competition*
el curso de formación – *the training course*
vecino – *here: neighboring*
la carpeta – *the folder*
el / la participante – *the participant*
la disposición – *the disposal, service*

a) Esta candidata ha (sido)/ estado / habido la mejor. Es / Está / Hay experta en márqueting y es / está / hay capacitada para realizar entrevistas en varios idiomas. Hace dos años fue / estuvo / hubo trabajando con la competencia.

b) Señores, el curso de formación será / estará / habrá en el salón de conferencias que es / está / hay en el edificio vecino. Ahora la secretaria ya les es / está / ha entregando las carpetas a los participantes.

c) • Señorita, ¿ sería / estaría / habría tan amable de ayudarnos?

  ○ Por supuesto. Soy / Estoy / Hay a su disposición, señores.

d) Lo que dijo el experto fue / estuvo / hubo muy interesante, pero no era / estaba / había bien. Soy / Estoy / Hay seguro de que los datos no eran / estaban / habían correctos, era / estaba / había varios errores.

7. An expert is talking about the prejudices that some people have regarding the character of the Andalusians. Complete the passage with **ser**, **estar**, or **hay**. ***

vago – *lazy*
mencionar – *to mention*
el alma – *the soul*
más bien – *rather*
la fama – *the fame*

a) ___Son___ muchas las opiniones que _____ acerca del carácter del andaluz: por ejemplo, se dice que _____ alegre, pero vago.

b) Posiblemente _____ cierto que _____ difícil no _____ alegre y no _____ de buen humor cuando siempre hace sol.

c) Sin embargo, _____ que mencionar que _____ muchos andaluces diferentes. **d)** La autora Luisa Moreno piensa que tal vez lo que _____ más cerca del alma del andaluz es el sol, la luz que siempre _____ presente y que explica por qué la mayoría de la gente _____ más bien optimista. **e)** Pero la autora no _____ de acuerdo con la fama de vago y opina que _____ muy injusta.

f) En Andalucía se trabaja como en todas partes, pero _____ importante trabajar para vivir, y el andaluz _____ alguien que vive intensamente.

Verbs with the Dative

> **A mí me encanta** la música latina... ¿Y **a ti, te gusta** la salsa?

①

> No, ese tipo de música **no me gusta nada**. Pero **me gusta mucho** el rock.

②

1. *I love Latin American music ... And you, do you like salsa?*
2. *No, I don't like that kind of music at all. But I like rock music very much.*

Many verbs of emotion form the following sentence structure:

(a mí)	**me**			viajar
(a ti)	**te**	gusta	(mucho)	
(a él, ella, usted)	**le**			el coche
(a nosotros /-as)	**nos**			
(a vosotros /-as)	**os**	gustan	(mucho)	los coches
(a ellos, ellas, ustedes)	**les**			

If the thing that pleases, displeases, is missing, etc. is a singular noun or an infinitive, the verb is in the third person singular. If the thing that pleases, etc. is plural or if an enumeration follows, the verb is in the third person plural.

The subject—that is, the noun or the infinitive—can also be the first element in the sentence, especially if the dative is not doubled:

Me gusta mucho **viajar**. = **Viajar** me gusta mucho.

Sometimes the Spanish object becomes the English subject, sometimes not.

Me duele.	*It hurts me. / I hurt.*
Me parece bien.	*It seems fine to me. / I think it's fine.*

Mucho is used to express a high degree; **no ... nada** lends emphasis to a negation:

Me gusta **mucho** la espinaca.	*I like spinach very much.*
No me gusta **nada** la espinaca.	*I don't like spinach at all.*

Many verbs of emotion, such as **gustar**, must be used with a dative pronoun. For emphasis, the dative is doubled, as here: **a mí**, **a tí**, etc.

▶ **Pronouns,** pp. 77 – 78

Exceptions: **amar** (*to love*), **odiar** (*to hate*), **preferir (ie)** (*to prefer*), **detestar** (*to detest*), and **soportar** (*to stand, tolerate*). For example: **Odio los deportes.**

Unlike English, Spanish uses the definite article here before the noun: **Me gusta <u>la</u> paella.**

With expressive verbs such as **encantar** and **fascinar**, neither **mucho** nor **nada** is used.

Reflexive Verbs

The verbs used with the dative include these:

1. *To love* is **querer** only when speaking of persons, as here: **¡Te quiero mucho!** Otherwise, use **encantar**: <u>Me encanta ir al cine</u>, <u>me encantan las películas</u>.
2. To ask whether someone agrees, use the preposition + dative pronoun construction: **A mí me gusta, ¿y a ti?** (*I like it, do you?*)

interesar	*to interest*
gustar	*to like, to enjoy, to taste*
encantar	*to like very much, love*
dar igual	*to be all the same*
parecer bien / mal	*to think [s.th. is] good / bad*
preocupar	*to worry*
molestar	*to bother*
enfadar	*to make angry*
pasar	*to happen*
doler (ue)	*to hurt*
bastar	*to be enough, suffice*
faltar	*to be missing / lacking*
salir bien / mal	*to turn out well / badly*
dar sueño	*to make sleepy*
dar miedo	*to scare*
hacer falta	*to be necessary*
hacer daño	*to harm, be harmful*

Reflexive Verbs

In the dictionary, you can recognize a reflexive verb by the ending –se.

▶ **Present Tense of Verbs**, p. 108

①   ¿Te diviertes en la playa?

②   No, **me aburro**. ¡No hay nada que hacer!

1. *Are you having fun at the beach? 2. No, I'm bored. There's nothing to do!*

Reflexive verbs always include a reflexive pronoun, which corresponds to the person of the verb. If a verb is irregular, you need to keep the irregularity in mind.

Many English verbs that are not reflexive are treated as reflexives in Spanish; that is, the subject and object are the same. Examples: **llamarse** (*to be called / named*), **casarse** (*to marry, get married*), **levantarse** (*to get up, rise*).

	aburrir**se**		divertir**se** (**ie**)	
(yo)	**me**	aburro	**me**	divierto
(tú)	**te**	aburres	**te**	diviertes
(él, ella, usted)	**se**	aburre	**se**	divierte
(nosotros / -as)	**nos**	aburrimos	**nos**	divertimos
(vosotros / -as)	**os**	aburrís	**os**	divertís
(ellos, ellas, ustedes)	**se**	aburren	**se**	divierten

Some verbs can be both reflexive or not, depending upon whether the subject acts upon itself. Examples include **lavar** (*to wash*), **lavarse** (*to wash o.s.*). In other cases, the reflexive has a different meaning: **ir** (*to go*) – **irse** (*to go away, leave*); **dormir** (*to sleep*) – **dormirse** (*to fall asleep*).

Reflexive pronouns normally precede the conjugated (finite) form of the verb. They may be attached to the present participle, the infinitive, and infinitive constructions; they must be attached to the affirmative imperative.

> Manuel **se** ducha todos los días.
> Ahora está duchándo**se**. = Ahora **se** está duchando.
> Después va a vestir**se**. = Después **se** va a vestir.
> Manuel, ¡láva**te** también el pelo!

Here are some reflexive verbs:

> ▶ **Placement of Pronouns**, p. 80

Regular Forms and Verb Groups

aburrirse	to be bored	levantarse	to stand up, rise
alegrarse	to be glad	llamarse	to be called
atreverse a	to dare to	llevarse	to take away
ducharse	to shower	marcharse	to leave, go away
casarse	to marry	quedarse	to stay, remain
dedicarse a	to do; to devote o.s. to	quejarse	to complain
enfadarse	to get angry	permitirse	to allow oneself

(ue)

acordarse de	to remember	dormirse	to fall asleep
acostarse	to go to bed	probarse	to try on

(ie)

arrepentirse	to regret	referirse a	to refer to
despertarse	to wake up	sentarse	to sit (down)
divertirse	to enjoy o.s.	sentirse bien	to feel good

(i)

despedirse	to say good-bye	vestirse	to get dressed, dress

(g)

ponerse algo	to put s.th. on

(ig)

caerse	to fall down

1. Many verbs of emotion have both a dative ("impersonal") and a reflexive construction, such as **me alegra** (*I'm glad*) and **me alegro** (reflexive).
2. The reflexive verbs **sentarse** (ie) and **acostarse** (ue) describe the action: *to sit down, to go to bed*. For the result of the action, use **estar sentado / -a** and **estar acostado / -a**.

Irregular Forms

	irse (to go away)		darse cuenta (to realize)		
(yo)	**me**	voy	**me**	doy	cuenta
(tú)	**te**	vas	**te**	das	cuenta
(él, ella, usted)	**se**	va	**se**	da	cuenta
(nosotros /-as)	**nos**	vamos	**nos**	damos	cuenta
(vosotros /-as)	**os**	vais	**os**	dais	cuenta
(ellos, ellas, ustedes)	**se**	van	**se**	dan	cuenta

Another expression with **dar** in the reflexive form is **darse prisa** (*to hurry*).

Translation of Modal Verbs

▶ Modal Verbs,
p. 104

① ¡**Déjame** ir a la fiesta, mamá!

② No, no **puedes** ir, ¡**tienes que** estudiar!

1. Let me go to the party, Mom! 2. No, you can't go, you have to study!

Generally, Spanish modal verbs are quite similar to English ones, but some constructions deserve a closer look. Modals clarify the relationship between the subject and its activity.

1. Must and should

Tengo que terminar hoy mismo.	
– obligation, compulsion (personal)	**tener que** + infinitive
En la esquina **hay que torce**r a la izquierda.	
– obligation (impersonal, general)	**hay que** + infinitive
Aquí no **es necesario pagar** aparcamiento. **No hace falta** pagar.	
– necessity (general)	**es necesario** / **hace falta** + infinitive
Es necesario que limpiemos la casa. ¡**Hace falta que** me **ayudes**!	
– necessity (personal)	**es necesario que** / **hace falta que** + subjunctive
Debes llamar a tu hermana; es su cumpleaños.	
– moral duty	**deber** + infinitive
Tú debes (de) ser Lucía, ¿verdad?	
– conjecture, surmise	**deber (de)** + infinitive
Hoy no **saldrás**, ¡y basta! Me **ayudarás** en casa.	
– commands or prohibitions	simple future
Deberías hacer más deporte.	
– advice, moral precept	**deber** in conditional + infinitive
Dígale a Pérez **que venga**.	
– rendition of a request	verb of telling + subjunctive

"Should / shall" as an expression of courtesy, as in *Shall I take you home?* is either not translated or rendered by a verb of wishing + subjunctive: **¿Te llevo a casa?** or **¿Quieres que te lleve a casa?**

2. Can and may

> • ¿**Puede venir** un momento, señorita?
> ○ Claro. ¿**Puedo** entrar?

| – possibility / permission | **poder** + infinitive |

> Tomás **sabe nadar** muy bien.

| – ability, acquired skill | **saber** + infinitive |

> ¿Me **permite fumar**? / ¿Me **permite que fume**?

| – polite request for permission | **permitir** + infinitive
permitir que + subjunctive |

> **No debes llegar** más tarde de las doce.

| – prohibition | **no deber** + infinitive |

> **No hay que decirle** nada a Ana.

| – suggestion (negative, impersonal) | **no hay que** + infinitive |

1. *Can* is not always translated with **poder** or **saber**. Compare *That can't be* = **No puede ser** with *I can't help it* = **No es culpa mía.**
2. *May / might* as an expression of politeness, as in *How may I help you?* must be rendered in terms of the context: **¿Qué desea/s?**, **¿Qué le/te sirvo?** or **¿Qué quieres tomar?**

3. Want and would like

> Hoy **quiero ir** con ustedes al cine.

| – strong wish, familiar | **querer** + infinitive |

> **Quería/Quisiera hablar** con usted un momento.

| – politely expressed wish | **quería/quisiera** + infinitive |

4. Need

> Para este puesto **hace falta tener** carnet de conducir.

| – demand | **hacer falta** + infinitive |

> **No necesitas explicar**me todo. **No tengo que saber**lo.

| – no necessity / obligation | **no necesitar**
no tener que + infinitive |

5. Let, cause

¡**Déja**me **ir** a la fiesta, mamá!	
– permission	**dejar** + infinitive

¿Para qué me **has hecho** venir?	
– compulsion, inducement	**hacer** + infinitive

Roberto **se ha operado** la nariz.	
– to let / cause something be done to oneself	reflexive verb

English mostly uses *get*, *become*, *turn* to express change; Spanish has a different system, taking into account how voluntary the change was.

▶ **Future**, p. 138

▶ **Passive**, p. 240

6. Expressing Changes

Spanish has various ways of expressing the notion of "becoming" or undergoing change, depending on the contexts. Here are some of the most important:

El terrorismo **se ha convertido en** un gran problema.	
– fundamental change	**convertirse en** + noun

El autor **se hizo** famoso después de su muerte.	
– change, development	**hacerse** + adjective / noun

Pepe **se ha vuelto** muy arrogante.	
– sharp change in disposition	**volverse** + adjective / noun

Con tanto ruido en la discoteca **me quedé** sorda.	
– change as result	**quedarse** + adjective

Julia **se ha puesto** roja como un tomate.	
– temporary change	**ponerse** + adjective

Yo de grande **quiero ser** actor. **Voy a ser** muy famoso.		
– intention, plan	**ir a ser** **querer ser** +	noun / adjective

En menos de un año **llegaré a ser** millonario.		
– attainment of a goal	**llegar a ser** +	noun / adjective

The development indicated by **volverse** is often negative, whereas the goal named with **llegar a ser** is usually positive.

Las fotos **salieron** muy bonitas. **Quedaron** muy bien.

– result   **salir / quedar** + adjective / adverb

The notion of *becoming / changing* is also expressed in Spanish by these additional verbs or verb constructions:

Simple verbs:

nacer	*to be born*
envejecer	*to grow old*
mejorar	*to improve, get better*
empeorar	*to get worse*
adelgazar	*to lose weight*
engordar	*to gain weight, get fat*
oscurecer	*to get dark (darken)*
amanecer	*to get light, dawn*
anochecer	*to get dark (nightfall)*

Reflexive verbs:

enfadarse	*to get angry*
enfurecerse	*to get furious*
calmarse	*to calm down*
cansarse	*to tire, get tired*
enfermarse	*to get sick*
curarse	*to get well*
desmayarse	*to become unconscious*
entristecerse	*to become sad*
marearse	*to get seasick*

Fixed expressions:

cumplir ... años	*to be (turn) ... years old*
ser de + person	*to become of someone*
ser hora de que + *subjuntive*	*to be time that (for)*

Examples:

El bebé va a nacer en mayo. – *The baby will be born in May.*
No quiero engordar. – *I don't want to get fat.*
¡No te enfades! – *Don't get angry!*
Mi nieto cumple hoy un año. – *My grandson is turning one year old today.*
Cuéntame qué es de ti. – *Tell me what has become of you.*
Ya es hora de que llegue Juan. – *It's time for Juan to come.*

Practice and Application

Special Verbs

1. Combine the following preferences with the correct verb form. *

la cerveza – los gatos – salir con mis amigos – las playas españolas –
el deporte y la naturaleza – el vino tinto – la cocina mediterránea –
las recetas prácticas – la col – el cine y el teatro

a) me gusta <u>la cerveza,</u>

b) me gustan _____

2. In a restaurant, people naturally talk about the ambiance and the
food, but about feelings as well. Translate the statements below. *

a) Do you like the photo?

   <u>¿Te gusta la foto?</u>

b) I don't like the fish at all.

c) We like this restaurant very much.

d) I think it's very good too.

e) I love Spanish wines!

f) Do you like the food, children?

g) Cheers! Darling, I like you very much ... I love you!

la comida – *the food*
el niño – *the child*
¡Salud! – *Cheers!*
cariño – *darling*

3. At the gym. Fill in the missing pronouns. *

a) • ¿Qué _os_ pasa, chicos? ¿ _____ molesta algo?

○ No, no, es que _____ duelen los brazos, este aparato es infernal.

b) • A mí _____ encanta venir al gimnasio todos los días. ¿Y a ___?

○ A ____ también, pero lamentablemente no siempre puedo.

c) • Vamos, Martha, ____ hace falta bajar un poco ese abdomen...

○ Pues _____ da igual. ¡Por hoy ya _____ basta de ejercicio!

d) • Claro, José, con tanto estrés, _____ duele la espalda.

○ Sí, lo sé. Eso _____ preocupa un poco. ¿Qué ejercicios me recomiendas?

e) • ¿Cuántas veces _____ faltan? Ya hemos perdido la cuenta.

○ _____ quedan cuatro veces más, pero tienen que ser este mes.

f) • Aaay, no Andrés, a mí este movimiento _____ hace daño.

○ ¡Qué va! Lo que _____ pasa a _____ es que no estás en forma.

me · mí

te · nos

ti · os

infernal –
hideous, dreadful
bajar – *here:*
to reduce, to tighten
el abdomen –
the abdomen
la espalda – *the back*
perder la cuenta –
to lose count
¡Qué va! –
Of course not!
estar en forma –
to be in shape, fit

4. Mark the correct verb. **

a) A los hispanohablantes ⟨les encanta⟩/se encantan/nos encanto decir cuando alguien se gusta/les gusta/nos gustan e incluso existe una palabra para ello: el piropo. **b)** Si a un chico o a una chica te gustais/se gustas/le gustas , escuchar un "Hola, guapa." o un "Adiós, guapo." no se molesto/nos molestan/le molesta a nadie.
c) No es necesario perder la calma, un piropo seguramente no te haces/te hace/se hacen daño. **d)** Claro que hay también expresiones más vulgares que no nos gustan/nos gustamos/nosotros gusta tampoco. **e)** Pero por lo general, a los hispanohablantes les parece/les parecen/se parecen normal tolerar una cierta dosis de flirteo en la vida cotidiana.

el/la hispanohablante –
the Spanish speaker
incluso – *even*
una cierta dosis –
a certain amount
la vida cotidiana –
the daily life

Practice and Application

Special Verbs

5. Practice makes perfect! Complete the missing parts of the table. *

Infinitive:

a) quedarse
b) marcharse
c) acordarse
d) vestirse
e) sentarse
f) irse
g) quejarse
h) despedirse

	yo	tú	él / ella	nosotros	vosotros	ellos / ellas
a)	me quedo	te quedas	se queda	nos quedamos	os quedáis	se quedan
b)			se marcha	nos marchamos		
c)		te acuerdas			os acordáis	
d)	me visto		se viste			
e)				nos sentamos		
f)					os vais	
g)		te quejas				
h)				nos despedimos		

6. Ricardo is a volunteer with the Red Cross. Complete this interview by adding the reflexive verbs. **

la persona mayor –
the older person
la movilidad –
the mobility
la mayor parte –
the majority
por una parte … por otra – *on the one hand … on the other*
ocuparse de –
to look after
por miedo – *out of fear*
tanto … como –
both … and
reunirse – *to meet*
de vez en cuando –
from time to time
a quien quise mucho –
whom I loved very much

a) ● Tú eres voluntario de la Cruz Roja, ¿a qué *(dedicarse)* <u>te dedicas</u> ?

b) ○ Ayudo a personas mayores que tienen poca movilidad y por eso

  (quedarse) _____ en casa la mayor parte del tiempo.

c) ● ¿Y qué problemas concretos tienen?

  ○ Bueno, por una parte yo *(ocuparse)* _____ de algunas cosas

  prácticas. Algunas personas no *(levantarse)* _____ si están

  solas por miedo a caerse. *(Relajarse)* _____ más si estoy

  yo cuando *(ducharse)* _____, por ejemplo.

d) ● Claro. ¿Y por otra parte …?

  ○ Por otra parte, algunos simplemente *(sentirse)* _____ un

  poco solos y *(alegrarse)* _____ cuando los visitamos.

e) ● ¿Y te gusta esta actividad?

  ○ Sí, me encanta. *(Sentirse)* _____ útil, conozco a gente

  interesante, tanto mayores como compañeros, porque también

  nosotros *(reunirse)* _____ de vez en cuando. Y *(acordarse)*

  _____ mucho de mi abuelo, a quien quise mucho.

7. Here you will learn something about the history and use of chewing gum. Fill in the blanks with the verbs provided. ******

a) El chicle ___se llama___ así porque viene del nombre de una

resina (tzicli) que mascaban los aztecas. **b)** Antes, los indígenas con

frecuencia _____ trocitos de chicle a todas partes.

c) En el siglo XIX, un científico norteamericano _____

del enorme potencial que tenía este material. **d)** En la selva de

Centroamérica, los "chicleros" _____ a reunir la resina,

que después _____ al sol para formar bloques, y así la

exportaban al extranjero. **e)** Hoy el chicle es sintético. A muchas

personas les gusta mascarlo cuando por alguna razón no _____

los dientes después de comer. **f)** Otros _____ cuando están

nerviosos o _____ mejor si mascan chicle.

g) Mascar chicle te ayuda porque, con el movimiento, tú _____

de la tensión muscular. **h)** Por otro lado, los soldados normalmente

llevan chicle en su ración militar porque mascando _____

despiertos.

se concentran
se dedicaban
se dio cuenta
se lavan
se llama
se llevaban
se mantienen
se relajan
se secaba
te liberas

mascar – *to chew*

8. Match the statements with the appropriate reactions. *****

a) No puedo ir con ustedes; debo terminar un trabajo para la
   Universidad.

b) ¿Me permite fumar? ¿Quiere que salga al balcón?

c) Tú debes ser la hija de Marisol, ¿verdad?

d) Señor Flores, quisiera hablar con usted un momento.

e) Si sabes esquiar bien, podemos subir al glaciar.

el glaciar – *the glacier*

( ) 1. No, no sé muy bien. Deberíamos quedarnos en pistas más fáciles.

(a) 2. Lo siento mucho, pero en este momento tengo que salir...

( ) 3. ¿Y tienes que terminarlo hoy? ¿No puedes dejarlo para mañana?

( ) 4. Sí, mi madre nos espera en casa. ¿Puedo llevar tu maleta?

( ) 5. No es necesario, puede hacerlo aquí si quiere.

Special Verbs

9. Connect the halves to form meaningful sentences. ******

a) Este cantante se volvió   (3)

b) La receta me salió muy   ( )

c) De pronto, el sapo se convirtió   ( )

d) La autora se hizo   ( )

e) No mires directamente al sol, ¡te   ( )

f) Cuando sea grande voy a   ( )

g) Cuando me encontré con el jefe en ese club nocturno   ( )
me puse roja

de pronto – *suddenly*
el sapo – *the toad*
ciego / -a – *blind*

1. en un príncipe guapísimo.

2. ser policía y a llevar uniforme.

3. famoso porque además de cantar bailaba muy bien.

4. como un tomate, porque la mujer con quien estaba no era su mujer.

5. bien, el pastel quedó exquisito.

6. rica cuando llevaron su novela al cine con un director buenísimo.

7. vas a quedar ciego!

10. Mark the correct expressions in this short biography of a famous Argentine woman. *******

a) Eva Perón (nació)/ fue nacida en 1919 en Argentina. **b)** En 1935 se fue a Buenos Aires y salió / se hizo actriz. **c)** Allí conoció a Juan Domingo Perón, quien en 1944 se puso / fue nombrado vicepresidente. **d)** Pronto, Evita se convirtió / se fue en su mejor colaboradora. **e)** Perón se hizo / fue elegido presidente en 1946, pero antes se casó con ella y así Evita llegó a ser / quería ser primera dama. **f)** Evita deseaba el poder para hacerse / quedarse aliada de los pobres. **g)** Aunque se volvió / se puso una figura de glamour, el pueblo siempre la perdonó porque salió / se convirtió en protectora de los humildes. **h)** Durante un viaje a Europa en plena Guerra Mundial, Evita se volvió enferma / se enfermó de cáncer. **i)** Murió en 1952. Sólo llegó a cumplir / fue 33 años.

humilde – *humble*
en plena Guerra
Mundial – *in the middle
of the World War*

Negation

¡Qué agradable es **no** hacer **nada**! ①

Sí, **no** trabajar **ni** limpiar la casa… ②

In addition to simple negation with **no**, several elements of negation can be combined in Spanish.

1. How pleasant it is to do nothing! 2. Yes, neither to work nor to clean the house …

If **no** stands alone, it means *no*. You can use it to give a negative answer to a question, perhaps followed by the correction.

Note:
¿Quieres café? –
No, gracias, and
- **¿No quieres café?**
○ **Sí, gracias.**

- ¿Eres economista?   ○ **No**, soy profesora.

To negate a statement, place **no** in front of the conjugated verb. Consequently, **no** precedes the modal or auxiliary verb in infinitive or present participle constructions or in compound tenses. If a sentence contains object or reflexive pronouns, **no** comes first. Then, depending on the context, **no** means *not* or *not any*.

- ¿Quieres bistec?   ○ **No, no** quiero, gracias.
      No como carne.

¡**No** puede ser! **No** ha llegado el correo. **No** me ha llegado la carta.

Multiple Negation

¡Aquí **nunca** cambia **nada**! ①

Tampoco puedes decir eso. ②

1. Nothing ever changes here! 2. You can't say that either.

Spanish sentences often contain more than one element of negation. **No** continues to precede the verb.

Juan **no** viene **nunca** a clase, por eso **ya no** nos vemos.

Multiple Negation

Elements of negation include:

nadie	*no one, nobody*	nunca / jamás	*never*
nada	*nothing*	ninguno / -a	*no, not ... any*
tampoco	*neither, not ... either*	todavía no / aún no	*not yet*
apenas	*hardly, scarcely*	ya no	*no longer*
ni	*or (in negation)*	de ningún modo	*in no way*
ni ... ni	*neither ... nor*	de ninguna manera	*in no way*

> 1. If **nadie** is an object, it is preceded by **a**:
> **No veo a nadie.**
> 2. Note:
>   - **¿Ya está listo.**
>   - ○ No, **todavía no.**
>   Compare:
>   - **¿Todavía está trabajando?**
>   - ○ No, **ya no.**

The most common structures with multiple elements of negation are:

No veo **nada**. **No** he visto **nada**.

– **no** + conjugated verb or auxiliary verb + element of negation.

No puedes hacer **nada**. Pepe **no** está haciendo **nada tampoco**. Y yo **no** voy a hacer **nada tampoco**.

– in infinitive or present participle constructions, **no** precedes the verb unit and other elements of negation usually follow it.

No quiero trabajar **ni** estudiar. **No** me gustan **ni** la oficina **ni** la Universidad.

– Instead of a second negation, **ni** is used with **no** in the same sentence. **Ni** can appear several times in the sentence.

A Paco **no** le gusta **nada**. = A Paco **nada** le gusta.
No ha venido **nadie**. = **Nadie** ha venido.
No me gustan **ni** el rock **ni** el jazz. = **Ni** el rock **ni** el jazz me gustan.

– If the verb is preceded by **nada**, **nadie**, **nunca**, **jamás**, **ni**, **ninguno**, or **tampoco** then **no** is omitted.

No he comido **todavía**. = **Todavía no** he comido.
No trabajo ya. = Ya **no** trabajo.

– If **todavía** or **ya** precede the verb, they are followed by **no**.

> In colloquial speech, a negation often is reinforced with additional words, as here: **No, ¡ni hablar!** (*No, certainly not!*), **No, ¡en absoluto!** (*No, not at all!*), **No, nada de eso.** (*No, nothing of the kind!*) or **No, ni idea.** (*No, I haven't a clue!*), etc.

In using the various elements of negation, you need to be careful when translating. **Nada** and **nadie** frequently will be rendered in English as *anything* and *anybody / anyone*.

Nadie sabe **nada**.	*Nobody knows anything.*
Aquí **no** hay **nunca nadie**.	*There's never anybody here.*
No veo a **nadie** en **ningún** lado.	*I don't see anybody anywhere.*

1. Answer the following questions with a negation. *

a) • ¿Tienes coche?   ○ <u>No, no tengo coche.</u>

b) • ¿Quieres café?   ○ _____

c) • ¿Sabes esquiar?   ○ _____

d) • ¿Te gusta el cine?   ○ _____

e) • ¿Han terminado?   ○ _____

2. A famous model is answering questions from reporters. Fill in the blanks with the elements of negation provided. *

a) • ¿Siempre estás a dieta?   ○ No, __nunca__ .

b) • ¿Alguien te escoge la ropa?   ○ No, _____ .

c) • ¿Haces todo sin consultar a tu agente?   ○ No, _____ .

d) • La otras modelos de tu agencia no llevan tatuajes. ¿Y tú?   ○ Yo _____ .

e) • ¿Todavía trabajas en un bar?   ○ No, _____ . Ahora gano suficiente como modelo.

nadie

tampoco

nunca

nada

ya no

3. In conclusion, a few more expressions. Match the columns. **

a) De nada.

b) ¡Claro que no!

c) De ninguna manera.

d) ¡Cómo no!

e) Ni sí ni no.

f) ¿Tienes ganas o no?

g) ¡Nada de eso!

h) ¡No quiero ni pensarlo!

i) Ni modo.

j) No es nada grave.

1. *In no way.*

2. *Yes and no.*

3. *Nothing of the kind!*

4. *Of course!*

5. *No matter.*

6. *Certainly not!*

7. *Don't mention it.*

8. *Do you want to or not?*

9. *It's nothing serious.*

10. *I don't even want to think about it!*

Types of Sentences

¿Cómo has dormido, Susana?

①

Mmmh, he dormido muy bien.

②

¡Qué pena que hoy sea lunes!

③

A sentence often consists of a subject and a predicate. The predicate consists of a verb and can include one or more complements (such as objects or indications of place or time).

1. How did you sleep, Susana? 2. Mmmh, I slept very well.
3. What a pity that today is Monday!

The Simple Sentence

1. The Declarative Sentence

In Spanish, a verb alone can constitute a sentence.

- • ¿Qué haces?　　　　　　　○ **Trabajo.**

If there are several elements, they appear in the sequence subject – predicate:

Subject	Object pronoun	Verb	Complements	
El cantante	les	ha dado	autógrafos	a todas las chicas.
		Han venido	al concierto	para verlo.

1. In Spanish, the indirect object follows the direct object.
2. For the third person, the indirect object generally is doubled with the pronoun **le** or **les**.

▸ **Personal Pronouns,** pp. 74–78

Complements are:

Escucha **esta canción.** ¿Conoces **a este cantante**?

▪ – a direct object. With persons, the preposition **a** must precede the object.

Esta canción **a mí me** encanta. **Le** he regalado **este CD a Lola.**

▪ – an indirect object alone or in addition to the direct object.

¿Te acuerdas **de ella?** La viste **en Caracas** cuando fuimos a ver a Rocío.

▪ – a prepositional, adverbial, or infinitive complement.

Adverbs and adverbial complements include indications of place, time, frequency, cause, manner, etc. They can appear as the first or last element in the sentence or can be spread out through the sentence:

A las ocho, en la Plaza Mayor, tengo una cita con Paco.
Tengo una cita con Paco **a las ocho en la Plaza Mayor**.
A las ocho tengo una cita con Paco **en la Plaza Mayor**.

2. The Interrogative Sentence

1. *Sir, do you live here?* 2. *Where is the beach?*

In interrogative sentences, the order of the subject and verb may be reversed.

¿Usted es el señor Pérez? = **¿Es usted el señor Pérez?**

If the subject pronoun is omitted because the context makes it clear who the subject is, then the word order is the same as in a declarative sentence.

● ¿Ha vivido en Madrid?   ▶   ○ Ha vivido en Madrid.

With questions containing an interrogative word or expression, the following word order is used:

Interrogative Word	Predicate	Subject
¿Quién	es	el cantante?
¿Dónde	están	todas las chicas?

Interrogative words always carry a written accent. Besides the interrogative determiners and pronouns **qué**, **quién**, **cuál**, **cuánto**, the following interrogative adverbs are important:

– **cómo** (*how*)	**¿Cómo está** tu madre?
– **dónde** (*where*)	**¿Dónde** estás?
– **adónde** (*where [to]*)	**¿Adónde** van?
– **de dónde** (*where [from]*)	**¿De dónde** eres?
– **cuándo** (*when*)	**¿Cuándo** estuviste en Trujillo?
– **desde cuándo** (*since when*)	**¿Desde cuándo** trabajas aquí?
– **para cuándo** (*for when*)	**¿Para cuándo** es la reservación?
– **cuánto tiempo** (*how long*)	**¿Cuánto tiempo** vas a trabajar?

The upside-down question mark **¿** directly precedes the question. Thus it can follow a comma and appear "in the middle of the sentence."

▶ **Interrogative Determiners** p. 32

▶ **Interrogative Pronouns**, p. 89

Use **a cómo** to inquire about a variable price:
¿A cómo están las sardinas?

In colloquial speech, **cómo** frequently is replaced by **¿qué tal?**. Examples: **¿Qué tal (está) la sopa?** (*How's the soup?*), **¿Qué tal (estuvo) el fin de semana?** (*How was the weekend?*).

Independent and Dependent Clauses

By connecting independent clauses and dependent clauses, you can express complex relationships.

He llegado tarde porque hoy es el cumpleaños de Víctor, que es mi nuevo colega.

I'm late because today is the birthday of Victor, who is my new colleague.

▶ **Conjunctions,** p. 253

▶ **Relative Pronouns,** p. 97

▶ **Use of the Subjunctive,** p. 158

Note the difference between **si** = *if* (conditional clause) and **cuando** = *when* (temporal adverbial clause): <u>**Si puedo, te llamo.** But **Cuando pueda, te llamo.**</u>

Clauses are linked by conjunctions (such as **porque**) or relative pronouns (such as **que**). The following can be linked:

– two independent clauses or – an independent and a dependent clause	María cocina **y** Pedro pone la mesa. María cocina **porque** Pedro no sabe.

There are various types of dependent clauses; depending on the meaning, their verb is in the indicative or the subjunctive.

– *that* clauses – relative clauses	Me gusta **que salgamos juntos.** El camino **por el que vamos** es muy bonito.
– adverbial clauses – conditional clauses	**Cuando sea grande**, voy a ser policía. **Si puedo**, voy a la fiesta el sábado.

Conditional Clauses

Conditional sentences name in the principal (independent) clause the consequence of a condition stated in the **si** clause. The order of the main clause and the dependent clause is unimportant. Also possible: <u>**Me llamas si quieres venir.**</u>

We distinguish two types of conditional clauses:

– open conditional clause – irreal (contrary-to-fact) conditional clause	**Si quieres venir**, me llamas. **Si tuviera dinero**, me iría de viaje.

Sequence of Tenses in a Conditional Sentence

The following combinations are possible, depending on how the speaker represents the condition.

1. Open Conditional Sentence

The condition is likely or reasonably likely to occur in the present or future:

Si clause in the present indicative	+ *main clause*
Si me **llamas**, te lo **cuento** todo.	– present indicative
te **contaré** en detalle.	– simple future indicative
coméntame todo.	– imperative

The condition has already been met in the past:

Si clause in the present perfect indicative	+ *main clause*
Si ya **ha llegado** Pepa, me **avisas**.	– present indicative
me **llamará**.	– simple future indicative
llámame.	– imperative

2. Contrary-to-fact (Irreal) Conditional Sentence:

The condition is unlikely or even impossible to fulfill in the present or future:

Si clause in the imperfect subjunctive	+ *main clause*
Si fuera / fuese rico, no trabajaría.	– conditional

The condition was not fulfilled in the past:

Si clause in the past perfect subjunctive	+ *main clause*
Si **hubiera / hubiese podido**, **habría ido.**	– conditional perfect
hubiera ido.	– past perf. subjunctive
hubiese ido.	

3. Conditional Sentences without *si*

Conditions also can be expressed by using certain subjunctive triggers, such as **en caso de que** (*if*), **a condición (de) que** (*on the condition that*), **siempre y cuando** (*as long as, provided that*), and **a menos que** (*unless*). In the open conditional clause, the present subjunctive is always used. Otherwise, the rules for *si* clauses apply.

Dependent clause in present subjunctive	+ *main clause in present indicative / future or imperative*
En caso de que me llames,	te lo **cuento / contaré** todo.
	coméntame todo.

1. The **si** clause never contains the present subjunctive, simple future, or conditional! Only in the main clause of an open conditional sentence will you find the simple future.

2. This does not apply to sentences in which **si** means *whether*, as here: **Avísame si vendrás**. This is not a conditional sentence, but an indirect question.

!

If a consequence in the present is described, in the latter case you can have the conditional in the main clause, as here: **Si no me hubiera quedado en la oficina, el reporte no estaría listo ahora.**

233

Practice and Application

Types of Sentences

1. Connect the two columns to form complete sentences. **

a) Si hubieras ido a la fiesta

b) Si conocieras a Juan

c) Si lo escuchas cantar

d) Si no lo has escuchado

e) Si puedo, lo

f) Si no pudiera venir,

1. entenderías por qué me gusta.

2. no sabes todavía lo que es bueno.

3. invitaré a cenar pronto.

4. habrías conocido a Juan.

5. me pondría muy triste.

6. te encantará.

2. In this psychological test, complete the contrary-to-fact conditional sentences with the verbs provided.

a) ser, ser
b) hacer, volver
c) ser, casarse
d) comprar, ganar
e) gustar, poder

a) ¿Qué animal __serías__ si _____ uno? ¿Por qué?

b) ¿Qué _____ de otra manera si _____ a vivir tu vida?

c) ¿Cómo __habría__ _____ tu vida si _____ con tu primer amor?

d) ¿Qué _____ si _____ muchísimo dinero en la lotería?

e) ¿Qué te _____ cambiar en tu vida actual si _____ cambiar dos cosas?

3. In life, there are both optimists and pessimists. Complete the dialogue below, using either **si** or **cuando**. **

a) • __Cuando__ tengamos dinero, haremos un viaje.

   ○ _____ algún día tenemos dinero, porque con lo que ganamos ...

b) • _____ haya vuelos baratos a Bolivia, los podemos aprovechar.

   ○ ¿Tú crees? _____ algún día una compañía aérea empieza con vuelos baratos a Bolivia, será un milagro.

c) • _____ seas más optimista, avísame, ¿eh?

   ○ ¡Hombre! _____ fuera tan optimista como tú, no sería realista.

Indirect Discourse

Mis amigos **me dijeron que era** muy fácil patinar...

①

¡Ay, hermanita, siempre te **he dicho que tengas** cuidado y **que no pruebes** todo lo nuevo!

②

> In direct discourse, other people's words are presented between quotation marks, dashes, or in a speech balloon. If they are not rendered literally, we call this indirect discourse.

1. My friends told me that it was very easy to ice skate … 2. Oh, Sis, I've always told you that you should be careful and not try everything new!

1. Discourse Markers and Change in Perspective

Indirect speech begins with a verb that serves as a discourse marker, that is, a "verb of saying" and **que** (*that*). If several sentences are reported, **que** is repeated each time. Indirect questions are introduced by **si** (*whether*) or an interrogative pronoun, such as **qué**, **quién**, etc.

In indirect speech, certain elements are adapted to the new perspective. The following may be changed:

> 1. Spanish sometimes uses **que** when it would be omitted in English, as here: **Dice que** sí / no / quizá. (*He says yes / no / maybe*).
> 2. Interrogative pronouns always have a written accent.

"**Yo he hecho** un flan." ▶ Irma dice que **ella ha hecho** un flan.

– the person of the verb and the subject pronoun.

"¿**Vienes** a visitar**me**?" ▶ Irma pregunta **si voy** a visitar**la**.

– the direction of the verbs **ir** – **venir**, **traer** – **llevar**, and the object pronouns.

"**Esta** receta es de **mi** amiga." ▶ Dice que **esa** receta es de **su** amiga.

– the demonstrative and possessive pronouns.

"**Aquí** la anoto para ti." ▶ Dice que **ahí** la anota para mí.

– the adverbs of place.

Depending on the speaker's intention, the appropriate verb of saying is chosen for the rendition:

decir *(to say, tell)*, comentar *(to comment, mention)*, responder / contestar *(to answer)*	– information and reports
opinar *(to think, give an opinion)*, comentar *(to comment, mention)*	– opinions, evaluations
explicar / aclarar *(to explain)*	– explanations
contar *(to tell)*, prometer *(to promise)*, exclamar *(to exclaim)*, gritar *(to shout)*	– accounts
preguntar *(to ask)*, no saber *(to not know)*, querer saber *(to want to know)*	– questions
pedir *(to request)*, decir *(to prompt)*, ordenar *(to order)*	– requests and commands
proponer *(to propose, suggest)*, recomendar *(to recommend)*, aconsejar *(to advise)*	– advice and suggestions

!

If the direct discourse contains an imperative, it is rendered with the present subjunctive, as here: "¡Avísenme!" ▸ "Me ha pedido que le <u>avisemos</u>."

In dependent clauses, therefore, the subjunctive also is used for requests and commands in the indirect discourse if an imperative is present in the direct discourse.

2. Indirect Discourse with Main Clause in the "Present"

The tense of the direct discourse is retained in the indirect rendition in the dependent clause, if the temporal conditions do not alter the statement (for example, if "mañana" still precedes it). This generally is the case when the verb of saying is in one of the following tenses:

- ● ¿**Van** a estar mañana? **Quisiera** organizar una fiesta.
- ○ Sí **estaremos**. ¿**Podemos** llevar algo?
- ● Sí, dile a Juan que **prepare** el flan que le sale tan bien.

Mi jefe pregunta si **vamos** a estar mañana.	– present
Ha explicado que **quisiera** organizar una fiesta.	– present perfect
Le diré que sí **estaremos**.	– future
Por mí, le preguntaría si **podemos** llevar algo.	– conditional
Me ha pedido que te diga que **prepares** un flan.	– present subjunctive

3. Indirect Discourse with Main Clause in the "Past"

If the verb of saying is in the *indefinido* (preterit), imperfect, or past perfect, the tense of the statement is "moved back a step."

Indirect Discourse with Main Clause in the "Past"

• Me **gusta** viajar. Ya **he viajado** mucho. **Recomiéndame** una ruta.
○ Dile a Juan que me **preste** su guía.

Mi jefe dijo que le **gustaba** viajar.	– *indefinido* (preterit)
Siempre contaba que ya **había viajado** mucho.	– imperfect
Me había pedido que le **recomendara** una ruta.	– past perfect

The sequence of tenses in indirect discourse with verbs in the past is as follows:

	Dijo / Decía / Había dicho ...
"Antes **viajaba** menos".	– que antes **viajaba** menos.
"De joven no **había podido**".	– que de joven no **había podido**.
"Me **gustaría** ir a Yucatán".	– que le **gustaría** ir a Yucatán.

The imperfect, past perfect, and conditional are retained.

"Ahora **tengo** la oportunidad".	– que ahora **tenía** la oportunidad.
present	▸ imperfect

"Ya **he viajado** mucho".	– que ya **había viajado** mucho.
present perfect	▸ past perfect

"En verano **fui** a Perú".	– que en verano **fue / había ido** a Perú.
indefinido remains or	▸ past perfect

"Pronto **iré** a Yucatán".	– que pronto **iría** a Yucatán.
future	▸ conditional

"**Recomiéndame** una ruta".	– que le **recomendara** una ruta.
imperative	▸ imperfect subjunctive

"Ojalá **haga** buen tiempo".	– que ojalá **hiciera** buen tiempo.
present subjunctive	▸ imperfect subjunctive

> If, in the direct statement, the future is replaced by **ir a** + infinitive in the present, it is expressed by **iba a** + infinitive, as here: **Voy a viajar mañana. Dijo que iba a viajar al día siguiente.**

If the speaker uses a verb of saying in the past in the rendition, then the expressions of time have to be adapted to the new temporal conditions. For example, **"hoy"** ▸ **ese día**, **"mañana"** ▸ **al día siguiente**, **"ayer"** ▸ **el día anterior**, etc.

Practice and Application

1. Since her grandmother is a bit hard of hearing, at the doctor's office the granddaughter repeats to her what the doctor has said. Complete the sentences below. **

débil – weak, feeble

a) • ¿Desde cuándo se siente débil?

   ○ El médico quiere saber desde cuándo te sientes débil , abuela.

b) • ¿Le duele algo, señora?

   ○ El médico pregunta _____, abuela.

c) • ¡Acuéstese ahí, por favor!

   ○ Dice _____, abuela.

d) • Respire profundamente y relájese.

   ○ Ha dicho que _____.

2. Some days later, the grandmother recounts what the doctor said to her. ***

la presión –
the (blood) pressure
con toda seguridad –
with certainty

a) • ¿Ha tenido la presión alta mucho tiempo?

   ○ El médico quiso saber si había tenido la presión alta mucho tiempo.

b) • ¿Toma algún medicamento para el corazón?

   ○ Preguntó _____ para el corazón.

c) • Tome estas pastillas y llámeme en una semana.

   ○ Me recomendó _____.

d) • No se preocupe. Estas pastillas le ayudarán con toda seguridad.

   ○ Dijo _____ con toda seguridad.

te pongas
los hiciéramos
~~nos vayamos~~
te la arregló
olvidáramos

a buena hora –
on time
los deberes –
the homework
arreglar – here: to
repair, fix

3. The younger brother always has to play back what Mom says. Choose the correct verb form. ***

Mamá: Vayan siempre a buena hora al colegio. No olviden los deberes, háganlos. Ah, y Laurita, ponte la falda del uniforme, ya te la arreglé.

a) Mamá ha dicho que nos vayamos siempre a buena hora al colegio.

b) Dijo que no _____ los deberes y que _____.

c) Laurita, mamá te recuerda que _____ la falda del uniforme, porque ya _____.

4. A lot of things are said in the stairwell. In the retellings below, choose the correct verb of saying. **

a) *Felipe:* "¿Cuándo cumples años?" "Yo, ¡mañana!" ▶ Felipe ordena / quiere saber cuándo es mi cumpleaños. Me ha dicho / ha propuesto que mañana es el suyo.

b) *Claudia:* "Daniela está saliendo ahora con Marcelo y está loca por él". ▶ Claudia me ha contado / aconseja que Daniela y Marcelo tienen una relación y pregunta / ha comentado que ella está enamoradísima.

estar loco / -a por alguien – *to be crazy about someone*

c) *Matilde:* "¿Pueden bajar la radio? Se oye en todo el edificio". ▶ Doña Matilde ha prometido / ha pedido que pongamos la radio menos fuerte, responde / opina que le molesta a todos los vecinos.

bajar – *here: to turn down (the volume)*

5. Sergio is listening to Maribel's answering machine and passing on the information to her. ***

a) Hola, soy Soledad. Maribel, llámame esta noche, por favor. Me urge que hables conmigo. ▶ Ha llamado Soledad y dice que la llames esta noche, que _____ .

me urge – *I urgently need*
el primo – *the cousin*
ir de copas – *to go out for a drink*

b) ¿Te acuerdas de mi primo Miguel? Pues está de visita y queremos ir de copas. ¿Te apetece venir con nosotros? Quedamos a las diez en el bar "Tango". Ah, soy yo, Raúl. ▶ Raúl pregunta si _____ _____ Miguel. Dice que está de visita y _____ ir de copas. Quiere saber si te apetece _____ y dejó dicho que _____ a las diez en el bar "Tango".

te apetece – *do you feel like*
quedar – *here: to meet*
fíjate – *imagine*
escanear – *to scan*

c) Hola, soy Agustín. Fíjate que tengo una crítica genial del grupo que fuimos a ver el otro día, así que te escaneé la página y te la envié por e-mail. Dime qué te parece. ▶ Agustín dice que _____ una crítica genial del grupo que _____ a ver el otro día, así que _____ la página y _____ por e-mail. Quiere que le _____ tu opinión.

Agentive and Stative Passive

The Passive Voice

¿Sabes tú cuántas fotos **han sido publicadas** de ese actor?

①

¡Miles! Ahora todas las revistas **están agotadas**.

②

> Spanish has two passive constructions: the agentive passive and the stative passive.

> The passive voice is used primarily in written Spanish. It is rarely used in colloquial speech. Instead, impersonal constructions are used.

1. Do you know how many photos of that actor have been published?
2. Thousands! Now all the magazines are sold out.

Only verbs that take a direct object can appear in a passive construction. In the passive voice the focus is not on the subject, but on the events or on the persons or things affected by the action.

▶ **Impersonal Sentences and Substitutes for the Passive**, p. 241

▶ **Past Participle**, p. 187

> The passive can be formed in all tenses and moods by conjugating **ser** appropriately, as here: **<u>son</u> publicadas**, **<u>han sido</u> publicadas**, **es malo que <u>sean</u> publicadas**, etc.

1. Agentive Passive

In the agentive passive voice, the occurrence of the events is important. The direct object of the active sentence becomes the passive subject; the agent disappears from the scene or is unnamed. The agentive passive is formed with **ser** and the past participle, which agrees with the subject in number and gender. The agent can be added by using the preposition **por**.

Active	Las revistas subject	publicaron verb	estas fotos. direct object
Passive	Estas fotos passive subject	**fueron publicadas** verb	(por las revistas). agent

2. Stative Passive

If the focus is not on the events but their result, use **estar** + past participle, with the participle agreeing in gender and number with the subject, as here:

- Mi vuelo, ¿ya **está confirmado**?
- ○ Sí, y su habitación de hotel ya **está reservada** también.

Impersonal Sentences

The following impersonal constructions have no subject:

¿Por qué **llueve** tanto?	*Why does it **rain** so much?*

- verbs referring to the climate or weather, such as **llover**, **hacer sol**, etc.

Hay mal tiempo.	***There is** bad weather.*
Hay que llevar paraguas.	***You have to** carry an umbrella.*

- **hay** *(there is / there are)* and **hay que** *(one must, you have to, it's necessary to)*

Se espera una mejora.	*An improvement **is expected**.*

- **se** + the third person of the verb. Generally the verb agrees in number with the noun that follows.

Dicen que va a hacer sol.	***They** say that **it** will be sunny.*

- verbs in the third person plural.

If the speaker includes himself / herself, then **uno / -a** is used as the subject. For example:

Uno siempre espera buen tiempo en las vacaciones.

Substitutes for the Passive

To place the direct object in the center of attention, make it the first element in the sentence and duplicate it with an accusative pronoun:

Las fotos las publicaron las revistas.
A la novia del actor, muchísimos reporteros **la** han entrevistado.

If the agent is not named, impersonal sentences are formulated:

Aquí **se construyen** nuevos centros comerciales.

- an impersonal construction with the reflexive pronoun **se**.

Dicen que será todo muy moderno.
Al alcalde lo **han entrevistado** en la radio sobre estos proyectos.

- an impersonal active sentence with the verb in the third person plural. By placement at the front and duplication, you can give further emphasis to the direct object.

Practice and Application

Passive Voice

1. Many Spaniards are extremely fond of going out with friends to eat tapas. Here you can read what that is like. Use the present tense form of the verb provided. *

la tapa – *(in Spain) the appetizer, savory snack*
la caña – *(in Spain) the small glass of draft beer*
la barra – *the bar*
la cáscara – *the shell*
el suelo – *the floor*

a) Según la costumbre, para ir de tapas en España, se *(ir)* __va__ con amigos.

b) Por lo general se *(recorrer)* _____ varios bares y se *(tomar)* _____ una caña o un vaso de vino en cada uno, con un par de tapas.

c) Normalmente no se *(mezclar)* _____ las bebidas.

d) Las tapas se *(poder)* _____ comer de pie en la barra del bar, y siempre se *(compartir)* _____.

e) Las cáscaras de las gambas se *(soler)* _____ tirar al suelo.

f) La cuenta no se *(pagar)* _____ por separado, sino que normalmente cada uno / -a paga una ronda.

2. What does it really take to lose weight? Put these sentences together correctly, and then number them in the right order. **

fijar – *to set*
bajar de peso –
to lose weight
el éxito – *the success*
el fracaso – *the failure*
de fuera – *from outside*

a) ( ) fijarse metas modestas. De ese modo se

b) (1) Uno no puede bajar de peso en un día. Hay que

c) ( ) que la única persona que puede bajar de peso es uno

d) ( ) posibilidad de realizarla.

e) ( ) logran éxitos pequeños y se gana

f) ( ) repetirse constantemente los fracasos anteriores. Dicen

g) ( ) mismo: si la decisión viene de fuera, no hay

h) ( ) motivación. Hay que pensar positivamente y no

3. Snow White has returned and has found things in a rather chaotic state. Complete the sentences with the stative passive. **

a) ¿Quién ha roto las lámparas? ¿Por qué ___están rotas___?

b) ¿Quién ha deshecho las camas? ¿Por qué _____?

c) ¿Quién ha abierto la nevera? ¿Por qué _____?

deshacer –
here: to mess up

d) ¿Quién ha desordenado todo? ¿Por qué _____?

4. Some episodes of history are completely unknown. Put the verbs provided in the passive voice. **

a) Cartagena de Indias <u>fue fundada</u> en la costa de Colombia en 1533 por Don Pedro de Heredia. **b)** Este importante puerto _____ contra frecuentes invasiones, por ser un importante centro comercial del Caribe. **c)** En el siglo XVIII, la "Armada Invencible" de los ingleses _____ en Cartagena de Indias, pero la noticia no _____ en Europa. **d)** 186 barcos _____ a Colombia. **e)** Después de la derrota, toda publicación sobre ella _____ por el rey Jorge II de Inglaterra. **f)** Durante el siguiente siglo, el Imperio español en América ya no _____ por los ingleses.

a) fundar
b) fortificar
c) vencer, difundir
d) enviar
e) prohibir
f) amenazar

fortificar – *to fortify*
invencible – *invincible*
difundir – *to spread*
la derrota – *the defeat*
publicar – *to publish*
amenazar – *to threaten*

5. Which explanation belongs with which proverb? ***

a) Cuando el río suena, agua lleva.   (4)
b) Poderoso caballero es don dinero.   ( )
c) Barriga llena, corazón contento.   ( )
d) No eches más leña al fuego.   ( )
e) Se hace lo que se puede.   ( )
f) Al pan pan y al vino vino.   ( )
g) Al mejor cazador se le va la liebre.   ( )
h) A lo hecho, pecho.   ( )
i) Agua que no has de beber, déjala correr.   ( )
j) Árbol que crece torcido nunca jamás se endereza.   ( )

1. Cada persona pone su mejor esfuerzo para hacer las cosas bien.
2. Si algo no es para uno, es mejor no tocarlo.
3. Es muy difícil que uno cambie sus costumbres.
4. Si se oyen rumores, hay algo de verdad.
5. Hay que aceptar la responsabilidad de los propios actos.
6. Cuando uno ha comido, está satisfecho de la vida.
7. No hay que polarizar más un conflicto.
8. Cuando se es rico, se tiene poder.
9. Si algo no sale bien, no significa que no seas bueno.
10. Hay que llamar a las cosas por su nombre.

la barriga – *the belly, tummy*
la leña – *the firewood*
la liebre – *the hare*
enderezarse – *to straighten up*

> Prepositions indicate the interrelationship between words or word groups.

The Prepositions

Sólo **por** este proyecto urgente he venido **a** la oficina. ①

Este calor es insoportable **para** mí. ②

¡Cómo me gustaría estar **en** la piscina! ③

---

1. I've come to the office only because of this urgent project. 2. This heat is unbearable for me! 3. How I would like to be in the swimming pool!

There are simple prepositions (**a**, **de**, **en**, etc.) and prepositional expressions that consist of several words (**al lado de**, **detrás de**, etc.). Here we treat only the most important of them.

1. *A*

> 1. **A + el = al**
> 2. Compare **querer** + thing = *want, would like*; **querer a** + person = *love,* as here: <u>**Quiero a Lupita.**</u>

▶ **Articles**, p. 21

• Pepe le ha prestado este CD **a** mi hermano.
○ ¡Qué bien! Y a propósito, ¿le has puesto pilas **al** toca-CD portátil?

The preposition **a** is used before the indirect object.

• Busco **a** Antonio para consultarle algo sobre este programa.
○ ¿Conoces **a** Dora? Ella sabe mucho de esto también.

– before the direct object with persons, groups of persons (for example, **Escucha <u>a la</u> orquesta**), or personified expressions (for example, **Busco <u>al</u> amor**). After **buscar**, **encontrar**, **necesitar**, and **tener**, the preposition **a** appears only when it refers to a specific person.

• ¿Adónde vas?   ○ Voy **al** sur. Mañana viajo **a** Santa Inés.
Simón ha venido **a** traerte un regalo para tu cumpleaños.

– to indicate a direction (*to*) or purpose (*in order to*), especially after verbs of motion (**ir**, **venir**, **volver**, etc.).

De aquí **a** Matamoros no es muy lejos. La ciudad está **a** 40 kilómetros.
De hoy **a** mañana descanso.

– with indications of distance or periods of time (*until*).

Tiene que torcer **a** la izquierda. **Al** lado del parque está el hotel.

– in prepositional expressions.

> The passage of a period of time is indicated with **a**:
> **A los cinco días nos volvimos a encontrar** (*After five days we met once again*).

Important prepositional expressions:

a la izquierda de	*to / on the left of*	a la derecha de	*to / on the right of*
a causa de	*because of*	debido a	*because of, due to*
a excepción de	*with the exception of*	a partir de	*from ... on*
a pesar de	*in spite of*	a través de	*through*
al lado de / junto a	*next to, beside*	al cabo de	*after (+ time)*

La discoteca abre **a** mediodía.
- ¿**A** qué estamos? ○ **A** cuatro de enero
A los 21 años empecé a trabajar en el taller.
Me lavo los dientes tres veces **al** día.

– with a point in time (*at*), statements of age, and indications of frequency, such as **... veces al día / a la semana / al mes**.

Las papas **a** la francesa son papas fritas.
Estos cuadros están pintados **a** mano.
A caballo son dos horas, **a** pie es medio día.

– to describe manner, as in style of preparation or production, and with certain types of movement (*on foot / horseback*).

Te invito **a** la conferencia. ¿Ya sabes **a** qué se refiere?
Vamos **a** practicar. Vuelva **a** repetir, por favor.

▶ Verbal Periphrasis, p. 191

– after certain adjectives such as **igual**, **parecido**, **inferior / superior**; after verbs such as **acostumbrarse, dedicarse, invitar, jugar, oler, saber**; and in the infinitive constructions **ir a, empezar / comenzar a, volver a, ponerse a**, etc., as well as **invitar a, aprender a, enseñar a**, and others.

▶ Adverbs, p. 53

A ver si podemos meter otro gol. **A veces** es mejor esperar.
Al final el equipo pasó a las finales.

– in numerous fixed adverbial phrases, such as **a veces, a menudo, a gusto, a lo mejor, a tiempo, a ver, al final**, etc.

2. *Con*

> Vivo **con** mis padres.
> ¿Vienes **con** nosotros al cine?

■ The preposition **con** (*with*) is used to indicate accompaniment or being together.

> La sopa se hace **con** champiñones.
> Mejor haz las cuentas **con** el programa Excel.

■ – for accompaniment or means.

> ¡No me mires **con** esa cara! Podemos hacerlo, aunque **con** dificultades.

■ – for manner.

> Sara **se** va a **casar conmigo**.
> ¿Estás **de acuerdo con** Luis?

■ – after certain verbs such as **casarse**, **enojarse** / **enfadarse**, **soñar** and in fixed expressions such as **estar de acuerdo con**, **con gusto**, **con cuidado**, etc.

!
> For the first and second person singular pronouns, there are special forms: **conmigo** and **contigo**.

3. *De*

> Esta foto es **de** Juanito. Es el hijo **de** la amiga **de** mi madre.
> ¿**De** quién es el libro **del** museo **de** Dalí? Es **de** la biblioteca.

■ The preposition **de** is used for relationship, possession, or agency.

> Es un sofá **de** cuero muy fino.   ¿Te gustan las novelas **de** amor?
> Quiero un bocadillo **de** queso.   Enrique es el chico **de** las gafas.
> Volamos a la ciudad **de** Quito.   ¿Conoces la costa **de** Almería?

■ – for more exact definition, to specify matter, contents, features, etc., and in general after **calle**, **ciudad**, **isla**, **parque**, **plaza**, etc. + name.

> Whereas English often adjectivizes nouns, Spanish generally links the two nouns with **de**. For example, *leather sofa* = **sofá de cuero**.

> Compare *the young man in glasses* = **el chico de gafas**.

> La habitación mide seis metros **de** largo y cuatro **de** ancho.
> Me trae un poco más **de** pan, por favor, y un vaso **de** vino tinto.

■ – for statement of measures and quantities.

Soy **de** la costa norte. Vengo **de** Ribadeo.

- to indicate origin.

Estamos a un km **de** la playa. **De** aquí al mar tardamos diez minutos.
La consulta cierra **de** dos a cuatro.

- to indicate the starting point for measuring a distance / a period of time.

Eran las once **de** la mañana del 25 **de** septiembre de 2004.
De joven vivía en la costa y trabajaba **de** noche en un bar.

- with the date or periods of time.

Antes de irte, mira esos papeles que están **delante de** ti.

- in prepositional expressions.

> **De + el = del**

▶ **Articles**, p. 21

Important expressions are:

alrededor de	*around*
antes / después de	*before / after*
cerca / lejos de	*close to / far from*
debajo / encima de	*under / on, over*
delante / detrás de	*in front of / in back of*
dentro / fuera de	*inside / outside*
enfrente de	*opposite, in front of*

¿**Te acuerdas de** Lorenzo? Se **acaba de** casar.

- after certain adverbs such as **capaz**, **fácil / difícil**, **lleno**, **seguro**; after verbs such as **acordarse**, **enamorarse**, **tratarse**; after nouns such as **ganas**, **miedo**; and in infinitive constructions such as **acabar de**, **dejar de**, **terminar de**, **tratar de**.

▶ **Verbal Periphrasis**, p. 191

Vamos, ¡camina **de prisa**! Tenemos que llegar **de una vez**.

- in numerous fixed phrases.

Also important:
- **Gracias.**
○ **De** nada.

de cerca / lejos	*closely / from a distance*
de día / de noche	*by day / by night*
de prisa	*quickly*
de pronto / de repente	*suddenly*
de una vez	*once and for all*
de verdad	*really*

4. *En*

With **entrar**, **en** is used, especially if you are in the space. For example: **Cuando entramos <u>en</u> la sala del cine ya estaba oscuro.**

1. *At someone's house* is rendered either with **en casa de** or with **con**, as here: **Pablito no está en mi casa, está con mis padres.** (*Pablito is not at my house, he is at my parents'.*)
2. *To work at / for a company* is normally rendered with **en**: **Trabajo en IBERFRUTAS, S.A.**

¡El pasaporte no está **en** el bolso!	– *in the purse*
Este fin de semana estoy **en** casa.	– *at home*
La maleta está **en** la cama.	– *on the bed*
Hay un cuadro **en** la pared.	– *on the wall*

The preposition **en** is used to specify the place in, on, or at which something or someone is located.

Siempre tomo vacaciones **en verano**, normalmente **en agosto**. Mi hermano nació **en 1974**. Lo voy a ver **en una semana**, **en Navidad.**

– with seasons, years, holidays, and stretches of time.

¿Cómo se dice **en alemán**: "Voy **en coche**"?

– with languages and means of transportation.

Cambia algo, **en lugar de** quejarte solamente.

– in prepositional expressions.

Important expressions are:

en dirección a	*in the direction of, toward*
en lugar de / en vez de	*in place of, instead of*
en medio de	*in the middle of*
en torno a	*around*

Siempre **pienso en** ti, no tardes **en** volver. No **insistas** más **en** esto, por favor. No **quedamos en** nada.

– after certain verbs such as **confiar en**, **pensar en**, **insistir en**, **quedar en**, **tardar en**.

En general no desayuno, aunque **en realidad** debería hacerlo. ¿**En serio** prefieres quedarte en casa?

– in fixed expressions, such as **en general**, **en realidad**, **en serio**, etc.

5. *Para*

> Estas flores son **para** ti. Estas son copas **para** vino tinto.
> Llamo **para** pedir una cita. ¡Nos vamos **para** Colombia!
>
> The preposition **para** is used to express designation, recipient, intention, purpose, or goal (*for*, *to*, *in order to*).
>
> **Para las 9** ya vamos a terminar.
> ¿Dejamos la discusión **para** mañana?
>
> – to express a specific point in time (deadline, appointment, etc.).
>
> Felipe está grande **para** un chico de su edad.
> Esto es fácil **para** ti, ¿verdad?
>
> – to express a comparison or reference.

> **Para** + infinitive must not be separated by a pronoun: **Haz yoga para relajarte.**

6. *Por*

> ¡Lo hice **por** tu culpa!
> No puedo venir **por** tener mucho trabajo.
>
> The preposition **por** is used to indicate a reason or a cause (*for*, *because of* ...).
>
> He sabido el resultado **por** el telediario; te mando los datos **por** fax.
>
> – to indicate means (*through*, *by*).
>
> Si das una vuelta **por** el centro, pasa **por** mi casa.
> Voy a hacer un viaje **por** Sudamérica.
> Te he buscado **por** todas partes.
>
> – to designate one or more points in an area (*through*, *past*).
>
> El toro saltó **por encima** de la barrera y se escapó **por detrás** de ella.
>
> – in prepositional expressions.

> 1. Compare **¿Por qué?** and **Pues porque sí.**
> 2. *To pick up* can be expressed with **ir por: Voy por ti.** In Spain, in colloquial speech you will hear the combination **ir a por: Voy a por ti.**

Important expressions are:

por aquí	*around here*
por encima / debajo de	*over / under*
por delante / detrás de	*ahead of / behind*
por dentro / fuera de	*(on the) inside / outside*

> **Por la mañana** no puedo, mejor **por la tarde**.
> Voy a quedarme aquí **por un mes** más. **Por junio** me tengo que ir.
>
> ▮ – to indicate a time span or give an approximate time.

▶ **Passive Voice**,
p. 240

> El Fausto fue escrito **por** Goethe.
>
> ▮ – to express agency with the passive voice.

> ¿**Por** cuánto se vende este terreno?
> Los incas cambiaban el oro **por** cosas sin valor.
> He pagado la cuenta **por** ustedes.
>
> ▮ – to state a price or indicate an exchange.

> Mi madre se interesa **por** la arqueología.
>
> ▮ – after some verbs, for example, **interesarse por**.

> ¡**Por** última vez! ¿Vas a venir o no?
>
> ▮ – in numerous fixed phrases.

Here are the most important:

por … vez	*for the …time*	por lo menos	*at least*
por casualidad	*by chance*	por lo tanto	*therefore*
por cierto	*by the way*	por poco	*almost*
por fin	*finally*	por fortuna	*fortunately*
por un lado	*on the one hand*	por otro lado	*on the other hand*

7. *Hacer* in Time Expressions

Antes de la una tenemos que estar allí, ¡pero el tren ya se fue **hace** una hora!	*before one o'clock* *one hour ago*
Vivo aquí **desde hace** dos meses, **desde** abril.	*for two months* *since April*

Some Spanish prepositions refer to a point in time; others refer to a span of time, elapsed between two events or periods of time:

<table>
<tr><td></td><td>*point in time*</td><td>*span of time*</td></tr>
<tr><td>*forward*</td><td>antes de</td><td>hace</td></tr>
<tr><td>*since*</td><td>desde</td><td>desde hace</td></tr>
</table>

points in time: **el verano, mi cumpleaños, las vacaciones, ayer**
spans of time: **un segundo, treinta minutos, dos días, mucho tiempo**

Expressions for spans of time always appear with words that designate "units of time," such as second(s), minute(s), hour(s), day(s), etc.

1. Bilbao is worth a visit! Choose the correct alternative. *

a) Mañana a/(por) la mañana vamos a/— ir por/en avión.

b) Volamos directamente en/a Bilbao. **c)** Bilbao está en el/del
norte de España, en/de el País Vasco. **d)** Por/Con supuesto,
queremos —/a ver al/el museo Guggenheim. **e)** Es obra del/al
arquitecto estadounidense Frank O. Gehry y es una —/de las
atraccciones más visitadas por/para los turistas. **f)** Pero Bilbao tiene
a / — muchos otros atractivos, además con/de una excelente
gastronomía. **g)** De/Por ejemplo, es muy agradable de/— caminar
a/por las calles del Casco Viejo, la parte antigua de/a la ciudad.
h) Los bilbaínos son muy amables y reciben —/a los visitantes
por/con esta frase: "Bienvenidos, ya estáis en/a casa."

*estadounidense –
U.S., from the U.S.A.
la atracción –
the attraction, place
of interest
el atractivo – the
appeal, attraction
el visitante – the visitor*

2. Some people are on a job hunt. Fill in the missing prepositions
a, **de**, **con**, **por**, or **para**. *

a) • Mira, aquí necesitan un ingeniero __de__ construcción _____
trabajar _____ La Paz. Le voy _____ decir _____ Manuel.

○ Sí, seguro que ese puesto es interesante _____ él.

b) Dicen _____ el periódico que las escuelas _____ idiomas _____
Santa Fe buscan profesores _____ experiencia _____ el verano. ¿No
quieres ir _____ Santa Fe? Podemos trabajar _____ las vacaciones
_____ la ciudad, _____ variar, en vez _____ siempre ir _____ la
playa.

c) • Aquí buscan practicantes _____ conocimiento _____ programas
_____ computadora _____ nivel usuario. Sólo hay que mandar los
papeles _____ esta dirección o contactar _____ la empresa
_____ e-mail.

○ Sí, pero quieren personas _____ menos _____ 30 años, no
es _____ mí.

*la construcción –
the construction
la experiencia –
the experience
el verano – the summer
para variar – for a
change
en vez de – instead of
a nivel usuario –
at user level*

Practice and Application

Prepositions

3. Match these halves to form complete sentences. ******

a) Llamo para

b) Para mí, este

c) ¡Muchas gracias

d) Me parece un precio

e) Mire, llamaba por lo de

1. por todo! Ha sido muy agradable.

2. muy alto por tan mala calidad.

3. confirmar mi vuelo a Caracas.

4. su reserva, es que nos falta un dato.

5. vino va muy bien con el pescado.

4. Granddad is telling about the 1960s. Fill in the blanks with **por** or **para**. ******

a) Hoy nos preocupan los emigrantes que vienen _para_ acá, pero no olvidemos la situación que había _____ los años 60... **b)** Recuerdo que un día pasó_____ el pueblo un Mercedes, _____ admiración de todos. **c)** ¡Era Ángel! Se había ido _____ Alemania y volvía _____ pasar el verano. **d)** ¡Y qué historias traía _____ nosotros! **e)** Sí, _____ allá había trabajo _____ miles de españoles, _____ ser mano de obra barata. **f)** Alemania era _____ ellos la tierra prometida. **g)** Se iban _____ trabajar duro y _____ ahorrar mucho, aunque recibían poco _____ su trabajo. **h)** La mayoría pensaba quedarse sólo _____ unos años y volver después _____ cumplir sus sueños... pero _____ muchos fue una nueva patria...

la mano de obra – *here: the manpower*
la tierra prometida – *the Promised Land*
ahorrar – *to save*
cumplir – *to fulfill*
la patria – *the homeland*

5. Two employees in a department store have a reunion. Fill in the blanks, using the words provided. ******

antes de

hace

desde

desde hace

a) • ¡Gloria! ¿ ___Desde___ cuándo trabajas aquí?

b) ○ _____ un mes. ¡Qué sorpresa verte aquí!

c) • Sí, creo que no nos hemos visto _____ varios años, ¿no?

d) ○ Es verdad, _____ la escuela. ¿Tomamos un aperitivo juntos _____ ir a casa hoy por la noche? ¿Quedamos en el bar "Paco"?

e) • ¡Excelente! Pero ahora me voy. Tengo que ver a mi jefe _____ las 10, y ya ha llegado _____ diez minutos. Es que hemos pedido unos escritorios _____ dos semanas y no han llegado. Los estamos reclamando _____ el jueves. Entonces hasta más tarde, ¿vale?

Conjunctions

Podemos ir al cine **y** ver la película de Goya.

①

Yo creo **que** llegamos a tiempo todavía.

②

Nos vamos **en cuanto** termine de lavar los platos.

③

> Conjunctions join words, phrases, clauses, or sentences. There are coordinating conjunctions and subordinating conjunctions.

1. We can go to the movies and see the film about Goya. 2. I think we'll still get there on time.
3. We'll leave as soon as I finish washing the plates.

Coordinating Conjunctions

Coordinating conjunctions link two elements of equal importance, such as two nouns, two adjectives, two independent clauses, etc.

Here are the most important:

• Estos son Inés **y** Octavio.	**y** *(and)*
Ni tú **ni** Pepe los conocen.	**ni ... ni** *(neither ... nor)*
○ ¿Quién es más simpático, Octavio **o** Inés?	**o** *(or)*
• Inés es más amable, **pero** Octavio es divertido.	**pero** *(but)*
Inés no es amiga de Octavio, **sino** su prima.	**sino** *(but)*
Octavio no tiene dinero, **pues** ahora no trabaja.	**pues** *(since, as)*
Sin embargo, es optimista.	**sin embargo** *(however, nevertheless)*
Por eso está tranquilo.	**por eso** *(therefore, for that reason)*
En cambio, Inés se preocupa.	**en cambio** *(on the other hand)*

> **!**
> Before words that start with **i-** or **hi-**, the conjunction **y** becomes **e**. Similarly, the conjunction **o** becomes **u** before words beginning with **o-** or **ho-**.
> • **Creo que Octavio e Inés van a venir, pero no sé si Inés u Octavio traerán el vino.**

Subordinate Conjunctions

Subordinate conjunctions appear between an independent clause and a dependent clause.

After some conjunctions, such as **para que**, the subjunctive is required. With others, the use of the subjunctive or indicative depends on the verb of the principal clause (for example, **pensar que** + indicative, **dudar que** + subjunctive), or on the time reference (for example, **cuando** + subjunctive refers to the future). Before certain conjunctions, especially before **que**, Spanish uses no comma.

Below are the most important subordinating conjunctions.

<u>Underlining</u> means that the conjunction is used with the indicative.
Bold means that it is used with the indicative or with the subjunctive, and red means that it is always used with the subjunctive.

▶ **Use of the Subjunctive**, p. 161

1. **Que** frequently is not translated into English. For example, **Digo <u>que</u> no.**
2. **Que** is preceded by a comma only in certain relative clauses, as here: **Mi amigo, <u>que</u> es de Cuba, no conoce la nieve.**

▶ **Relative Pronouns**, p. 97 ff

Como si is always followed by the imperfect subjunctive or the past perfect subjunctive.

Espero **que** esté bien, señorita Julia. El señor Lugo dice **que** va a llegar a las dos.	**que** *(that)*
Prepare los papeles **para que** estén listos. Llame al cliente **a fin de que** venga más tarde.	para que, a fin de que *(so that)*
Estos son productos nuevos, **así que** los ponemos en la lista. Ese precio está mal, **de modo que** hay que corregirlo. Estoy en mi oficina, **de manera que** puede traerme las cartas.	<u>así que</u> **de modo que** **de manera que** *(so that)*
Si llama el señor Roa, que venga personalmente. Ha preguntado **si** le hacemos un precio especial.	**si** *(if)* <u>si</u> *(whether)*
En caso de que llame, no quiero hablar con él.	en caso de que *(in case)*
Podemos darle un descuento **con tal de que** pida mucho. Ahora quiero trabajar en paz, **a menos que** haya algo urgente.	con tal de que *(provided that)* a menos que *(unless)*
Como es mediodía, vamos a comer. **Como** me llame ahora mi jefe, ¡renuncio! ¡Actúa **como si** fuéramos sus esclavos!	<u>como</u> *(since, as)* como *(if)* como si *(as if)*

Cuando llega, empieza a dar órdenes. **Cuando** vuelva de comer, va a tener más trabajo para mí. **En cuanto** empiece, me va a interrumpir otra vez. **Tan pronto como** hago algo, quiere otra cosa.	cuando *(whenever)* cuando *(when, as soon as)* **en cuanto** *(as soon as)* **tan pronto como** *(as soon as)*
Tengo que concentrarme **mientras** trabajo. **Mientras** el jefe esté en la reunión, estoy tranquila.	mientras *(while)* mientras *(as long as)*
Aunque no he terminado, ya me voy. **Aunque** el jefe no quiera, hoy no me quedo más.	**aunque** *(although, though, even if)*
Normalmente espero a mi novio **hasta que** llega a casa. Hoy no lo voy a esperar **hasta que** llegue. Tengo hambre.	**hasta que** *(until)*
Antes de que venga, voy a prepararme unos espaguetis. **Después de que** coma, me voy a sentir mejor.	antes de que *(before)* después de que *(after)*
A pesar de que mi jefe es difícil, el trabajo me gusta.	**a pesar de que** *(although)*
Desde que lo conozco, no ha cambiado.	desde que *(since)*
Por más que trato, siempre es muy duro conmigo.	**por más que** *(no matter how much)*
No puedo trabajar **sin que** me critique.	sin que *(without)*
Ya que es así, tengo que guardar la calma. Pero no es difícil, **porque** soy una persona tranquila.	ya que *(since)* **porque** *(because)*

A number of Spanish prepositions become conjunctions by adding **que**. **Durante**, however, is used only prepositionally, with a noun: **Me concentro durante mi trabajo.**

In colloquial speech, **que** takes the place of **es que** or **porque**: **Habla más fuerte, que no te oigo.**

Practice and Application

Conjunctions

1. Ana is describing her nieces. Choose the correct conjunction. *

a) Eugenia, Ofelia y/(e) Isabel son las hijas de mi prima. **b)** No estoy segura de si Eugenia o/u Isabel es mayor, pero Ofelia es la pequeñita. **c)** Es una niña alegre y/e inquieta, tiene siete o/u ocho años.

2. Eduardo works in a textile factory and is always on the phone. Complete his statements below with **porque, pero,** or **sino.** **

a) Yo no dije que iba a hacer la presentación, __sino__ sólo las transparencias, _____ el jefe es quien va a presentar.

b) Claro que el márqueting es importante, _____ tenemos que elaborar una mejor estrategia de ventas _____ la competencia es muy fuerte.

c) Ese material no es para todos los clientes, _____ sólo para algunos, _____ es muy caro.

3. Connect the two columns to form complete sentences. **

a) Si el profesor no viene pronto,

b) Cuando hagas el pastel de la receta,

c) Si no mejora en dos días,

d) Cuando vayas a Figueres,

1. no dejes de ver el museo de Dalí.
2. me llama para hacer otra cita.
3. nos vamos a casa.
4. ¿me traes un trozo para probarlo?

4. The main characters of the novel, before their first night together ... Fill in the conjunctions provided on the left. ***

Antes de que
aunque
~~En cuanto~~
ni
pero
por eso
porque
que
y

a) *(As soon as)* En cuanto entraron en el piso, él supo *(that)* _____ sería algo muy especial. **b)** *(Before)* _____ subieran, habían ido a cenar *(and)* _____, *(although)* _____ por lo general era tímido, con ella era distinto, *(because)* _____ parecía sinceramente interesada. **c)** Quizá *(for that reason)* _____ ahora era todo tan natural. **d)** Se besaron, *(but)* _____ sin muchas palabras *(noch)* _____ prisas...

Numbers, Quantities, and Time Expressions

En casa éramos **once** hermanos, **cinco** hombres y **seis** mujeres.

①

Y en la escuela había el **doble** de chicos que de chicas.

②

1. At home there were eleven of us siblings, five boys and six girls.
2. And at school there were twice as many boys as girls.

Cardinal Numbers

> Most cardinal numbers are invariable. A period is used to indicate thousands, and a comma is used as a decimal point.

0 cero	20 veinte	201 doscient**os uno**, **un**,
1 **un/o**, **una**	21 veint**iuno**,	doscient**as una**
2 dos	**-ún**, **-una**	240 doscient**os/-as** cuarenta
3 tres	22 veint**i**dós	300 trescient**os/-as**
4 cuatro	30 treinta	400 cuatrocientos/-as
5 cinco	31 treinta **y** uno,	412 cuatrocientos/-as doce
6 seis	un, una	500 **quinientos/-as**
7 siete	32 treinta **y** dos	600 seiscientos/-as
8 ocho	40 cuarenta	700 **sete**cientos/-as
9 nueve	50 **cincuenta**	800 ochocientos/-as
10 diez	55 cincuenta y cinco	900 novecientos/-as
11 **once**	60 **sesenta**	1.000 **mil**
12 **doce**	70 **setenta**	1.999 mil novecientos/-as
13 **trece**	80 ochenta	noventa y nueve
14 **catorce**	90 noventa	2.001 dos mil uno, un, una
15 **quince**	100 **cien**	15.000 quince mil
16 diecis**é**is	101 cien**to uno**,	500.000 quinientos/-as mil
17 diecisiete	**un**, **una**	1.000.000 un millón
18 dieciocho	110 cien**to** diez	100.000.000 cien millones
19 dieci**n**ueve	200 doscient**os/-as**	1.000.000.000 mil millones

> 1. To make big numbers easier to read, groups of three are separated by a decimal point.
> 2. Note: Year dates are masculine and are read like any other number. For example, 1968 = **mil novecientos sesenta y ocho.**

Cardinal Numbers

The numbers 16–29 are contracted to form single words, with the original **y** becoming **diez y seis** ▸ **dieciséis**. From 31 on, tens and ones are written separately and linked by **y**.

¿Es **un** tres o **un** nueve? Es que ya no veo muy bien.

Numbers are masculine in Spanish.

Before numbers and quantities, **unos / -as** means *approximately*.

Veintiún, **veintidós**, and **veintitrés** have a written accent.

• Tengo veinti**una** monedas y veinti**ún** billetes… Sí, son veinti**uno**.

Uno agrees in gender with the noun. Before masculine nouns, use **un**. This also applies to 21, 31, 41, etc.

• Hay **cien** competiciones y la entrada cuesta **ciento** cincuenta euros.

One hundred is **cien**. From 101 on, however, use **ciento**.

Percent is rendered as follows: 100% = el / un cien por cien / ciento.

Doscient**as** competidoras van a correr los quinient**os** metros. Trescient**as** diez mil cadenas de televisión transmiten las Olimpíadas.

The hundreds agree in gender and number with the noun. This is true even when another invariable number separates them (**trescientas diez mil cadenas**).

Las Olimpíadas en México fueron en **mil** novecientos sesenta y ocho.

Mil is invariable, between 1,100 and 9,999 as well.

The preposition **de** precedes the noun also with **millón / millones** + fractional numbers. Compare **un millón y medio de productos** with **un millón quinientos mil productos**.

• México D.F. tiene unos veinte **millones de** habitantes.
○ Aquí dice que ya hay **un millón ochocientos cincuenta mil** más.

Between **millón / millones** and the following noun, the preposition **de** is used if no other number appears between them.

• Este negocio puede ganar **mil millones / un millardo** de dólares.

Spanish has the term **millardo** for *billion*, but **mil millones** is used far more frequently.

The Date

The date is abbreviated with hyphens: **22-4-2005** or **22-IV-2005**. Note that the day of the month goes in first place.

1. *The first* is **el uno** or **el primero**.
2. In a letter, no article is used in the date.

For the days of the month, use the cardinal numbers. Generally the definite article is used before the day, and the preposition **de** appears between the day and the month and between the month and the year:

La carta es del 22 (**veintidós**) de abril **de** 2005 (dos mil cinco).

Ordinal Numbers

> Es la **cuarta** vez que vengo, ¡y todavía no sé en qué piso vives!

①

> Vivo en el **quinto** piso. Hay que subir uno más.

②

> Ordinal numbers agree in number and gender with the noun.

1. It's the fourth time I've come, and I still don't know what floor you live on! 2. I live on the fifth floor. You have to go one higher.

In Spanish, ordinal numbers are represented numerically as:

> In Spanish, ordinal numbers are written in the form shown on the left, with a superscript. This corresponds to the English 1st, 2nd, 3rd, 4th, etc.

1°, 1er , 1ª	primero, primer, primera	6°, 6ª	sexto/-a
2°, 2ª	segundo/-a	7°, 7ª	séptimo/-a
3°, 3er, 3ª	tercero, tercer, tercera	8°, 8ª	octavo/-a
4°, 4ª	cuarto/-a	9°, 9ª	noveno/-a
5°, 5ª	quinto/-a	10°, 10ª	décimo/-a

Es la **cuarta** vez que pregunto y usted es la **cuarta** que no lo sabe.

Ordinal numbers usually precede the noun or take its place.

El **primer** día escuchamos el **tercer** concierto de Albéniz.

Primero and **tercero** drop the **-o** before a masculine noun.

La oficina está en el **piso once**.

From "eleventh" on, the ordinal numbers are rarely used. Instead, Spanish generally uses the cardinal numbers after the noun.

> 1. In colloquial speech, starting with "11th," the ending **-avo / -a** is often used. For example: **Es la veinteava vez que te llamo.**
> 2. *For the umpteenth time* = **por enésima vez.**

Centuries, Rulers, and Names

Centuries, names of rulers, certain historical events, and the like are designated numerically with Roman numerals. This is the general rule: up to ten, read them as ordinal numbers, and after that as cardinal numbers.

> Ordinal numbers over ten are used only for special occasions. For example: **el vigésimo quinto aniversario.**

written	*spoken*
el siglo V a.C.	el siglo quinto antes de Cristo
el siglo XXI	el siglo veintiuno
Felipe II	Felipe Segundo
Luis XIV	Luis Catorce
la II Guerra Mundial	la Segunda Guerra Mundial

Percentages and Decimal Numbers

El/Un 50% (cincuenta por ciento) de las chicas estudia una carrera.

Before percentages, the article (definite or indefinite) generally is used. The verb usually is singular.

Sólo **un 8,5% (ocho coma cinco por ciento)** recibe una beca.

Unlike English, Spanish uses a comma as a decimal point.

Expressions of Quantity

1/2 kg	medio kilo	1/2 h	media hora

Medio, media are used without an article.

1/3 l	un tercio de litro	la tercera parte de los alumnos
1/4 kg	un cuarto de kilo	la cuarta parte del profesorado

The preposition **de** is used between **tercio** and **cuarto** and the noun. If you want to refer to one-third or one-fourth of a certain quantity, you usually use the construction **la tercera** or **cuarta parte de**.

1-1/2 l	un litro y medio	2-3/4 h dos horas y tres cuartos

With mixed numbers, use this formula: whole number + **y** + fractional number.

Hoy logramos sólo **la mitad**, mañana tenemos que trabajar **el doble**.

These are also useful: **la mitad** (*half*), **el doble** (*double*), and **el triple** (*three times as much*).

The following expressions of quantity are related to numbers:

una docena de actrices	*a dozen actresses*
un centenar de modelos	*a hundred models*
cientos de reporteros	*hundreds of reporters*
un millar de revistas	*a thousand magazines*
miles de entrevistas	*thousands of interviews*
millones de fotos	*millions of photos*

Una quincena and **quince días** both mean *14 days = two weeks*.

Telling Time

① ¿A qué hora empieza la película?

A las nueve. ②

③ ¿Y ya **son las nueve**?

1. *What time does the film start? 2. At nine. 3. And is it nine yet?*

The 24-hour system is used only for official statements of time, for example, in railroad stations and airports, in television and radio broadcasts, etc. For example: **El tren sale a las veinte horas y diez minutos. El avión llega a las dieciséis quince.**

¿Qué hor**a es**?

Generally, the singular is used in asking the time of day.

Es la una. Ya casi **es** mediodía.

With 1 o'clock, 12 noon (**mediodía**), and midnight (**medianoche**), use **es**; otherwise, use **son**. The hours are given with the feminine definite article + the cardinal numbers from 1 to 12.

Son las once **de la noche**. ¡Qué tarde!

To state the time more precisely, add **de la mañana** (1 A.M. –12 P.M.), **de la tarde** (1 P.M. until dusk), or **de la noche** (from dusk until midnight).

Son las cuatro **y cinco**.
- ¿Ya son las dos **y media**? ○ No, son las dos **y cuarto**.

The minutes up to the half hour are joined by **y** to the preceding hour. Likewise: **media** (*half past the hour*) and **cuarto** (*quarter past*).

- ¿Ya es la una menos **cuarto**? ○ No, es la una **menos veinte**.

After *half past*, the minutes of the next full hour are subtracted with **menos**. Likewise: **menos cuarto**.

- ¿**A qué hora** empieza la película? ○ **A las** nueve y media.

To ask the time when something begins (*At what time / When*), use **¿A qué hora? ... A la / -s ...** (*At ... o'clock*).

1. **Hora / s** is not included when the time is given.
2. **Por la mañana / tarde / noche** is used without giving the time.

In LA, the expression **falta / ... para** is used after the half hour. For example: **Faltan diez para las cinco.**

Practice and Application

Numbers

1. How would you translate these quantities given in your cookbook? *

a) 1/2 kg potatoes   _medio kilo de papas_

b) 1/4 kg ham   _____

c) 100 g cheese   _____

d) 1-1/2 l white wine   _____

2. Read and write these times seen on a digital watch. *

a) 01:30   _la una y media de la mañana_

b) 17:15   _____

c) 05:40   _____

d) 00:10   _____

3. Write out the numbers, currencies, weights, etc. *

el euro – *the euro*
la fecha de nacimiento – *the date of birth*

a) Este hotel tiene **54** habitaciones dobles que cuestan por noche **91 €**.

_cincuenta y cuatro,_____

b) Mi fecha de nacimiento es el **30-X-1965**.

_____

c) En **1987** Ecuador tenía **9.008.474** habitantes. Hoy son un **13,2 %** más.

_____

4. Translate the following. *

el céntimo – *the cent*
Hace ... grados – *It's ... degrees*

a) I need 50 cents.   _Necesito cincuenta céntimos._

b) It is the third time.   _____

c) I live on the second floor.   _____

d) Today it is 25 degrees.   _____

e) The film starts at 10 o'clock.   _____

f) My teacher (*fem.*) is 44 years old.   _____

g) Tomorrow is Friday the 13th.   _____

Answers

Nouns (pp. 17–19)

1. el: libro, Danubio, sistema, ocho, agua, avión; **la:** oficina, mano, catedral, luna, libertad, mujer;
los: hoteles, problemas, camareros, sofás, coches, mapas;
las: ciudades, noches, habitaciones, farmacias, decisiones, llaves.

2. a) los vecinos; b) las jóvenes;
c) los programas;
d) los coordinadores;
e) las discusiones;
f) los domingos; g) las llaves;
h) los análisis.

3. a) la madre – el padre –
los padres; b) el hijo – la hija –
los hijos; c) la hermana –
el hermano – los hermanos;
d) el señor Roca – la señora
Roca – los señores Roca;
e) la abuela – el abuelo –
los abuelos; f) el hombre –
la mujer – el niño/el hijo.

4. a) la mujer; b) la actriz;
c) la cantante; d) la gata;
e) la yegua; f) la dependienta;
g) la princesa; h) la modelo;
i) la vaca; j) la gallina.

5. a) El; b) los; c) el; d) las;
e) el; f) La; g) los.

6. a) el capital; b) la policía;
c) del grupo; d) los medios;
e) la guía; f) la capital; g) la
bolsa; h) las medias.

7. a–3; b–5; c–2; d–1; e–4.

Determiners, Articles (pp. 26–27)

1. a) los, —, los; b) —, —; c) El,
el, El; d) —, la, —; e) del, el.

2. a) ¡Por favor, otra cerveza!
b) Perdón, ¿dónde están los
servicios? c) Lo mejor es la
paella. d) La paella me gusta
mucho. e) ¿Tiene/n agua
mineral con gas? f) Y, por favor,
otro medio litro de vino tinto.
g) ¡La cuenta, por favor!

3. a) un; b) Los; c) —; d) —;
e) El; f) lo; g) la.

4. a) el señor Lozada; b) otra
solución; c) Lo que dices;
d) la señora Reyes; e) el abrigo;
f) El jueves.

5. a) La, los, el, un; b) el, al,
—, el, las, la; c) el, —, un/el;
d) al, lo; e) los, un;
f) la, —/un.

Demonstrative, Possessive, and Interrogative Determiners (pp. 34–36)

1. a) ¿De quién es esa maleta?
¿De aquel señor? b) Aquí está
este paraguas. ¿Es de aquella
joven? c) Ese turista ha dejado
este mapa.

2. a) esta, Estos; b) estas, esta;
c) esta, este; d) este, este.

3. a) esa, ese; b) esa, Ese; c) esas,
ese; d) Ese, esa; e) esos.

4. a) 7; b) 1; c) 3; d) 5; e) 4; f) 6;
g) 8; h) 2.

5. a) ese, Este; b) aquella; c) este,
aquel, esa; d) Estos, esa; e) ese,
esta; f) Estos, aquellos; g) esa,
este.

6. a) *unstressed:* **su** coche,
su vecina, **sus** hijos;
stressed: Dios **mío**,
una vecina **mía**;
b) *unstressed:* **vuestros** amigos,
nuestros amigos;
stressed: una compañera
suya.

7. a) tus; b) mis, nuestros;
c) tuya; d) su; e) tus, tuya, su;
f) sus, mi.

8. a) Cuántos; b) Qué/Cuántos;
c) cuántas; c) Qué; d) Cuánta.

Indefinite Determiners (pp. 43–44)

1. a) mucha, algún, varios;
b) ninguna; c) cualquier,
demasiada, tantas.

2. a) otra; b) otro; c) otras;
d) otros; e) otra.

3. a) Todo el; b) Todos los;
c) todas las; d) toda la, todos
los; e) todas las, todos los;
f) toda la.

4. a) alguna, ningún; b) algún,
ninguna, algunas; c) alguna,
ningún; d) alguna, ningún.

5. a) Cada, mismo, mismo,
diferentes; b) muchas, todos,
varias, misma, ningún;
c) suficiente, bastante;
d) algunas, muchas, varias;
e) Todas, ningún; f) Algunas,
alguna, otra, ningún;
g) algunas, otras, tantas.

Adjectives (pp. 50–52)

1. a) negro; b) viejo; c) alegre;
d) pequeño; e) rico; f) barato;
g) interesante; h) feo;
i) moderno; j) corto.

2. papas picantes, aceitunas
negras, ensalada mixta, jamón
serrano, queso manchego,
sardinas fritas con tomate.

3. a) encantadora, amables,
cariñosa, alegre, rubia, azules,
medio, mayor; b) serio,
conservador, hostil, alto,
delgado, económicas, inter-
nacional, importante;
c) pequeños, inquietos, activos,
catastrófico, monos, moreno,
gordito, rubia, preciosos,
ocupada.

4. a) tres blusas y unos pantalones
rojos; b) dos pantalones azul
marino; c) una chaqueta marrón;
d) cinco camisas blancas;
e) una blusa y un suéter verdes;
f) un vestido naranja.

5. a) nueva, trabajadora;
b) holgazanes, científico;
c) triste, cansado;
d) fáciles, útiles y divertidos.

6. a – 6; b – 1; c – 4; d – 3; e – 7;
f – 5; g – 2.

7. a) Es la primera vez que estoy
aquí. b) Este es un buen
restaurante. c) ¡Eso me parece
un mal chiste! d) ¡Mmmh! ¡Qué
buena receta! e) Pare por favor
enfrente del tercer edificio a la
izquierda. f) ¡No tengo ningún
problema! g) ¡Esa es una gran
película!

8. a) verde; b) rojas; c) amarillos;
d) negra; e) blancos; f) rosa,
azules; g) roja, amarilla, verde;
h) rojos; i) verde.

Adverbs (pp. 59 – 61)

1. a) buen, bien; b) alegremente, alegre; c) rápidas, rápido/rápidamente; d) tranquilo, tranquilamente; e) malo, mal, mal.

2. 1) Buenos días, Srta. Perea.
2) ¿Está aquí el Sr. Salgado?
3) Sólo traigo ... 4) No, lamentablemente ... 5) Está en una reunión urgente. 6) Pero por supuesto ... 7) Yo se los doy ...
8) Está bien ...

3. *Adjektive:* muchas, amable, Buenos, urgente.
Adverbien: aquí, bien, por supuesto, Sólo, lamentablemente, pronto, luego, probablemente.

4. a) Buen; b) bien, buen; c) bien, Buenos, bien; d) buenos.

5. a) Los domingos, por la tarde, totalmente; b) Pronto, a menudo; c) Hoy, rápido, todavía; d) mucho, bien; e) Por fin, a tiempo; f) Por lo general, caóticamente, con mucho gusto; g) Casi, de repente; h) Por supuesto, también; i) lamentablemente, al final; j) En realidad, sobre todo.

6. a) Ya, tarde, todavía, de pronto; b) mañana, enseguida; c) antes, mucho, perfectamente; d) Así, constantemente, siempre, amablemente; e) Poco a poco, pronto.

7. a) temporales; b) temporalmente; c) activamente; d) activa; e) regulares; f) regularmente; g) profesionalmente; h) profesionales.

Comparisons (pp. 68 – 71)

1. a) que, tanto, como;
b) que, tantas, como;
c) tantas, como, tantos, como.

2. a) bonita que; b) anticuado que; c) fresca como; d) cómodos que; e) horrible como.

3. a) mejor; b) menos, que; c) más, que; d) más, que.

4. a – 3; b – 5; c – 6; d – 2; e – 1; f – 4.

5. a) más; b) más malo/peor; c) menos; d) mejor; e) más grande; f) el mayor.

6. a) que; b) mucho, igual; c) de; d) muy; e) de, que; f) que, más; g) de.

7. a) más silenciosamente que; b) menos tranquilamente que; c) tan rápido/rápidamente como; d) mejor que; e) tanto como, más duro/duramente.

8. a) Enrique canta mejor. b) Sonia hace menos deporte que Sara. c) Juliana hace más deberes que Carlitos. d) Pedro ha hecho más presentaciones que María. e) La letra de Eduardo es más fea / peor que la de Gonzalo.

9. a) altísimo; b) clarísimo; c) rarísimamente; d) prontísimo; e) tantísimo.

10. a) mucho, muchas; b) muy, mucho; c) muchas, mucho; d) muy, muchas; e) muy; f) muy, muchas, muy; g) muy, muy, mucha, Muchas, mucho.

Personal Pronouns (pp. 81–86)

1. a) ¿Dónde está el coche? ¿No funciona? b) Señor Mata, usted vive lejos, ¿verdad? Yo también. c) Jesús y María trabajan desde hace un mes. Ella trabaja en un banco y él en un supermercado.
   d) • Este cuadro es muy intere-sante. ▸ ○ Sí, es muy moderno.
   e) • ¿La nueva colega? ▸ ○ Yo no lo soy, es ella. Yo sólo estoy de visita.

2. a) ellos; b) contigo; c) tú, yo; d) ti, ella.

3. a–4; b–3; c–6; d–5; e–2; f–1.

4. a) a ella, a ti; b) conmigo, entre tú y yo; c) contigo, Para mí; d) detrás de nosotros, delante de ti.

5. a) las; b) las; c) lo, los; d) La, La, los.

6. Vamos a hacerla. Queremos hacerla, vais a conocerlos.

7. a) les; b) me; c) le; d) te; e) os; f) les; g) nos; h) le; i) les.

8. a) se; b) nos; c) me, me; d) os, nos; e) te, te; f) me, se.

9. a) A Laura ya no la veo.
   b) Estas cuentas las pagamos enseguida/inmediatamente.
   c) ¡Sólo a ustedes los quiero tanto!

10. a) te lo; b) se las; c) te lo; d) se las; e) se lo; f) se los.

11. a) se los; b) se las; c) nos las; d) se la; e) se las.

12. a) Me lo he comprado;
    b) se las está probando;
    c) te lo puedo regalar;
    d) se ha ido con él; e) se la voy a llevar.

13. b) está probándoselas;
    c) puedo regalártelo;
    e) voy a llevársela.

14. a) te; b) ellas, entender**los**;
    c) —, la; d) lo; e) —, noso-tros, ellos; f) —, se; g) ella;
    h) —;
    i) ti, te, visitar**lo**.

15. a) le, sí, la; b) con**migo**, se/le;
    c) se lo, sí; d) ella, con**migo**, me, con**sigo**; e) mand**ársela**;
    f) convertir**la**, ella; g) se, sí.

Demonstrative, Possessive, and Interrogative Pronouns (pp. 91–92)

1. a) V; b) C; c) V; d) V; e) C; f) C; g) C.

2. a) esas; b) Ese; c) aquel; d) ese, este; e) ese; f) Esto, esto.

3. a) suyo, mío; b) vuestras, nuestras, mía; c) tuya, mía, mías; d) tuyo, mío.

4. a) mi, mis; b) sus, nuestras, sus, nuestras; c) míos, tuyos; d) mi, suyo, tu; e) vuestras; f) mío.

5. a) cuál; b) Cuánto; c) Quién; d) qué.

6. a) Qué; b) qué, qué; c) Cuál; d) Cuál; e) Qué; f) Cuál.

Indefinite and Relative Pronouns (pp. 100–102)

1. a) nadie, alguien; b) algo, nada; c) alguien, alguna; d) algo, nada.

2. a) nada; b) otra; c) uno; d) nadie; e) suficiente; f) mismo.

3. a) Las dietas no ayudan a nadie. b) Uno no debe preocuparse por reducir el consumo de azúcar. c) Las vitaminas de los alimentos naturales no son suficientes. d) ¿Ejercicio? La mayoría de la gente hace demasiado, ¡no es necesario tanto! e) A cualquiera le ayuda tomar tres aspirinas diarias.

4. a) muchos, cada uno; b) Algunos, suficientes, nadie; c) Cualquiera, pocos, tantas; d) demasiado, otros; e) nadie, nada, alguien.

5. a) un cocinero famoso que vive … b) El restaurante donde trabaja … c) Su mujer, quien trabaja … d) es un lugar adonde van …

6. a) ¡Por fin estoy en el apartamento con el que he soñado tanto tiempo! b) Una vecina, a quien he encontrado en el pasillo, me ha saludado muy amablemente. c) Ahora estoy en el salón, desde donde se escucha el ruido de los pájaros del parque que está enfrente del edificio.

7. a) cuya, como; b) que, cuyo, que/quienes; c) lo que ; d) que; e) cuyos, que.

Verbs: Present Indicative (pp. 113–117)

1. a) sonrío, sé, puedo, voy; b) sueñas, bebes, encuentras; c) prefiere, sigue, habla; d) recordamos, vamos, vemos; e) vivís, distribuís, dais, conocéis; f) ven, hacen, trabajan.

2. a) estar, ganar, poder, comprar; b) regalar, construir; c) significar, ofrecer; d) medir, costar; e) tener, parecer.

3. a) destruir; b) encontrar; c) responder; d) cerrar; e) bajar; f) vender; g) salir; h) despertar; i) llevar; j) terminar.

4. a) *regelmäßig:* buscar, preguntar, responder, abrir, subir, bajar, comprar, vender, entrar, llevar, terminar; b) *o ▶ ue:* encontrar, dormir; c) *e ▶ ie:* cerrar, despertar, empezar; d) *y:* construir, destruir; e) *g:* salir; f) *ig:* traer.

5. a) estamos, tiene, tiene; b) tengo, veo, viene, quiere, duerme; c) son, es; d) sigue, juego, quiere; e) sois, dice; f) creo, son, aprenden, salgo, doy, significa, cuesta, es, come; g) oyen, pueden, cuentan, repito, llaman, escuchamos, vuela.

6. a) estudiar, estudio, estudias, estudia, estudiamos, estudiáis, estudian; b) vender, vendo, vende, vendemos, vendéis, venden; c) escribir, escribes, escribe, escribimos, escribís, escriben; d) estoy, estás, está, estamos, estáis, están; e) hacer, hago, haces, hace, hacéis, hacen; f) venir, vengo, vienes, venimos, venís, vienen;

g) ir, voy, vas, va, vamos, vais;
h) saber, sé, sabes, sabe,
sabemos, saben.

7. a – 2; b – 5; c – 6; d – 1; e – 4;
f – 3.

8. a) tener hambre / sed; b) tener
ganas de; c) tener sueño;
d) tener... años; e) tener
prisa.

9. 1) • ¿Qué te ofrezco? Tengo
cerveza, vino, licor...
2) ○ Primero prefiero algo fresco, porque hace mucho
calor. 3) ¿Tienes algún jugo?
4) • Claro, te puedo dar jugo
de piña, de melocotón...
5) ○ Entonces, ¿por favor me
das de piña? 6) Es que soy
alérgico al melocotón.
7) • Claro, aquí lo tienes.
8) ¿Te importa si yo bebo jugo
de melocotón?
9) ○ Hombre, no hay ningún
problema si eres tú quien lo
bebe.

10. a) mira; b) paga, manda;
c) van; d) es, tiene, quiere;
e) suena, lleva; f) dicen;
g) hace, puede; h) muere;
i) cae; j) cuesta, vale.

11. a) son, guardan, conoces;
b) llevan, simboliza, visten;
c) tiene, es, dura, representa;
d) arrojan, salen, deben.

12. a) está; b) se va, participa,
hieren, queda; c) Pasa, es,
permanece; d) consigue,
puede; e) ocupa, se casa,
escribe, tienen; f) publica,
deja; g) muere.

Verbs: Past Indicative, Present Perfect / Imperfect (pp. 123 – 125)

1. a) habéis terminado, hemos
cosido; b) ha habido, ha traído,
ha dicho; c) has visto,
he puesto; d) ha guardado;
e) ha empezado, han salido.

2. a) ha tocado; b) Ha venido,
hemos sido; c) hemos estado,
hemos pasado; d) ha estado,
ha contado; e) ha hecho,
hemos llorado; f) se han ido,
nos hemos quedado; g) ha
resultado, ha empezado.

3. 1) • Hola Carmencita, ¿ya...
2) ○ Estupendamente...
3) • ¡Qué bien!...
4) ○ Pues... No, pero...
5) • ¡Qué guay! ¿Entonces...
6) ○ Sí, sí. Ha sido realmente...

4. volver, pasar, viajar, llover,
hacer, haber, gustar, ver, ser.

5. a) llego, espera, he encontrado;
b) cocina, ha preparado, ha
limpiado; c) ha dicho, ha leído,
ha abierto, sabe, es, trabajan,
llevan; d) ha decidido, quiere;
e) he quedado, he dado.

6. a) estaba; b) Llevaba; c) sabía;
d) hacía; e) Tenía.

7. a) he hecho, hacía; b) He
pelado, pelaba; c) He preparado,
preparaba; d) ha salido, salía.

8. a) volvían, estaban; b) tenía;
c) podía, veía, se aburría;
d) trabajaba, hacía; e) llamaba;
f) era; g) se preocupaban,
visitaban; h) se sentaban, se
sentían; i) estaban, pasaban,
echaban.

Verbs: Past Indicative, *Indefinido*, Contrast with Imperfect (pp. 133–137)

1. a) repetí, empecé, tuve;
   b) escribiste, viste, tomaste;
   c) dio, fue, siguió; d) hicimos,
   recordamos, comimos;
   e) pusisteis, estuvisteis,
   limpiasteis; f) dijeron, pidieron,
   pudieron.
2. a) nacer, llegar; b) realizar,
   fundar; c) estar, dedicarse,
   decidir, irse; d) empezar;
   e) hacerse, seguir, recibir,
   publicar; f) mudarse.
3. a–3; b–5; c–4; d–1; e–2.
4. a) fuiste; b) Viajé, Fue;
   c) conocieron; d) Visitamos,
   vimos; e) vivieron; f) pasamos;
   g) volamos, nos quedamos, nos
   ahorramos, pagamos.
5. a) asesinó, encontró, dijo, vi,
   respondió, hablaron, dijeron,
   fue; b) iba, trabajaba, tenía,
   odiaba, era; c) He pasado, he
   dicho, hemos preguntado, ha
   habido, ha hecho, ha sido;
   d) había visto, había muerto,
   habían sido.
6. a) vi, veía, he visto, había visto,
   ver; b) fuiste, eras, habías sido,
   ser; c) siguió, seguía, ha
   seguido, seguir; d) estuvimos,
   hemos estado, habíamos estado,
   estar; e) dijisteis, decíais,
   habéis dicho, habíais dicho;
   f) tuvieron, han tenido, habían
   tenido, tener; g) ponía, he
   puesto, había puesto, poner.
7. a) encontré, estaba; b) he
   pensado, Estuvo, trabajó,
   aprendió, ha tenido; c) has
   hecho, hice, salimos, Fuimos,
   conocíamos.

8. a) Tuve, había perdido;
   b) Llamé, había llegado;
   c) habían cobrado, fui.
9. a–4; b–1; c–6; d–5; e–2;
   f–3.
10. a) llegó, vivían, eran;
    b) conquistaron, obligaron;
    c) dejaron, eran, iniciaron;
    d) murieron, tenían, trajeron;
    e) sufrió, llegaban; f) hubo;
    g) dependía; h) perdió,
    se convirtió.
11. a) vivía, tenía; b) se llamaba;
    c) mandó, era, se perdieron;
    d) dijo, se subió; e) Descubrió,
    había, caminaron; f) llegaron,
    vieron, era, se habían imagi-
    nado; g) dijeron, empezaron,
    habían comido, estaban;
    h) habían visto, llegó; i) Se
    trataba, era, sabían; j) saludó,
    invitó; k) se pusieron,
    aceptaron; l) cenaron, se
    durmieron, había dado;
    m) cambió, despertó, tuvo;
    n) terminó, han leído.

Verbs: Future + Conditional (pp. 146–149)

1. a) hará; b) iremos;
   c) Saldremos; d) haré;
   e) traerá; f) pasaremos.
2. a) habrá pasado; b) nos habremos relajado; c) habré vuelto;
   d) Habrá sido.
3. a) saldrás; b) estará; c) irás;
   d) pedirán, harás; e) tendrás;
   f) llevará; g) se alegrará;
   h) Te saludará, dirá.
4. a) habrás salido; b) habrá
   estado; c) habrás ido;
   d) habrán pedido, habrás
   hecho; e) habrás tenido;
   f) habrá llevado; g) se habrá

alegrado; h) Te habrá saludado, habrá dicho.

5. a – 5; b – 3; c – 1; d – 6; e – 2;
f – 4.

6. a – 7; b – 5; c – 2; d – 6; e – 1;
f – 4; g – 3.

7. a) guardaría; b) pondrían;
c) gastarías; d) compraríamos;
e) tendría.

8. a – 4; b – 8; c – 5; d – 6; e – 7;
f – 2; g – 3; h – 1.

9. poder, encantar, deber, gustar,
decir, importar, tener, hacer.

10. a) me sentaría; b) me comería;
c) pediría; d) pagaríamos;
e) dejaría; f) pensaría;
g) llegaría; llevaría;
h) ofrecería.

11. a) C; b) I; c) I; d) C; e) I; f) I;
g) C; h) C.

12. a) habría pagado; b) habrían
podido; c) habría tenido;
d) habríamos dicho.

Verbs: Imperative (pp. 155 – 157)

1. a) ven, escribe, sal; b) repita,
baile, sea, recuerde; c) hagamos, hablemos; d) poned,
seguid, id; e) den, oigan,
tomen.

2. a – 5; b – 3; c – 2; d – 1; e – 4.

3. a) ponerse, subir, quedarse;
b) corregir, dar, mandar;
c) hacer, hacer, poner;
d) mostrar, traer;
e) andar, enfadarse, mirar, dar.

4. a) tú; b) tú; c) usted;
d) usted; e) usted; f) tú; g) tú;
h) usted.

5. a) pise; b) Introduzca; c) Tire
– Empuje; d) haga; e) Ponga;
f) aparque.

6. a) pisen; b) Introduzcan;
c) Tiren – Empujen; d) hagan;
e) Pongan; f) aparquen.

7. a) empezar, empieza, empiece,
empecemos, empezad, empie-
cen; b) vender, venda, venda-
mos, vended, vendan; c) subir,
sube, suba, subamos, suban;
d) ve, vaya, vayamos, id,
vayan; e) decir, di, digamos,
decid, digan.

8. a) dejen, levántense;
b) ayúdame, sube; c) te
quejes, Acomódalo; d) hagan,
pongan, pónganse;
e) Vámonos / Vayámonos.

9. a) ¡Acércate! b) ¡Vete!
c) ¡Dígamelo! d) ¡No os las
pongáis! e) ¡No se rían!
f) ¡No lo hagas!

10. a) servidlo; b) síguela;
c) Leámosla; d) pídesela;
e) no se lo compre;
f) no se lo traigáis; g) ponte-
los;
h) terminémoslo.

Verbs: Present Subjunctive (pp. 166 – 170)

1. a – 2; b – 5; c – 1; d – 6; e – 3;
f – 4.

2. a) necesitan que - construyan;
b) dudan que - puedan;
c) piden que – sea; d) teme
que – aumente; e) no piensan
que – paguen; f) es hora de
que – bajen; g) Es necesario
que – digan; h) Es natural
que – vaya.

3. a) construir; b) poder;
c) ser; d) aumentar; e) pagar;
f) bajar; g) decir; i) ir.

4. a) mande, tarden; b) ponga,
responda; c) reenvíe; d) sean,
escriban.

5. a) viajar, viaje, viajes, viaje, viajemos, viajéis, viajen;
b) volar, vuele, vueles, volemos, voléis, vuelen;
c) conocer, conozcas, conozca, conozcamos, conozcáis, conozcan; d) esté, estés, esté, estemos, estéis, estén; e) ir, vaya, vayas, vaya, vayáis, vayan; f) quedarse, me quede, te quedes, se quede, nos quedemos, os quedéis;
g) vuelva, vuelvas, vuelva, volvamos, volváis, vuelvan.

6. a) comunicarse; b) escuche, ofrezca; c) solucionar, hablar;
d) hacer, distraiga, interrumpa;
e) pueda; f) acepten, hablen, sepan.

7. a – 3; b – 1; c – 5; d – 2; e – 4.

8. a – 7; b – 3; c – 1; d – 6; e – 8;
f – 2; g – 5; h – 4.

9. a) esperes, vuelvas; b) comprenda, expliquemos, se dé;
c) termines, pueda, acabe, empiece; d) estés, sea, esté, salga, sea.

10. a) gustan; b) leen; c) conserven; d) son, adquieran; e) expliquen; f) tienes/tengas, aumenten; g) ganan, se identifiquen, desarrollen; h) sean;
i) parecen/parezcan, dan, sufran; j) dejan, son, esté, haya, duren; k) tienen, voy, tenga, lea, juguemos.

11. a) llegas, va, haya; b) cita, seas; c) se retrase, pierdas, llames; d) llegue, planee;
e) existan, siga; f) está, sean, venga; g) sea; h) cumplan, hagas; i) hay, tire, recuerde;
j) haga; k) interrumpa, quieren, termine; l) pierden, hablan, está; m) miren, parezca; n) gusten, seas.

Verbs: Subjunctive, Other (pp. 177 – 181)

1. a) haya habido; b) hayan ocurrido; c) haya llovido;
d) haya recogido; e) haya revelado; f) hayan pasado.

2. a) fueron, pidieron, tuvieron; fuera, pidiera, tuviera; b) se enteraron, leyeron, dijeron; te enteraras, leyeras, dijeras;
c) conocieron, pusieron, bebieron; conociera, pusiera, bebiera; d) hicieron, trabajaron, se divirtieron; hiciéramos, trabajáramos, nos divirtiéramos;
e) vieron, se acostaron, siguieron; vierais, os acostarais, siguierais; f) consultaron, dieron, oyeron; consultaran, dieran, oyeran.

3. a) hubiera; b) me aburriera, tuviera; c) pudiera; d) me dedicara, tocara; e) hiciera;
f) propusiera, faltara, fuera;
g) estuvieras; h) vinierais;
i) dijeras / dijerais.

4. a – 3; b – 5; c – 8; d – 6; e – 1;
f – 2; g – 4; h – 7.

5. a) el hecho de que – publicaran;
b) fue un escándalo que – hicieran; c) había sido un gran avance que – hubiera; d) les pareció pésima idea que – presentaran; e) Temieron que – fomentaran; f) criticaron que llevaran, aunque – fueran;
g) Les molestó que – mostraran;
h) les gustó que – posaran;
i) fue agradable que – dejaran.

6. a) publicar; b) hacer; c) haber;
d) presentar; e) fomentar;
f) ser, llevar; g) mostrar;
h) posar; i) dejar.

7. a) trabaje, trabajara;
b) queráis, explicaras;
c) vivieran, cambiaran, vivamos; d) fuera, presente,
vayamos.

8. a – 2; b – 7; c – 3; d – 5; e – 8;
f – 1; g – 6; h – 4.

9. a) terminara; b) limpiara,
hiciera; c) estaba/estuviera,
tuviera; d) fuera; e) solicitara;
f) ofrecían, eran, estaban;
g) fuera; h) pidiera, llegara;
i) llegó, se diera; j) cambiaba;
k) descansara.

10. a) hubiera hecho; b) hubiera
hablado; c) se hubiera imaginado; d) hubiera dicho;
e) hubiera llegado; f) hubiera
abierto; g) hubiera escrito.

11. a) como si fuera; b) temían
que (yo) no pudiera; c) Digas
lo que digas; d) se haya/n
podido (usted/es) ir; e) mi
hermana se hubiera puesto mis
zapatos; f) cuando hayan
llegado a casa; g) hagamos las
cosas; h) te hubieras quedado
con nosotros.

Unconjugated Forms of the Verb (pp. 196 – 201)

1. a) gustar, quitar, cantar, llorar,
escuchar; b) tener, caer, llover,
saber, entender; c) discutir,
salir, pedir, dormir.

2. a) voy a; b) vas a; c) vais a;
d) voy a; e) vamos a; f) va a.

3. a – 3; b – 5; c – 1; d – 2; e – 4.

4. a) de; b) a; c) —; d) por;
e) para; f) a; g) —.

5. a) acaba de terminar; b) Suelo
trabajar, trato de aprender;
c) lograr hablarlo, he decidido
vivir; d) dejó de ser, empezó a
trabajar; e) Pienso combinar,
ponerte a pensar; f) he intentado encontrar; g) dejar de
jugar; h) volver a vivir;
i) acabas por no ser.

6. a) decidimos; b) Nos pusimos
a; c) te atreverías a; d) conseguiremos, lograr; e) quedamos
en; f) Nos echamos a; nos las
arreglábamos para; g) llegó a;
h) Solíamos, se ponía a;
i) hizo; j) llegado a, acabamos por.

7. a) Al llegar; b) Nada más
aclarar; c) Teniendo; d) hasta
conseguir; e) siendo/por ser;
f) Antes de irnos.

8. a) se está duchando; b) está
hablando; c) estamos cenando;
d) están esquiando; e) Está
vendiendo, estoy alquilando.

9. b – 1; e – 2; g – 3; c – 4; f – 5;
d – 6; a – 7.

10. b) estuvo llorando; e) se fue
consolando; g) llevaba años
dedicándose; c) se había pasado los días cuidando; f) sigo
llorando; d) voy aprendiendo;
a) limpiándose las lágrimas.

11. a) rebajados, envueltos;
b) sido, cansado, tenido,
acaloradas, solucionado;
c) escrita, puesto, distraída,
estado, sentada, concentrada,
corregido; d) cerrada, abierta.

12. a) trabajando, obtenido;
b) jubilarse, haciendo, aprendiendo, leyendo; c) termina-
dos, organizarse; d) Trabajando, conseguir, fijado;
e) ponernos, quedándonos,
comiéndonos.

13. a) han ido; b) que tuvieron que salir, así llamados, siguen hablando; c) fueron expulsados, reconquistada, era tolerada; d) Contando, acabó por ser; e) llevaron – a establecerse; f) se fueron adaptando, manteniendo; g) sigue siendo hablada, ha cambiado; h) ha ido tomando, prestadas; i) va a poder entender.

Special Verbs: *ser, estar, hay* (pp. 211–214)

1. a) es, está; b) es; c) hay; d) está; e) es, hay, hay; f) hay, es; g) es.
2. a–3; b–5; c–2; d–6; e–1; f–4.
3. a) hay, está, Es, Está/Es. b) estás, estoy, estoy, hay, soy; c) está, hay, hay, es, Está; d) están, es, está, es, está, ser; e) Hay, estamos, estoy, es, Es, estás; f) están, Están, hay/son, hay/es, hay, Están, Hay, está.
4. 1–c; 2–e; 3–f; 4–d; 5–a; 6–b.
5. a) son; b) hay, tienen; c) están, son; d) Hay, está, tiene, es; e) Hay, están; f) es; g) Es, tiene; h) ser, tiene, es, está; i) tienen, estar; j) está, está; k) hay, tiene.
6. a) ha sido, Es, está, estuvo; b) será, está, está; c) sería, Estoy; d) fue/ estuvo, estaba, Estoy, estaban, había.
7. a) Son, hay, es; b) es, es, ser, estar; c) hay, hay; d) está, está, es; e) está, es; f) es, es.

Special Verbs: Verbs with the Dative, Reflexive Verbs, Modal Verbs, Verbs of Change (pp. 222–226)

1. a) la cerveza, salir con mis amigos, el vino tinto, la cocina mediterránea, la col; b) los gatos, las playas españolas, el deporte y la naturaleza, las recetas prácticas, el cine y el teatro.
2. a) ¿Te gusta la foto? b) (A mí) no me gusta nada el pescado./ El pescado no me gusta nada. c) Este restaurante nos gusta mucho/nos encanta. c) A mí también me parece muy bien. e) ¡Me encantan/me gustan mucho los vinos españoles! f) ¿Les gusta la comida, niños/hijos? g) ¡Salud! Cariño, me gustas mucho... ¡Te quiero!
3. a) os, Os, nos; b) me, ti, mí; c) te, me, me; d) te, me; e) nos, Os; f) me, te, ti.
4. a) les encanta, les gusta; b) le gustas, le molesta; c) te hace; d) nos gustan; e) les parece.
5. a) me quedo, te quedas, se queda, nos quedamos, os quedáis, se quedan; b) me marcho, te marchas, os marcháis, se marchan; c) me acuerdo, se acuerda, nos acordamos, se acuerdan; d) te vistes, nos vestimos, os vestís, se visten; e) me siento, te sientas, se sienta, os sentáis, se sientan; f) me voy, te vas, se va, nos vamos, se van; g) me quejo, se queja, nos quejamos, os quejáis, se quejan; h) me despido, te despides, se despide, os despedís, se despiden.

6. a) te dedicas; b) se quedan; c) me ocupo, se levantan, Se relajan, se duchan; d) se sienten, se alegran; e) Me siento, nos reunimos, me acuerdo.

7. a) se llama; b) se llevaban; c) se dio cuenta; d) se dedica-ban, se secaba; e) se lavan; f) se relajan, se concentran; g) te liberas; h) se mantienen.

8. a – 3; b – 5; c – 4; d – 2; e – 1.

9. a – 3; b – 5; c – 1; d – 6; e – 7; f – 2; g – 4.

10. a) nació; b) se hizo; c) fue nombrado; d) se convirtió; e) fue elegido, llegó a ser; f) hacerse; g) se volvió, se convirtió; h) se enfermó; i) llegó a cumplir.

Negation (p. 229)

1. a) No, no tengo coche. b) No, no quiero café. c) No, no sé esquiar. d) No, no me gusta el cine. e) No, no hemos terminado.

2. a) nunca; b) nadie; c) nada; d) tampoco; e) ya no.

3. a) a – 7; b – 6; c – 1; d – 4; e – 2; f – 8; g – 3; h – 10; i – 5; j – 9.

Types of Sentences, the Conditional Sentence (p. 234)

1. a – 4; b – 1; c – 6; d – 2; e – 3; f – 5.

2. a) serías, fueras; b) harías, volvieras; c) habría sido, te hubieras casado; d) comprarías, ganaras; e) gustaría, pudieras.

3. a) Cuando, Si; b) Cuando, Si; c) Cuando, Si.

Indirect Discourse (pp. 238 – 239)

1. a) desde cuándo te sientes débil; b) si te duele algo; c) que te acuestes ahí (por favor); d) respires profundamente y te relajes.

2. a) si había tenido la presión alta; b) si tomaba algún medica-mento; c) que tomara esas/unas pastillas y lo llamara en una semana; d) que no me pre-ocupara y que estas pastillas me ayudarían.

3. a) nos vayamos; b) olvidáramos, los hiciéramos; te pongas, te la arregló.

4. a) quiere saber, ha dicho; b) ha contado, ha comentado; c) ha pedido, opina.

5. a) la llames, le urge que hables con ella; b) te acuerdas de su primo, que quieren, ir con ellos, quedaron; c) tiene, fueron/fuisteis, te escaneó, te la envió, digas.

Passive Voice + Impersonal Sentences (pp. 242 – 243)

1. a) va; b) recorren, toma;
c) mezclan; d) pueden, compar-
ten; e) suelen; f) paga.
2. a – 2; b – 1; c – 6; d – 8; e – 3;
f – 5; g – 7: h – 4.
3. a) están rotas; b) están des-
hechas; c) está abierta; d) está
desordenado.
4. a) fue fundada; b) fue fortifi-
cado; c) fue vencida, fue difun-
dida; d) fueron enviados; e) fue
prohibida; f) fue amenazado.
5. a – 4; b – 8; c – 6; d – 7; e – 1;
f – 10; g – 9; h – 5; i – 2; j – 3.

Prepositions (pp. 251 – 252)

1. a) por, a, en; b) a; c) en el, en;
d) Por, —, el; e) del, de, por;
f) —, de; g) Por, —, por, de;
h) a, con, en.
2. a) de, para, en, a, a, para;
b) en, de, de/en, con, para, a,
en, en, para, de, a; c) con, de,
de, a, a, a/con, por, de, de,
para.
3. a – 3; b – 5; c – 1; d – 2; e – 4.
4. a) para, por; b) por, para;
c) para, para; d) para; e) por,
para, por; f) para; g) para, para,
por; h) por, para, para.
5. a) Desde; b) Desde hace;
c) desde hace; d) desde, antes
de; e) antes de, hace, hace,
desde.

Conjunctions (p. 256)

1. a) e; b) o; c) e, u.
2. a) sino, porque; b) pero, porque;
c) sino, porque.
3. a – 3; b – 4; c – 2; d – 1.
4. a) En cuanto, que; b) Antes de
que, y, aunque, porque; c) por
eso; d) pero, ni.

Numbers, Quantities, and Time Expressions (p. 262)

1. a) medio kilo de papas;
b) un cuarto de kilo de jamón;
c) cien gramos de queso; e) un
litro y medio de vino blanco.
2. a) la una y media de la mañana;
b) las cinco y cuarto de la tarde;
c) las seis menos veinte de la
mañana; d) las doce y diez de la
noche.
3. a) cincuenta y cuatro, noventa
y un euros; b) treinta de
octubre de mil novecientos
sesenta y cinco; c) mil novecientos ochenta y siete, nueve
millones ocho mil cuatrocientos
setenta y cuatro, trece coma dos
por ciento.
4. a) Necesito cincuenta céntimos.
b) Es la tercera vez. c) Vivo
en el segundo piso. d) Hoy
hace / tenemos veinticinco
grados. e) La película empieza
a las diez. f) Mi profesora tiene
cuarenta y cuatro años.
g) Mañana es viernes trece.

Overview of Grammatical Terms

The terms used in this book appear in **bold**.

English	Spanish
accusative	acusativo
accusative object	objeto directo
adjective	adjetivo
adverb	adverbio
article	artículo
auxiliary verb (helping verb)	verbo auxiliar
cardinal number	número cardinal
comparative	comparativo
conditional	condicional
conditional sentence	oración condicional
conjugation	conjugación
conjunction	conjunción
consonant	consonante
dative	dativo
dative object	objeto indirecto
demonstrative pronoun	pronombre demostrativo
direct object	objeto directo
feminine	femenino
future perfect	futuro perfecto
future, simple future	futuro
gender	género
genitive	genitivo
imperative	imperativo
imperfect	imperfecto
indefinite pronoun	pronombre indefinido
indicative	indicativo
indirect object	objeto indirecto
infinitive	infinitivo
interrogative pronoun	pronombre interrogativo
masculine	masculino
modal verb	verbo modal
near future	futuro próximo
negation	negación

English	Spanish
nominative	nominativo
noun	sustantivo
number	número
object	objeto
object pronoun	pronombre de objeto
ordinal number	número ordinal
passive voice	voz pasiva
past participle	participio perfecto
past perfect	pluscuamperfecto
personal pronoun	pronombre personal
plural	plural
possessive pronoun	plural
predicate	predicado
preposition	preposición
present	presente
present participle	gerundio
present perfect	(pretérito) perfecto
preterit	indefinido
progressive	presente continuo
pronoun	pronombre reflexivo
reflexive pronoun	pronombre relativo
reflexive verb	verbo reflexivo
relative pronoun	pronombre relativo
singular	singular
subject	sujeto
subject pronoun	pronombre sujeto
subjunctive	subjuntivo
superlative	superlativo
tense	tiempo
verb	verbo
vowel	vocal

Index

Index

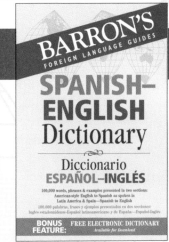

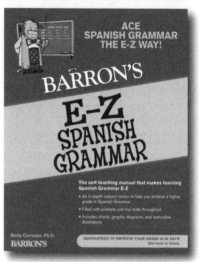